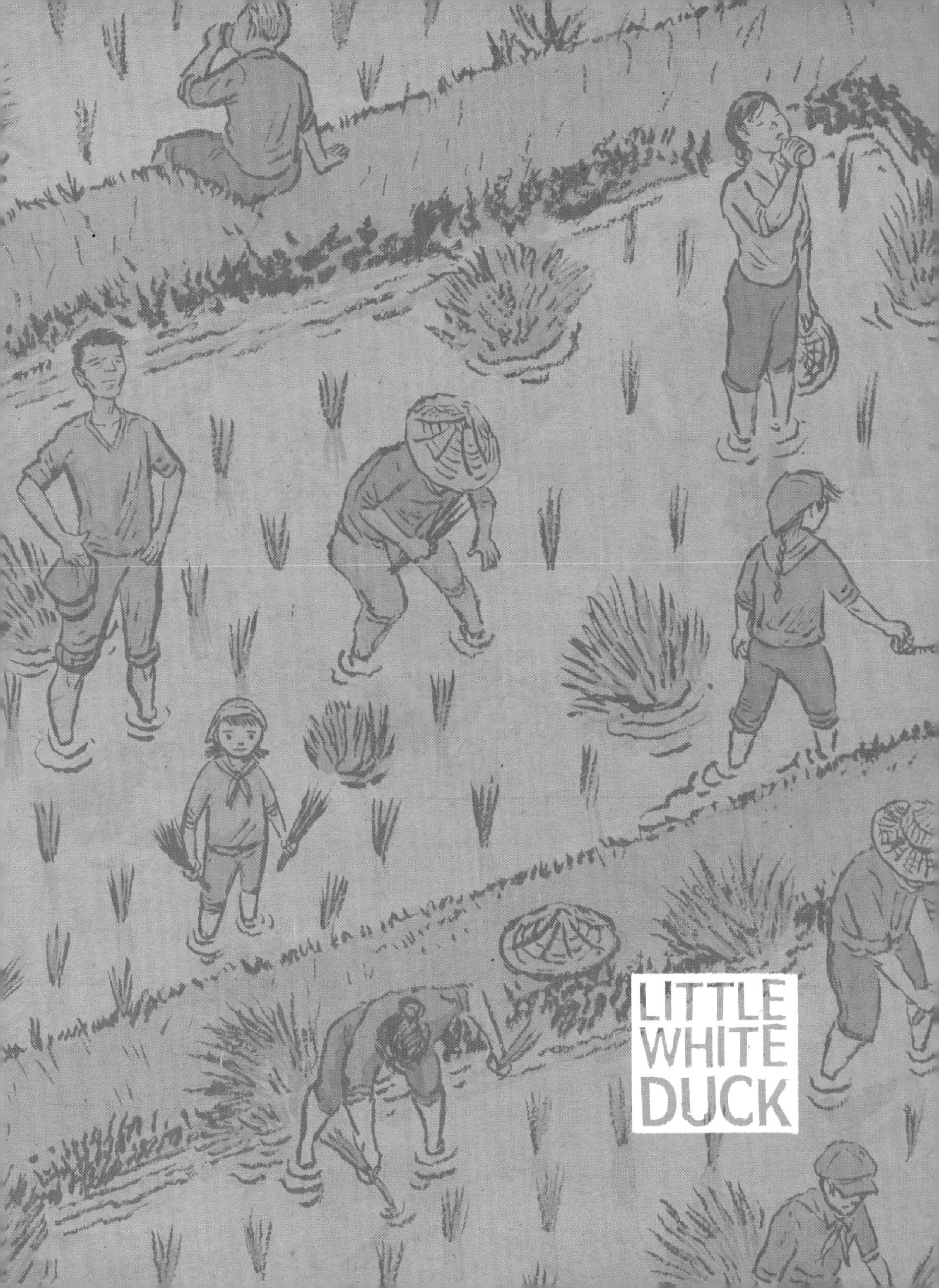
LITTLE
WHITE
DUCK

LITTLE WHITE DUCK

A CHILDHOOD IN CHINA

NA LIU AND
ANDRÉS VERA MARTÍNEZ

GRAPHIC UNIVERSE™ • MINNEAPOLIS • NEW YORK

We would like to thank Valerie Cabrera, Bob Mecoy, David Sandlin, Tao Nyeu, Qi Wu, and Carol Burrell; and the art students of Mr. A. D. Lucero's class at Mills Elementary School in Austin, TX, for their help in choosing the cover of this book.

—Andrés and Na

Story by Andrés Vera Martínez and Na Liu
Illustrations by Andrés Vera Martínez
Lettering by Andrés Vera Martínez and Na Liu

Graphic Universe™
A division of Lerner Publishing Group, Inc.
241 First Avenue North
Minneapolis, MN 55401 U.S.A.

Website address: www.lernerbooks.com

Library of Congress Cataloging-in-Publication Data

Martínez, Andrés Vera.
   Little White Duck : a childhood in China / by Andrés Vera Martínez and Na Liu ; illustrated by Andrés Vera Martínez.
       p.   cm.
       Summary: A young girl describes her experiences growing up in China, beginning with the death of Chairman Mao in 1976.
       ISBN: 978-0-7613-6587-7 (lib. bdg. : alk. paper)
       ISBN: 978-0-7613-7963-8 (eBook)
       1. China—History—1976-2002—Juvenile fiction. 2. China— History—1976-2002—Comic books, strips, etc. 3. Graphic novels. [1. Graphic novels. 2. China—History—1976-2002—Fiction.] I. Liu, Na, 1973- II. Title.
   PZ7.7M373Whi 2012
   741.5—dc22   2011005347

Manufactured in the United States of America
3 — BP — 3/1/13

謹以此书献给

我们在中国的

家人们和我们的

宝贝女儿美兰

We would like to dedicate this book to
our family in China and daughter Mei Lan.

—Andrés and Na

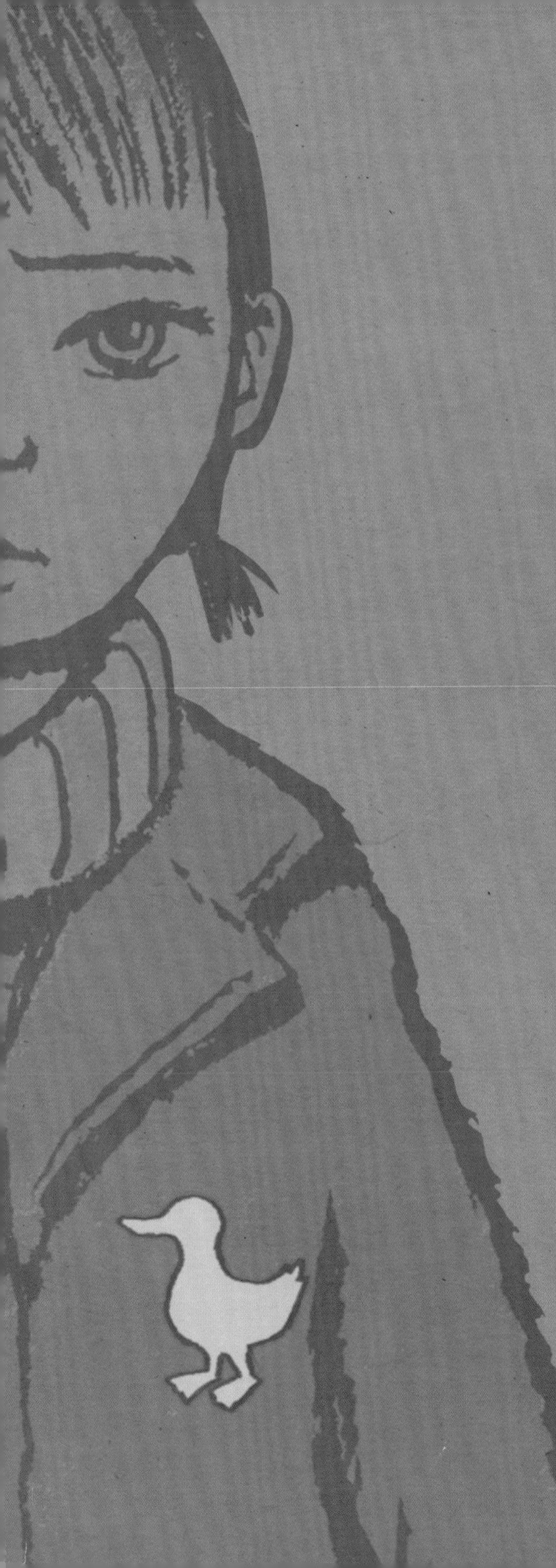

TABLE OF CONTENTS

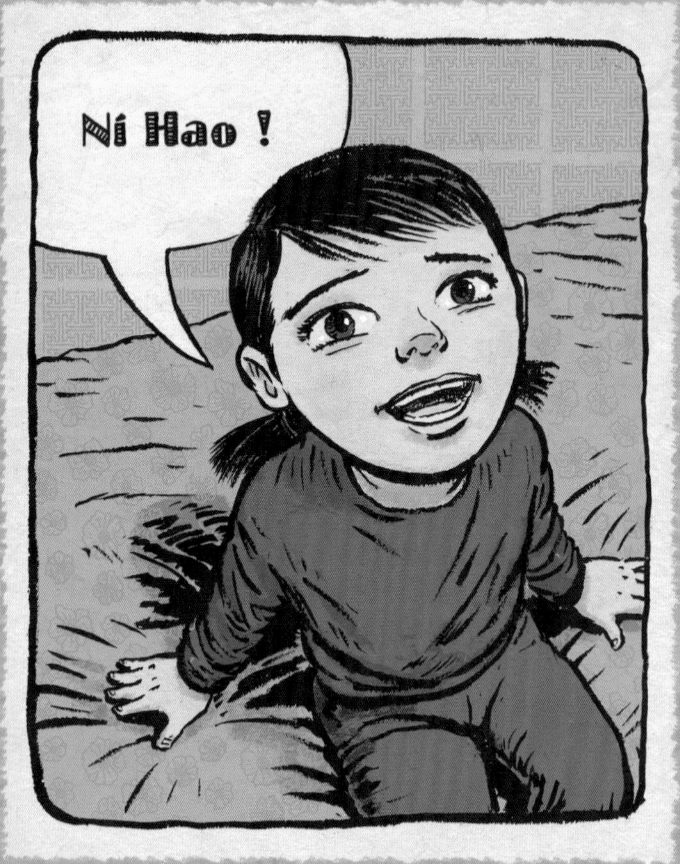
Ni Hao !

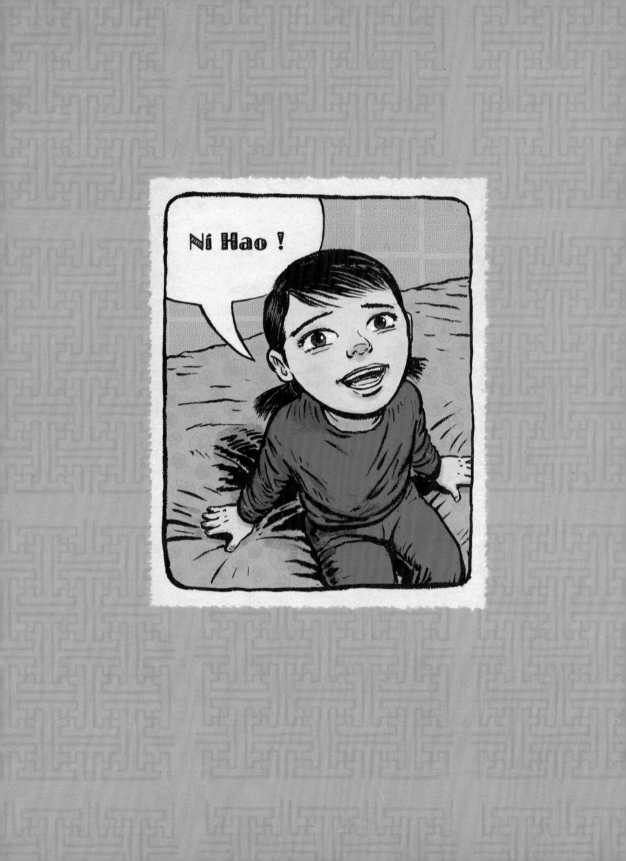

Hello,

THAT'S ME, NA, IN THE PICTURE ON THE LEFT. I WAS BORN IN ZHIFANG, A SUBURB OF WUHAN, CHINA, IN 1973. WUHAN IS A VERY LARGE CITY NEAR THE CENTER OF THE COUNTRY, NEXT TO THE FAMOUS CHANG RIVER (YANGTZE).

IN FACT, THE RIVER GOES RIGHT THROUGH THE CITY, LIKE THIS . . .

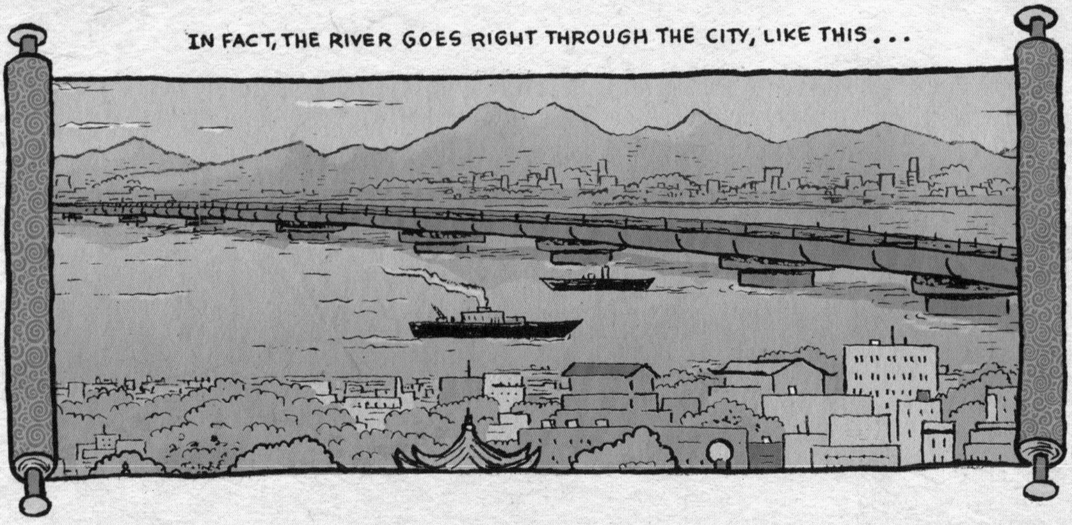

LIU IS MY FAMILY NAME. NA IS MY GIVEN NAME. IN CHINA THE FAMILY NAME COMES FIRST: LIU NA.

BUT CHILDREN IN CHINA ARE HARDLY EVER CALLED BY THEIR REAL NAMES. ALL CHILDREN ARE GIVEN NICKNAMES. THE TRADITION BEGAN THOUSANDS OF YEARS AGO, BECAUSE IT WAS THOUGHT THAT BAD LUCK AND SPIRITS COULDN'T FIND YOU IF YOUR TRUE NAME WAS NEVER SPOKEN OUT LOUD.

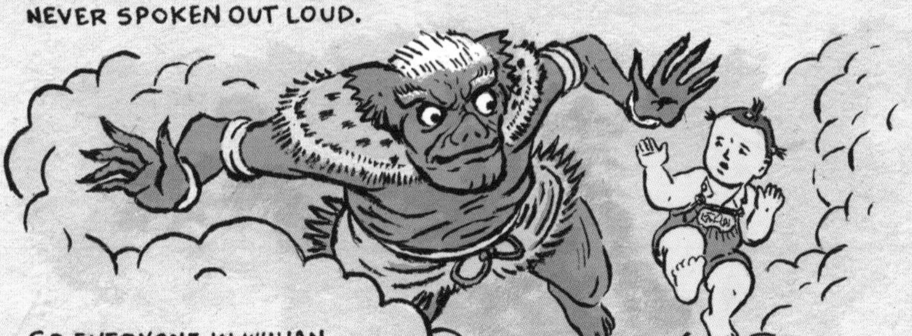

SO EVERYONE IN WUHAN CALLS ME QIN. IT MEANS PIANO.

A **CHINESE** PIANO LOOKS LIKE THIS.

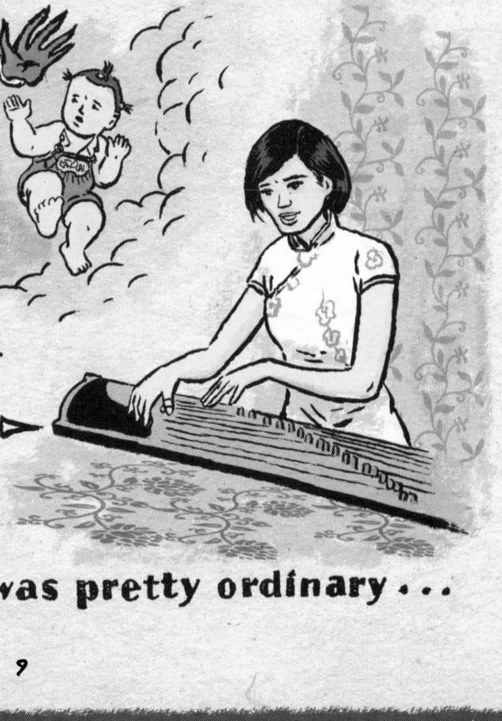

AFTER MY LITTLE SISTER WAS BORN, MY NICKNAME CHANGED TO DA QIN (BIG PIANO), AND MY SISTER'S WAS XIAO QIN (LITTLE PIANO).

I think my life in China was pretty ordinary . . .

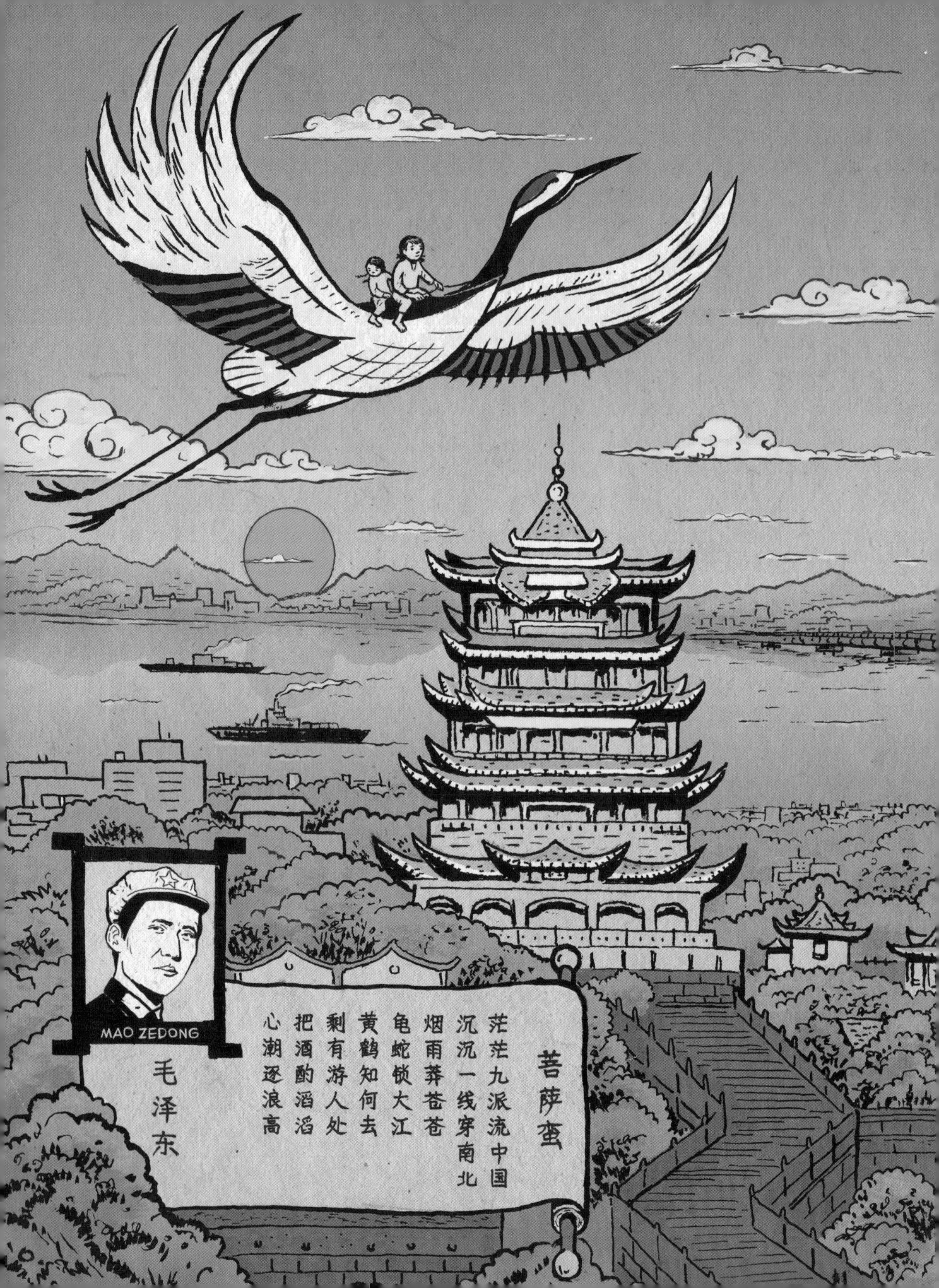
MAO ZEDONG
菩萨蛮
茫茫九派流中国
沉沉一线穿南北
烟雨莽苍苍
龟蛇锁大江
黄鹤知何去
剩有游人处
把酒酹滔滔
心潮逐浪高
毛泽东

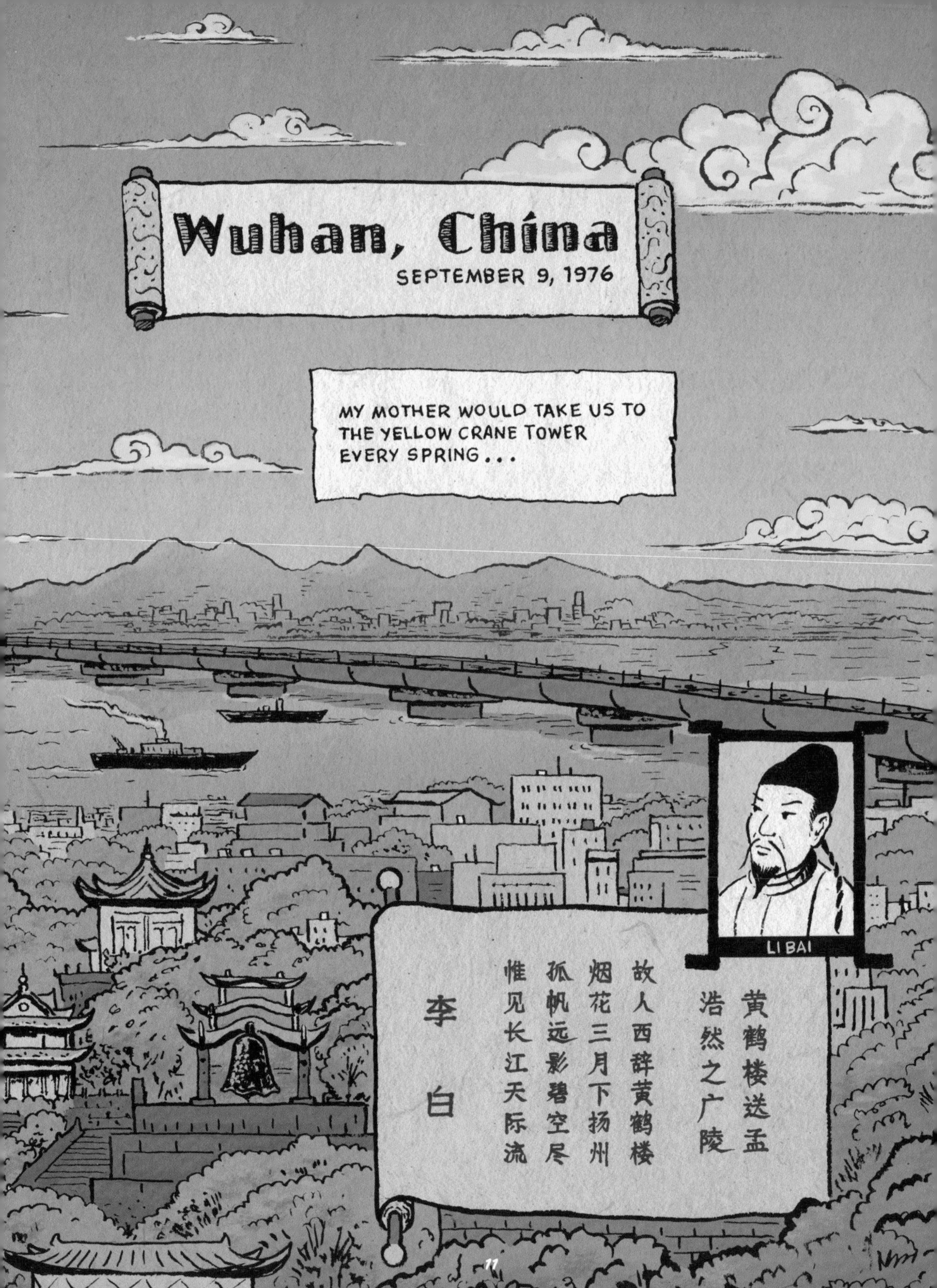
Wuhan, China
SEPTEMBER 9, 1976
MY MOTHER WOULD TAKE US TO THE YELLOW CRANE TOWER EVERY SPRING . . .
LI BAI
黄鹤楼送孟
浩然之广陵
故人西辞黄鹤楼
烟花三月下扬州
孤帆远影碧空尽
惟见长江天际流
李白

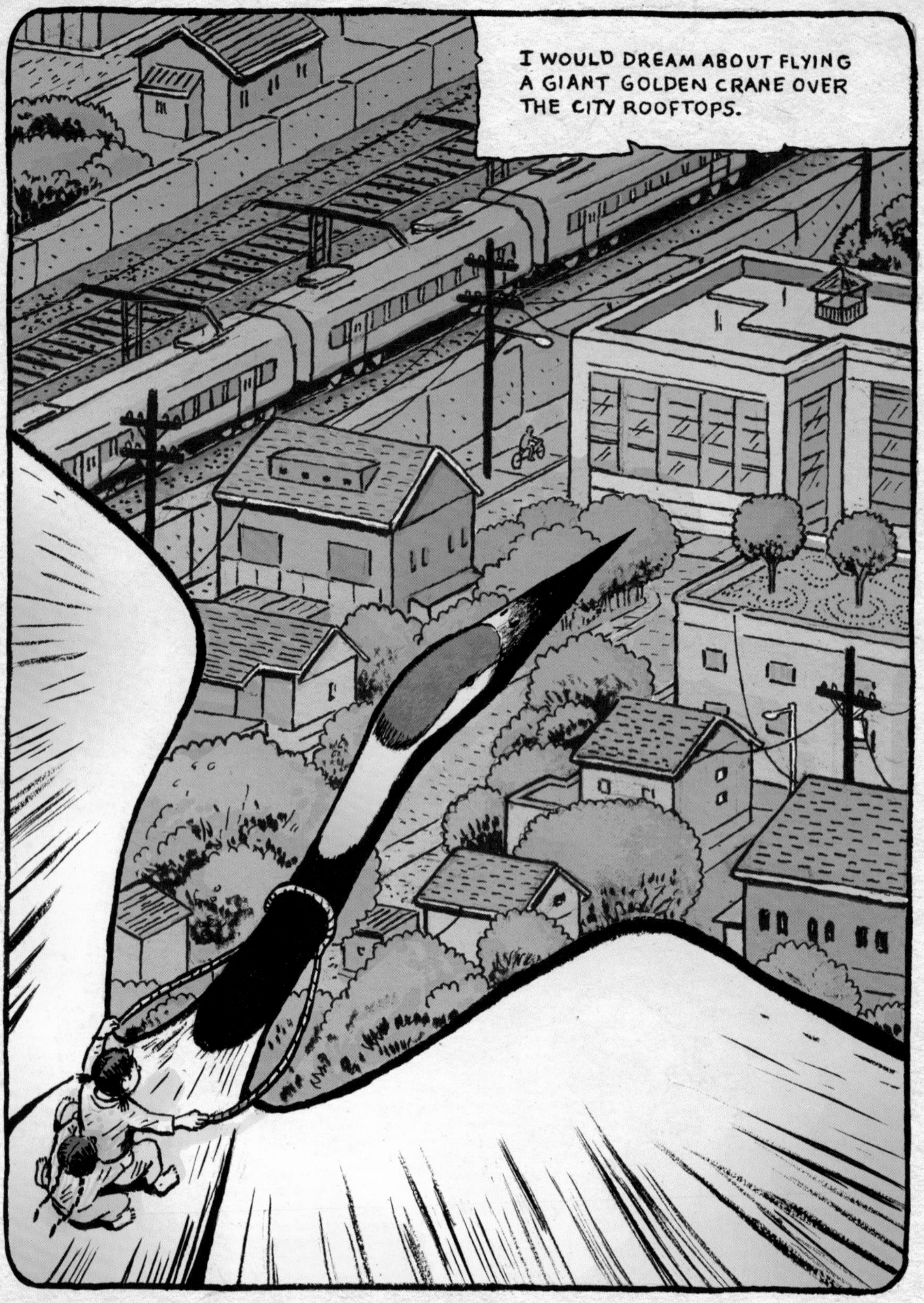
I WOULD DREAM ABOUT FLYING A GIANT GOLDEN CRANE OVER THE CITY ROOFTOPS.

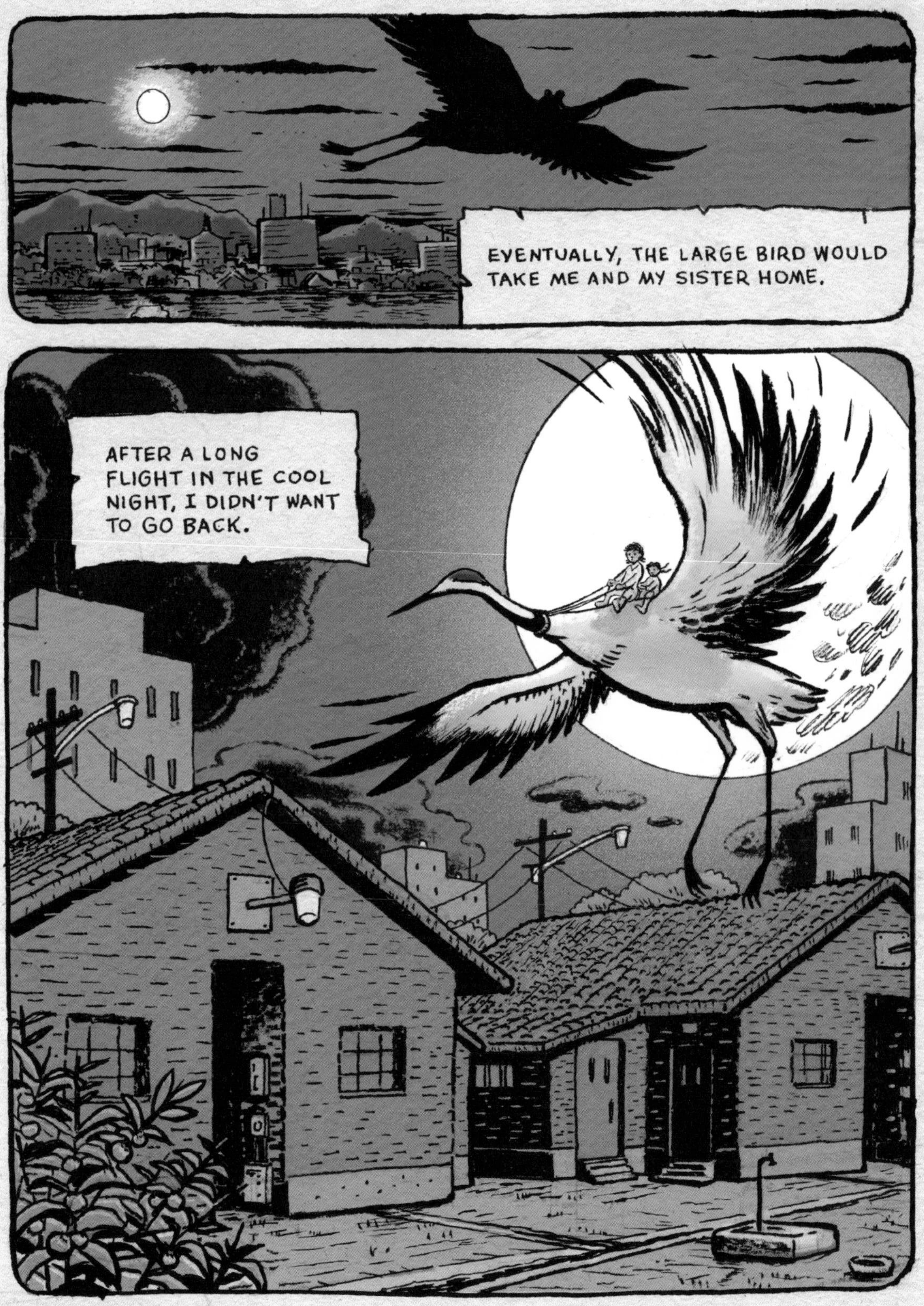
EVENTUALLY, THE LARGE BIRD WOULD TAKE ME AND MY SISTER HOME.
AFTER A LONG FLIGHT IN THE COOL NIGHT, I DIDN'T WANT TO GO BACK.

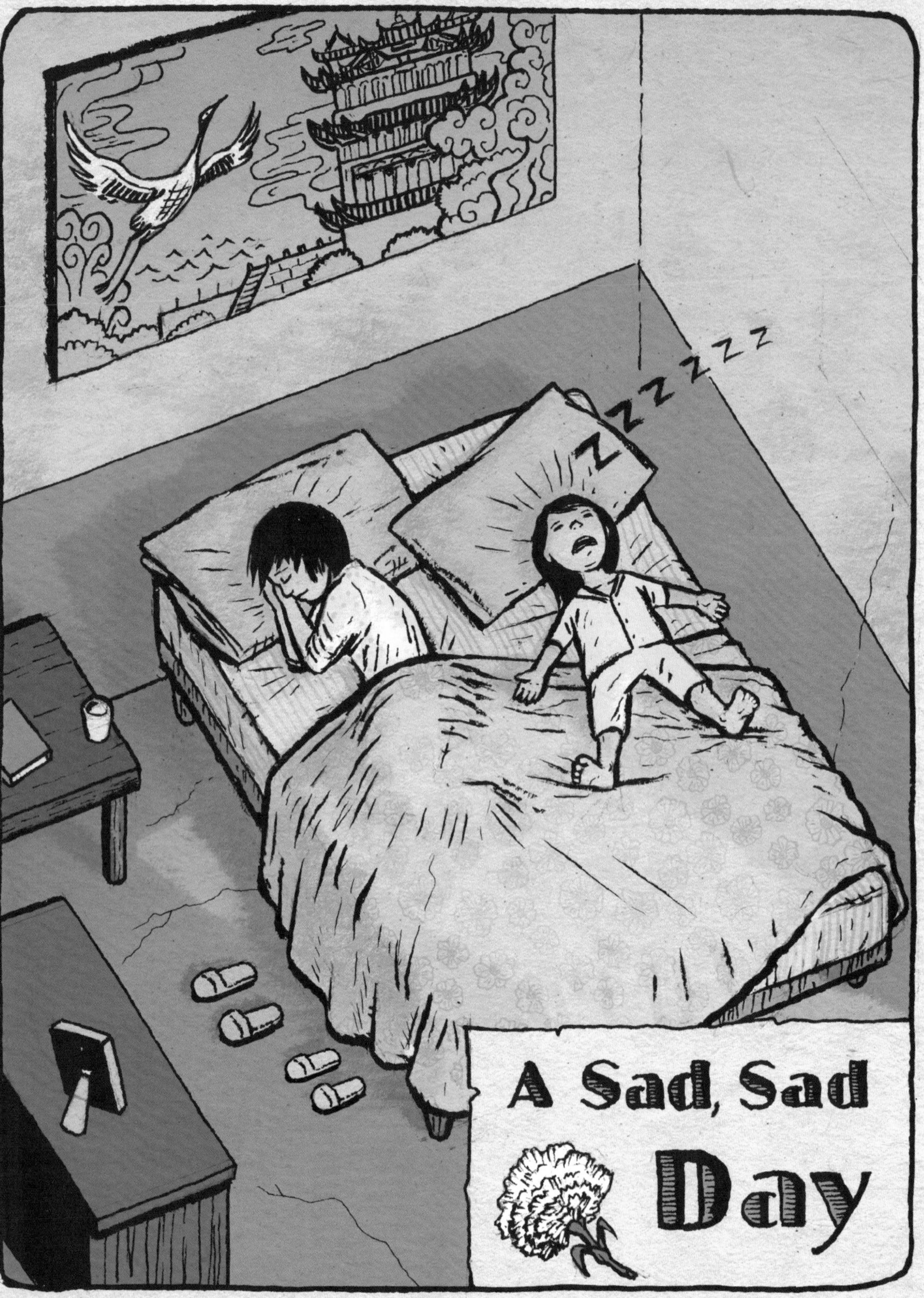
ZZZZZZZZ
A Sad, Sad
Day

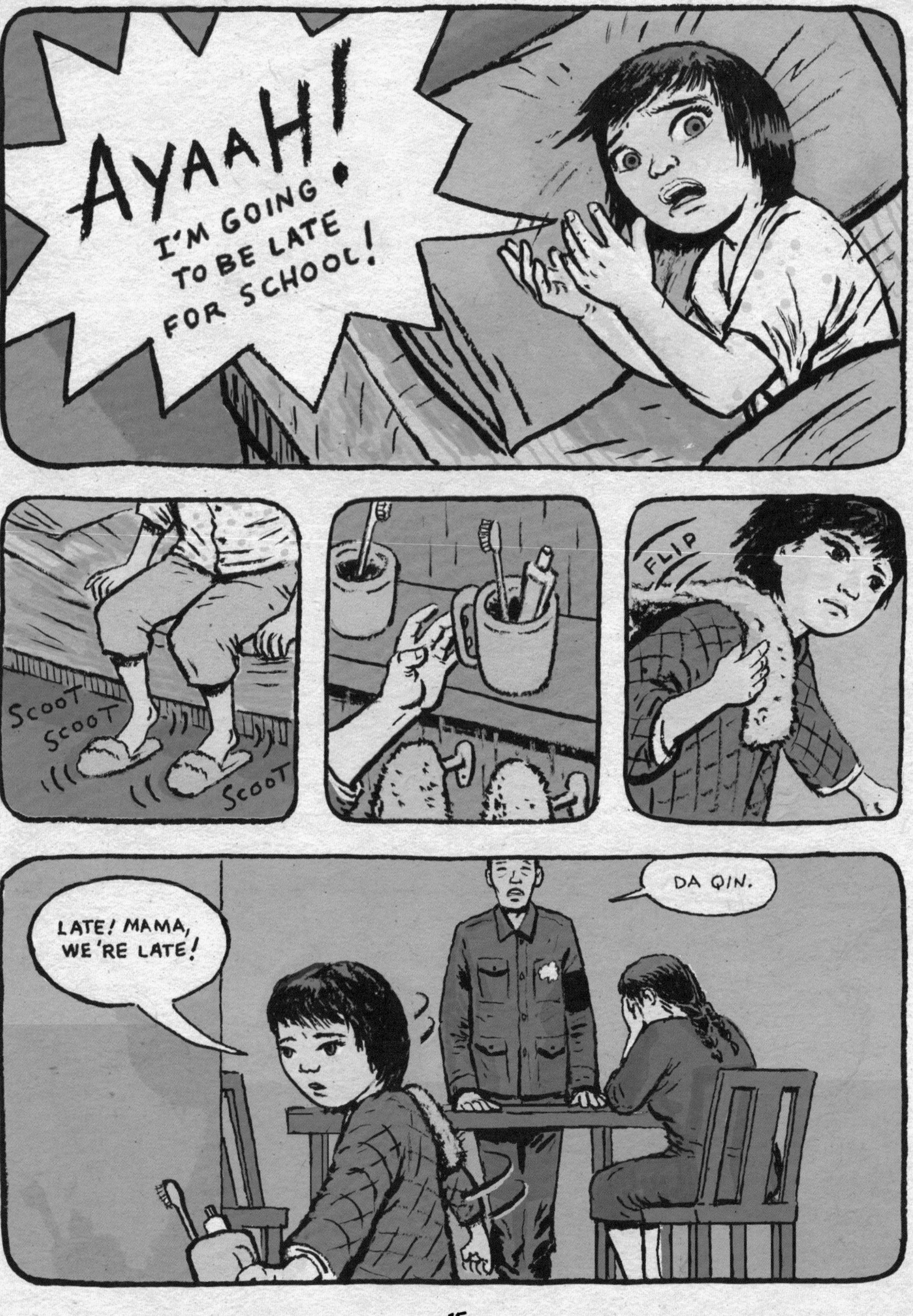
AYAAH!
I'M GOING TO BE LATE FOR SCHOOL!
SCOOT SCOOT SCOOT
FLIP
LATE! MAMA, WE'RE LATE!
DA QIN.

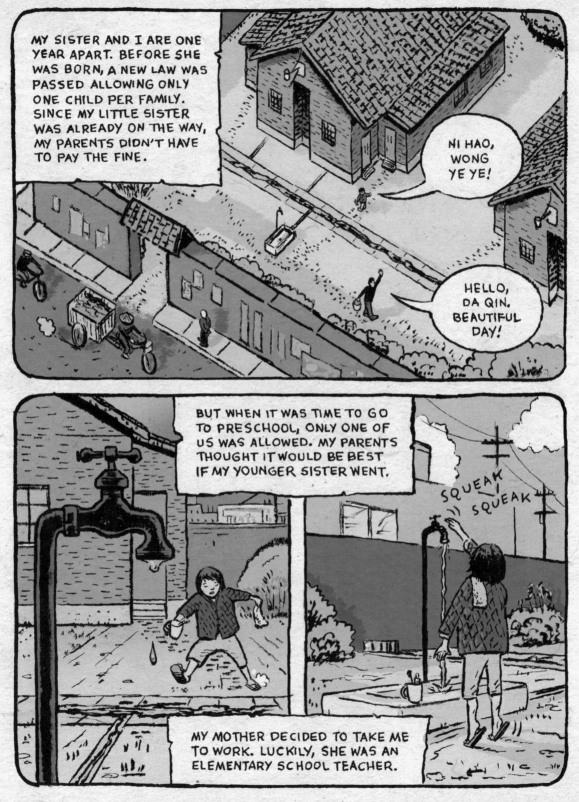

MY SISTER AND I ARE ONE YEAR APART. BEFORE SHE WAS BORN, A NEW LAW WAS PASSED ALLOWING ONLY ONE CHILD PER FAMILY. SINCE MY LITTLE SISTER WAS ALREADY ON THE WAY, MY PARENTS DIDN'T HAVE TO PAY THE FINE.

NI HAO, WONG YE YE!

HELLO, DA QIN. BEAUTIFUL DAY!

BUT WHEN IT WAS TIME TO GO TO PRESCHOOL, ONLY ONE OF US WAS ALLOWED. MY PARENTS THOUGHT IT WOULD BE BEST IF MY YOUNGER SISTER WENT.

SQUEAK SQUEAK

MY MOTHER DECIDED TO TAKE ME TO WORK. LUCKILY, SHE WAS AN ELEMENTARY SCHOOL TEACHER.

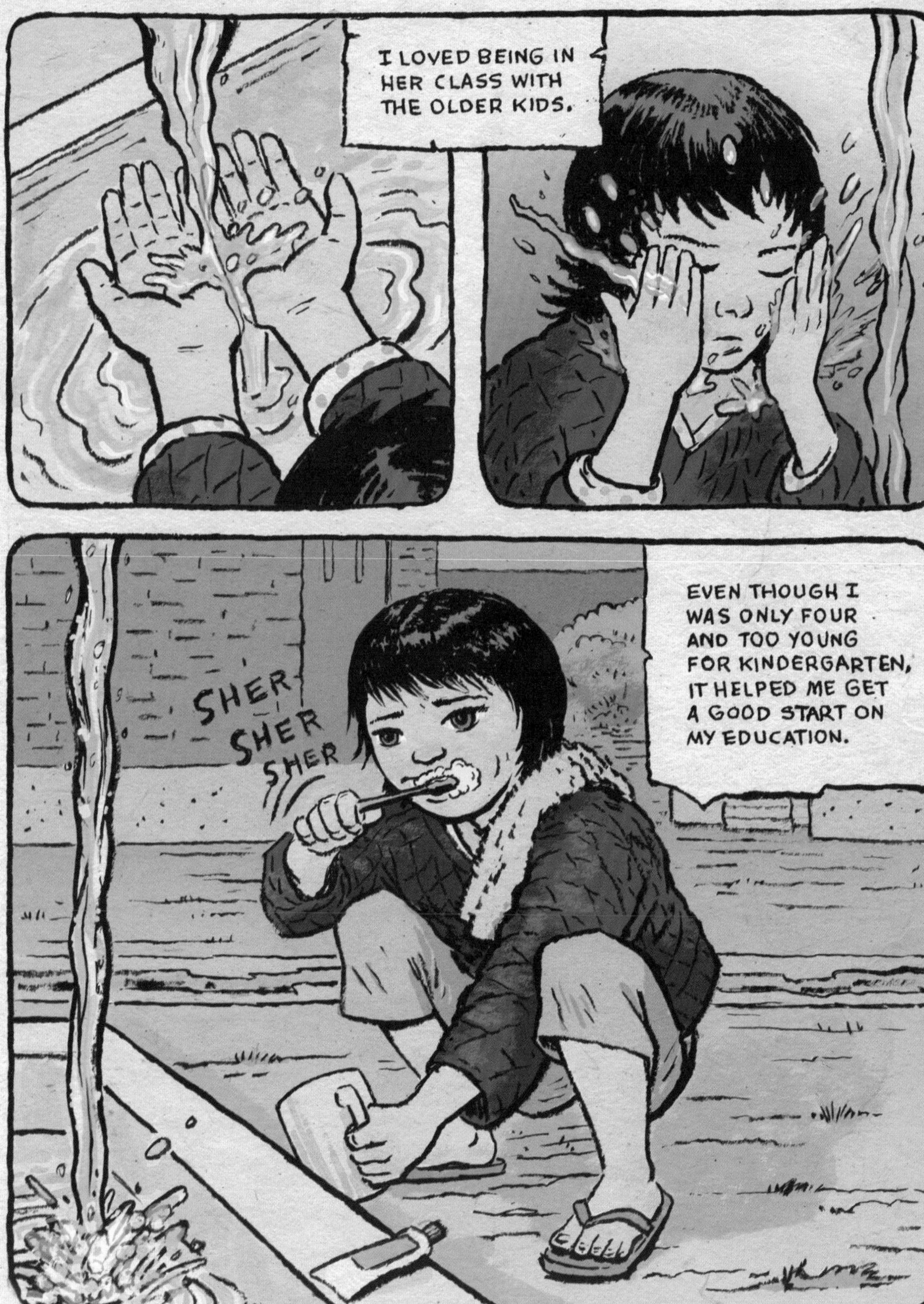

I LOVED BEING IN HER CLASS WITH THE OLDER KIDS.
EVEN THOUGH I WAS ONLY FOUR AND TOO YOUNG FOR KINDERGARTEN, IT HELPED ME GET A GOOD START ON MY EDUCATION.
SHER SHER SHER

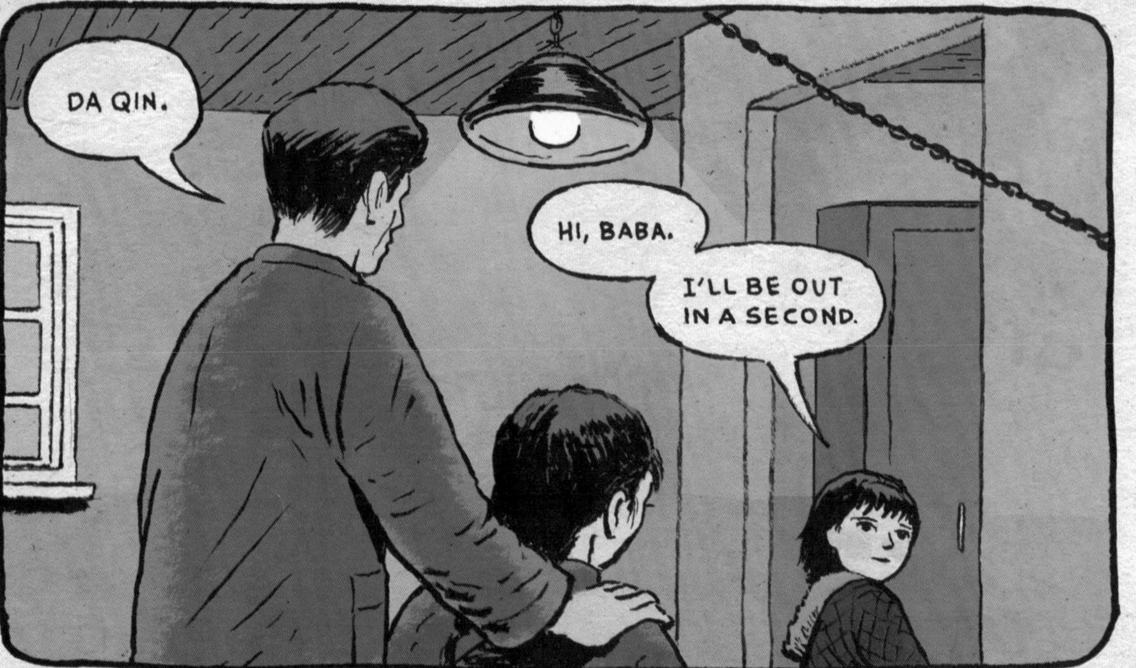
DA QIN.
HI, BABA.
I'LL BE OUT IN A SECOND.

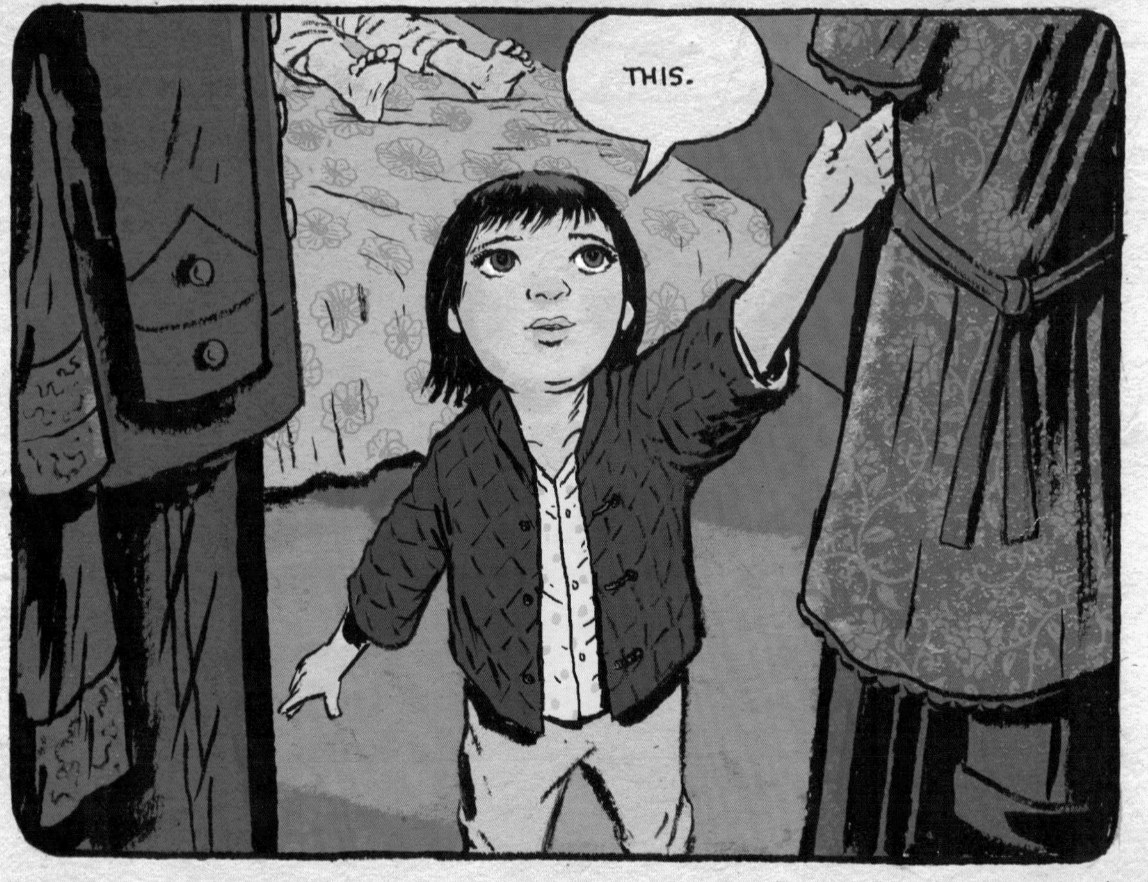
THIS.

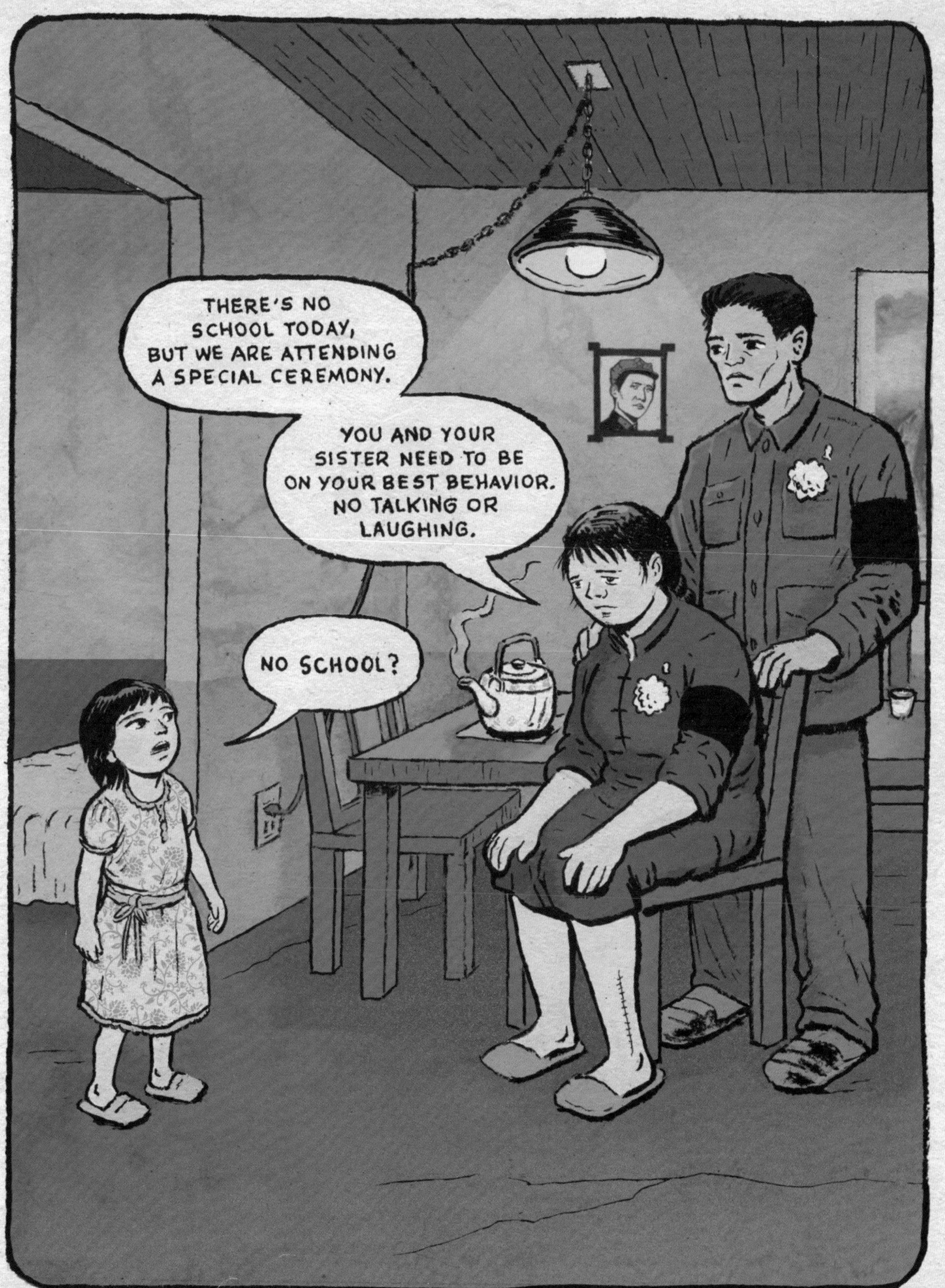
THERE'S NO SCHOOL TODAY, BUT WE ARE ATTENDING A SPECIAL CEREMONY.
YOU AND YOUR SISTER NEED TO BE ON YOUR BEST BEHAVIOR. NO TALKING OR LAUGHING.
NO SCHOOL?

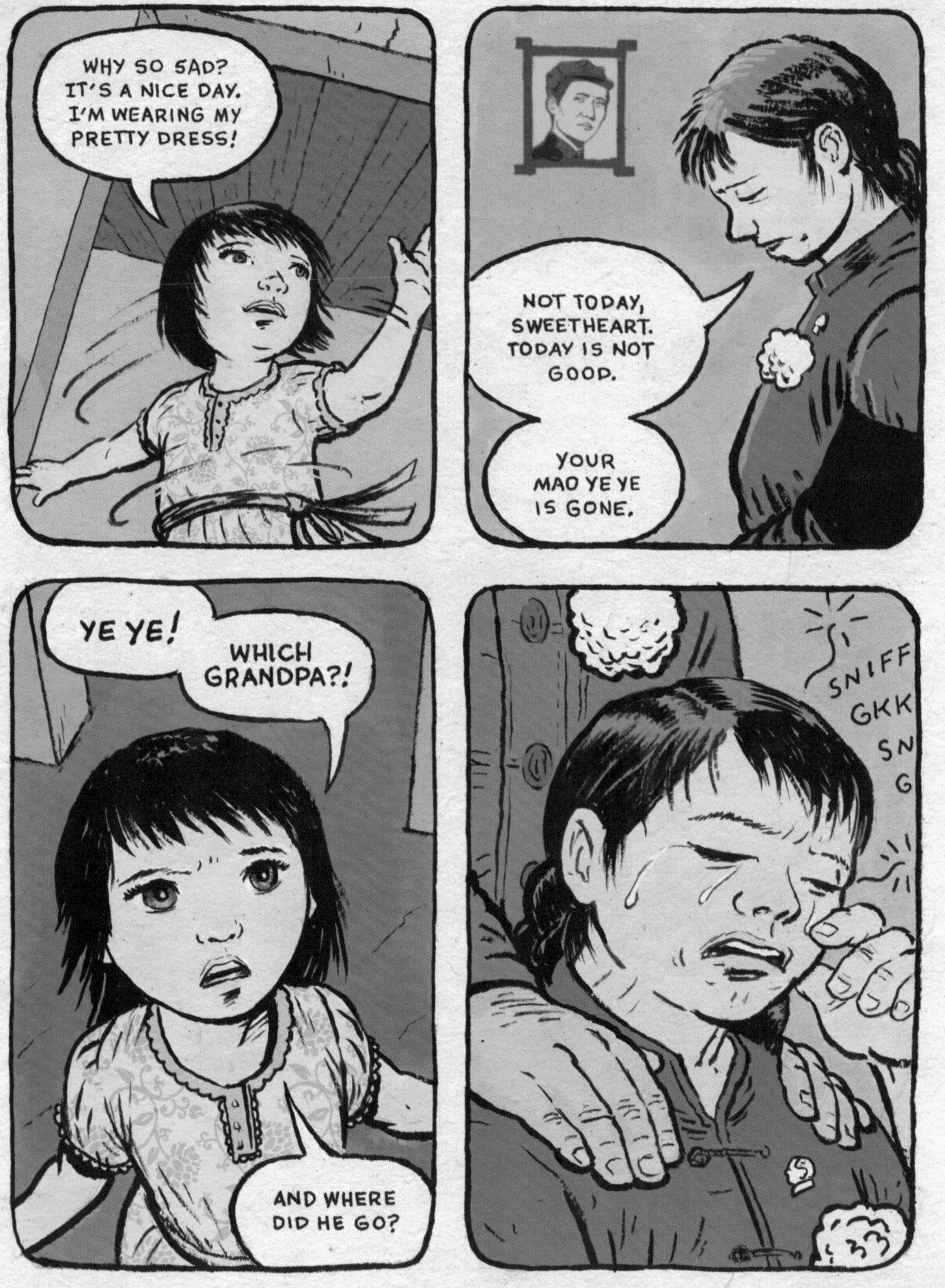
WHY SO SAD? IT'S A NICE DAY. I'M WEARING MY PRETTY DRESS!
NOT TODAY, SWEETHEART. TODAY IS NOT GOOD.
YOUR MAO YE YE IS GONE.
YE YE!
WHICH GRANDPA?!
AND WHERE DID HE GO?
SNIFF
GKK
SN
G

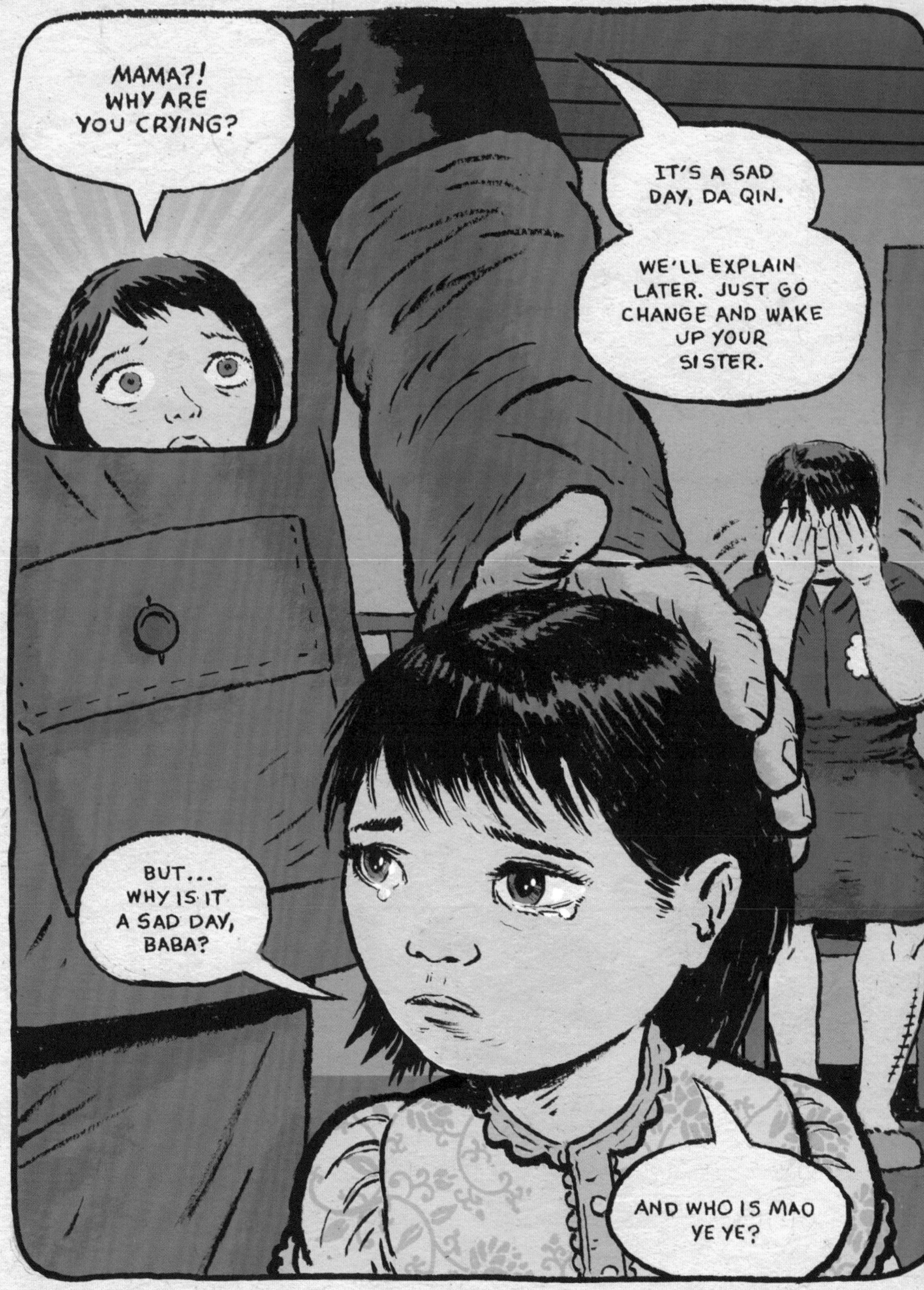
MAMA?! WHY ARE YOU CRYING?
IT'S A SAD DAY, DA QIN.
WE'LL EXPLAIN LATER. JUST GO CHANGE AND WAKE UP YOUR SISTER.
BUT... WHY IS IT A SAD DAY, BABA?
AND WHO IS MAO YE YE?

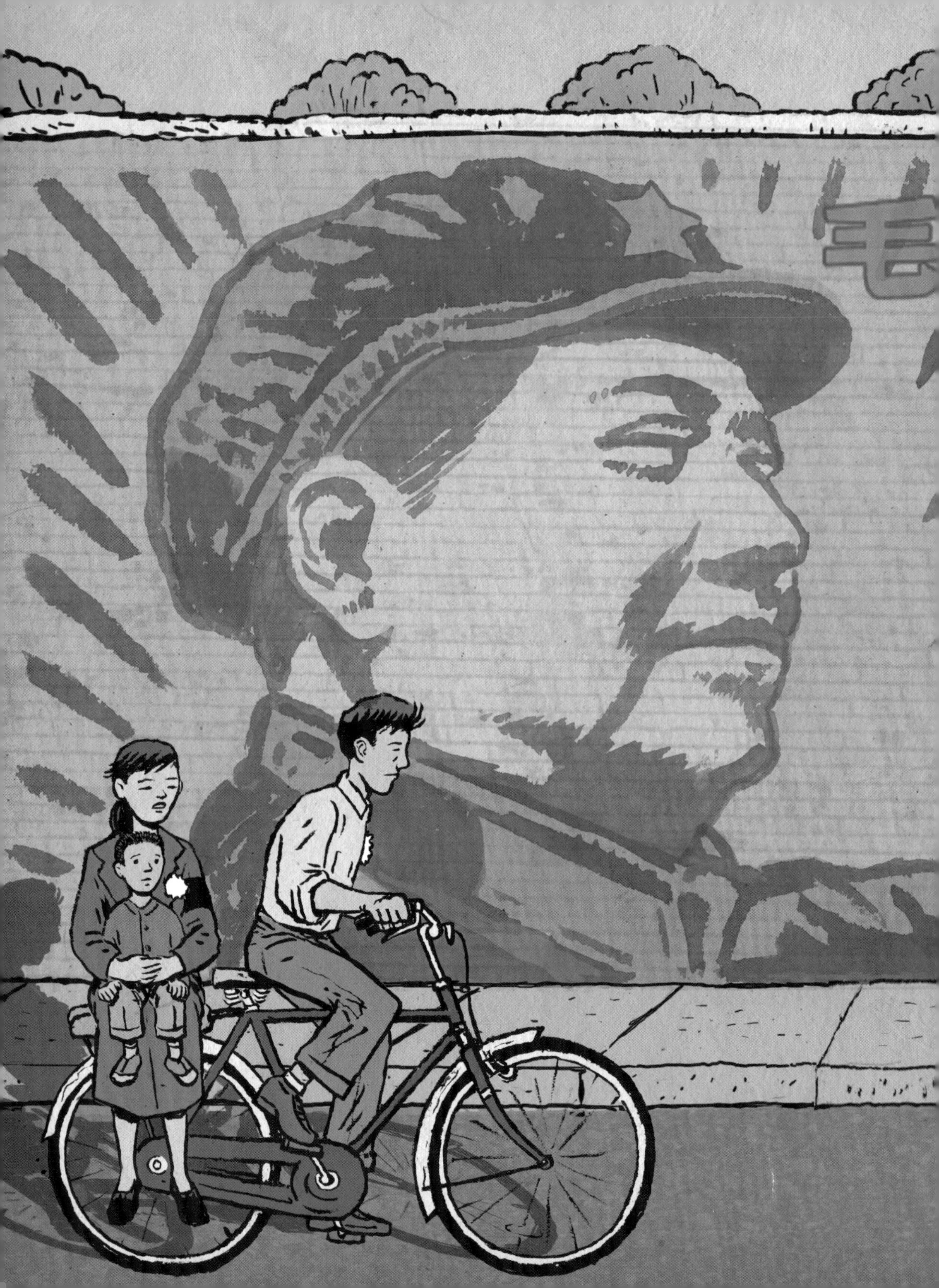
毛

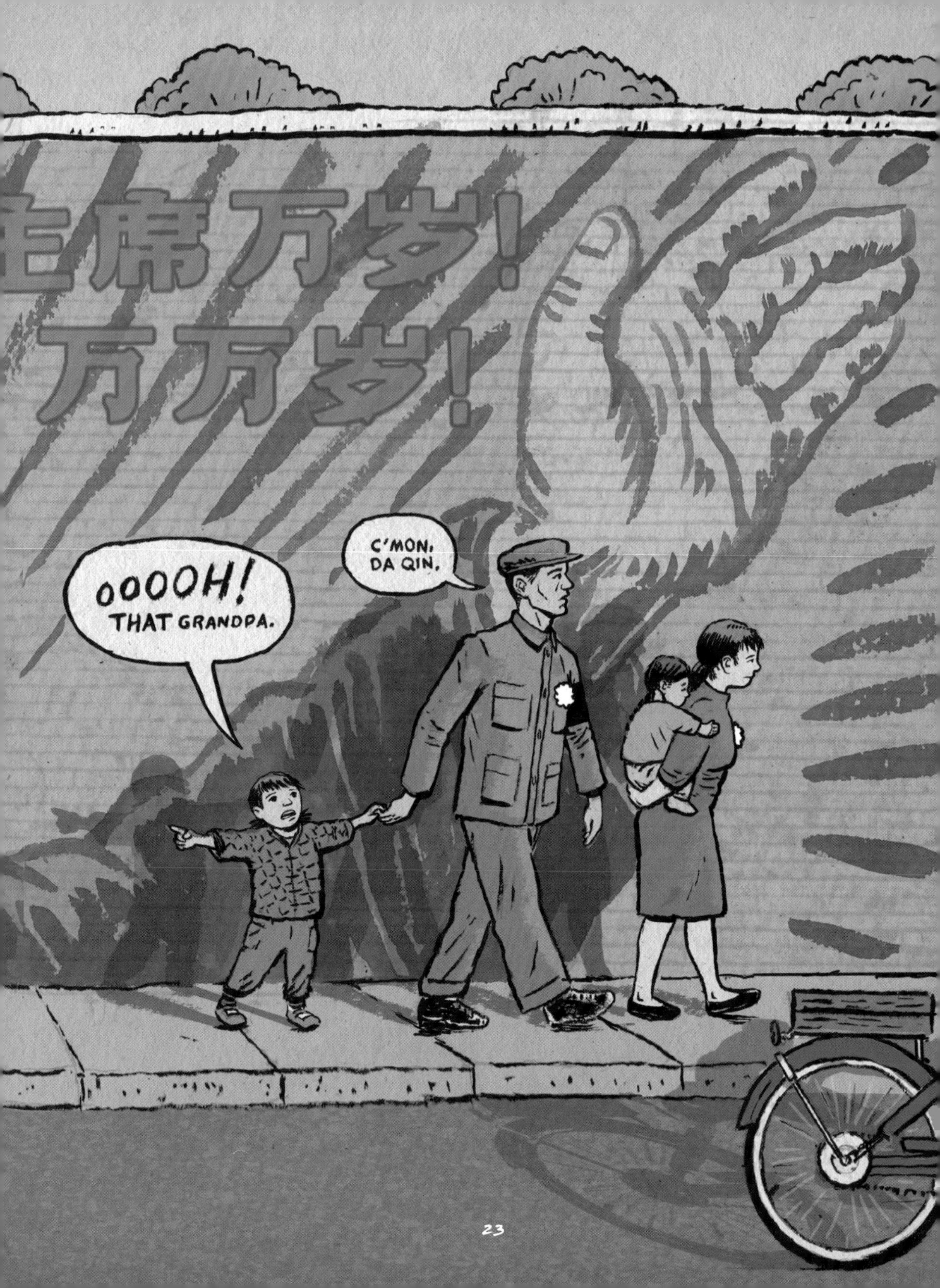
席万岁!
万万岁!
OOOOH! THAT GRANDPA.
C'MON, DA QIN.

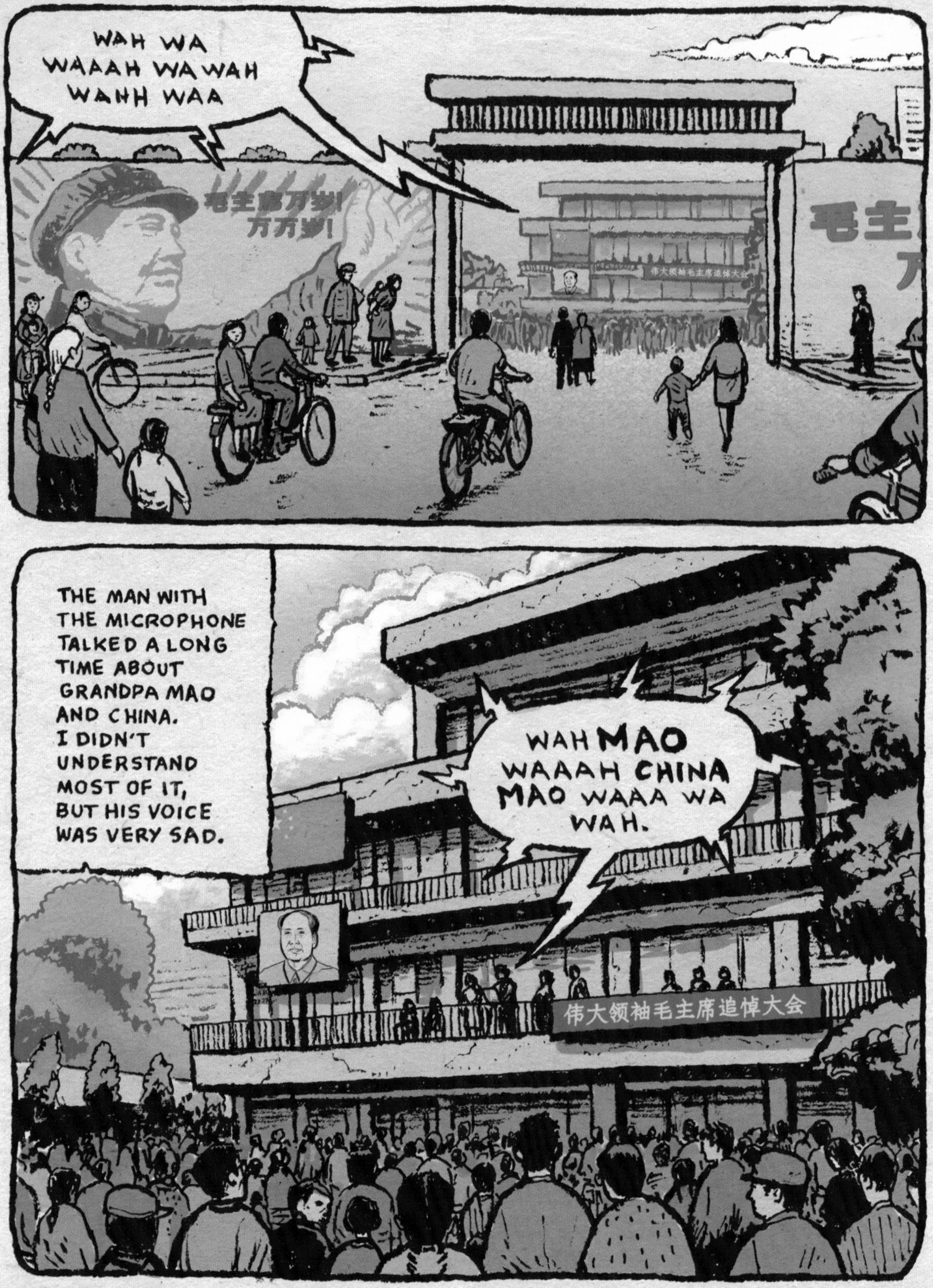
WAH WA
WAAAH WA WAH
WANH WAA
毛主席万岁！
万万岁！
伟大领袖毛主席追悼大会
THE MAN WITH THE MICROPHONE TALKED A LONG TIME ABOUT GRANDPA MAO AND CHINA. I DIDN'T UNDERSTAND MOST OF IT, BUT HIS VOICE WAS VERY SAD.
WAH MAO WAAAH CHINA MAO WAAA WA WAH.
伟大领袖毛主席追悼大会

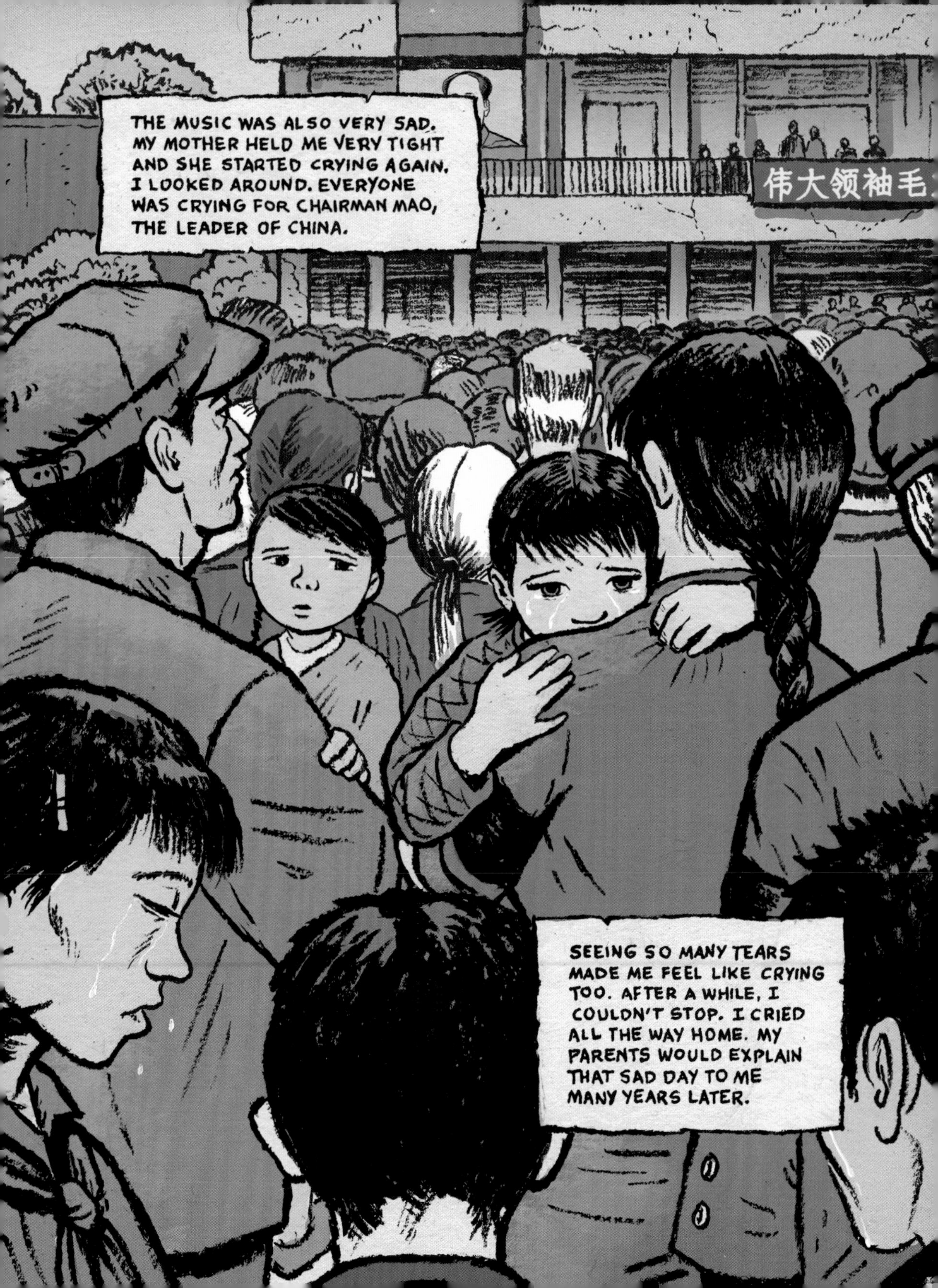
THE MUSIC WAS ALSO VERY SAD. MY MOTHER HELD ME VERY TIGHT AND SHE STARTED CRYING AGAIN. I LOOKED AROUND. EVERYONE WAS CRYING FOR CHAIRMAN MAO, THE LEADER OF CHINA.
伟大领袖毛
SEEING SO MANY TEARS MADE ME FEEL LIKE CRYING TOO. AFTER A WHILE, I COULDN'T STOP. I CRIED ALL THE WAY HOME. MY PARENTS WOULD EXPLAIN THAT SAD DAY TO ME MANY YEARS LATER.

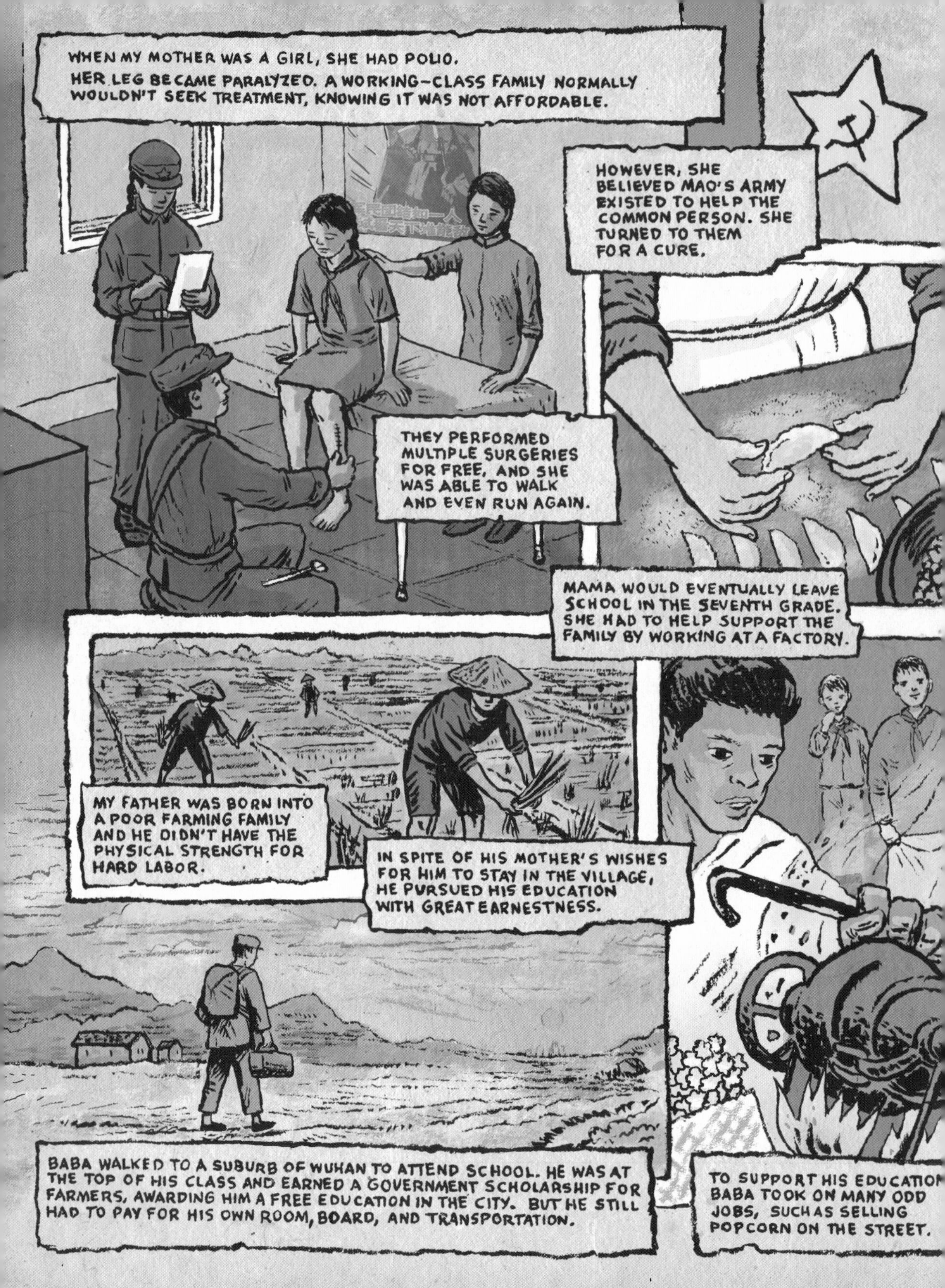
WHEN MY MOTHER WAS A GIRL, SHE HAD POLIO.
HER LEG BECAME PARALYZED. A WORKING-CLASS FAMILY NORMALLY WOULDN'T SEEK TREATMENT, KNOWING IT WAS NOT AFFORDABLE.
HOWEVER, SHE BELIEVED MAO'S ARMY EXISTED TO HELP THE COMMON PERSON. SHE TURNED TO THEM FOR A CURE.
THEY PERFORMED MULTIPLE SURGERIES FOR FREE, AND SHE WAS ABLE TO WALK AND EVEN RUN AGAIN.
MAMA WOULD EVENTUALLY LEAVE SCHOOL IN THE SEVENTH GRADE. SHE HAD TO HELP SUPPORT THE FAMILY BY WORKING AT A FACTORY.
MY FATHER WAS BORN INTO A POOR FARMING FAMILY AND HE DIDN'T HAVE THE PHYSICAL STRENGTH FOR HARD LABOR.
IN SPITE OF HIS MOTHER'S WISHES FOR HIM TO STAY IN THE VILLAGE, HE PURSUED HIS EDUCATION WITH GREAT EARNESTNESS.
BABA WALKED TO A SUBURB OF WUHAN TO ATTEND SCHOOL. HE WAS AT THE TOP OF HIS CLASS AND EARNED A GOVERNMENT SCHOLARSHIP FOR FARMERS, AWARDING HIM A FREE EDUCATION IN THE CITY. BUT HE STILL HAD TO PAY FOR HIS OWN ROOM, BOARD, AND TRANSPORTATION.
TO SUPPORT HIS EDUCATION BABA TOOK ON MANY ODD JOBS, SUCH AS SELLING POPCORN ON THE STREET.

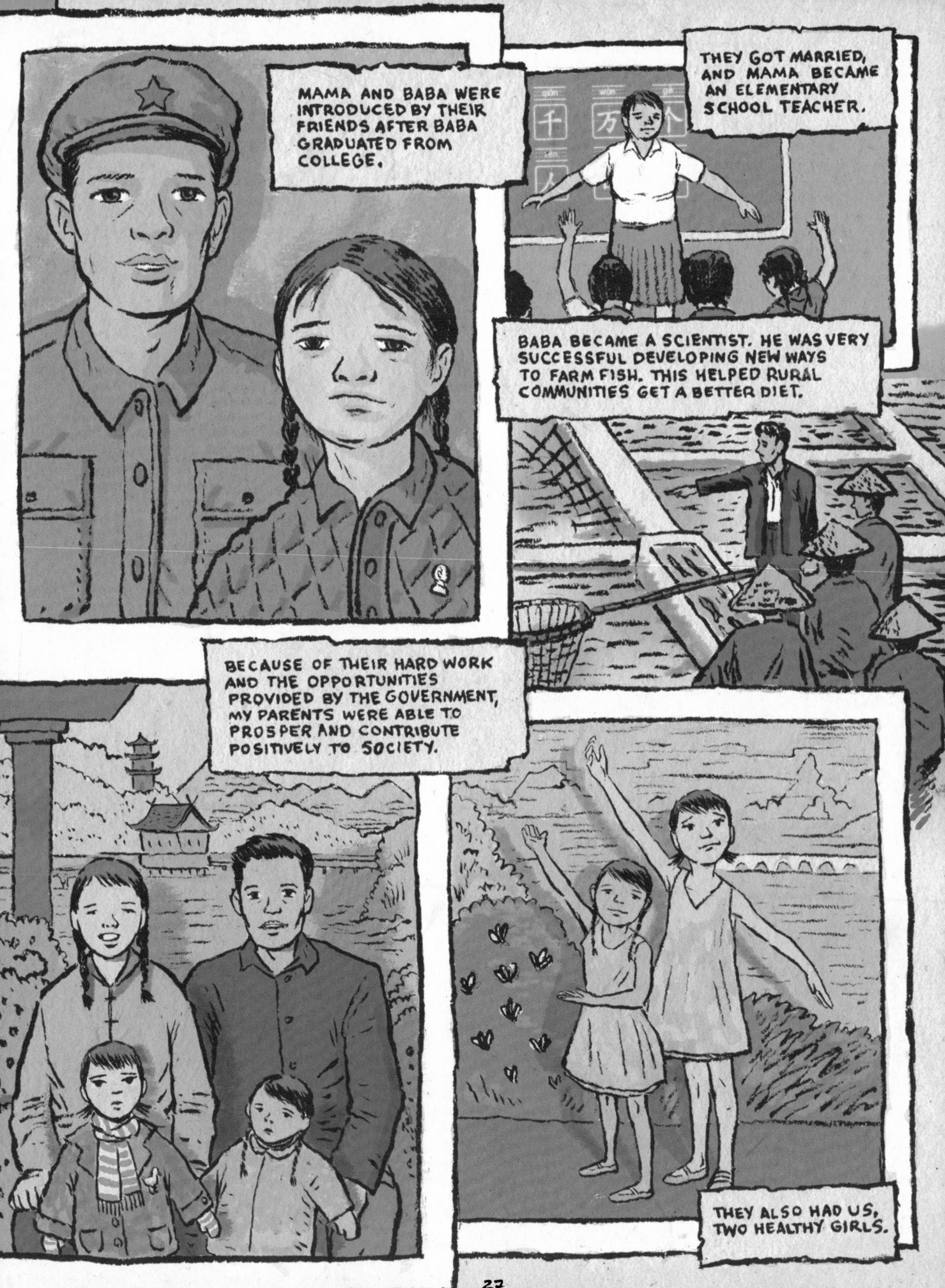
MAMA AND BABA WERE INTRODUCED BY THEIR FRIENDS AFTER BABA GRADUATED FROM COLLEGE.
THEY GOT MARRIED, AND MAMA BECAME AN ELEMENTARY SCHOOL TEACHER.
BABA BECAME A SCIENTIST. HE WAS VERY SUCCESSFUL DEVELOPING NEW WAYS TO FARM FISH. THIS HELPED RURAL COMMUNITIES GET A BETTER DIET.
BECAUSE OF THEIR HARD WORK AND THE OPPORTUNITIES PROVIDED BY THE GOVERNMENT, MY PARENTS WERE ABLE TO PROSPER AND CONTRIBUTE POSITIVELY TO SOCIETY.
THEY ALSO HAD US, TWO HEALTHY GIRLS.

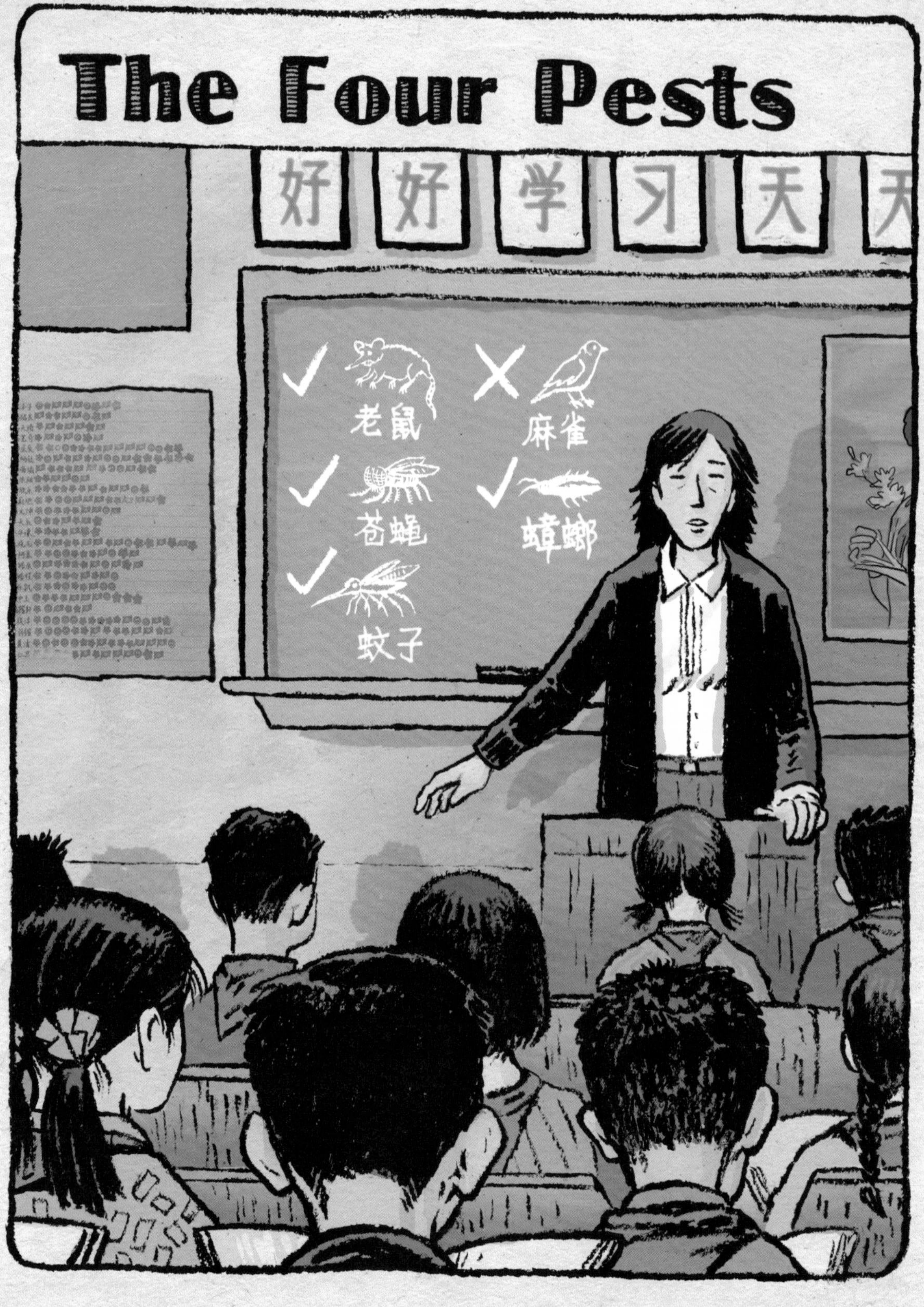
The Four Pests
好好学习天
老鼠
麻雀
苍蝇
蟑螂
蚊子

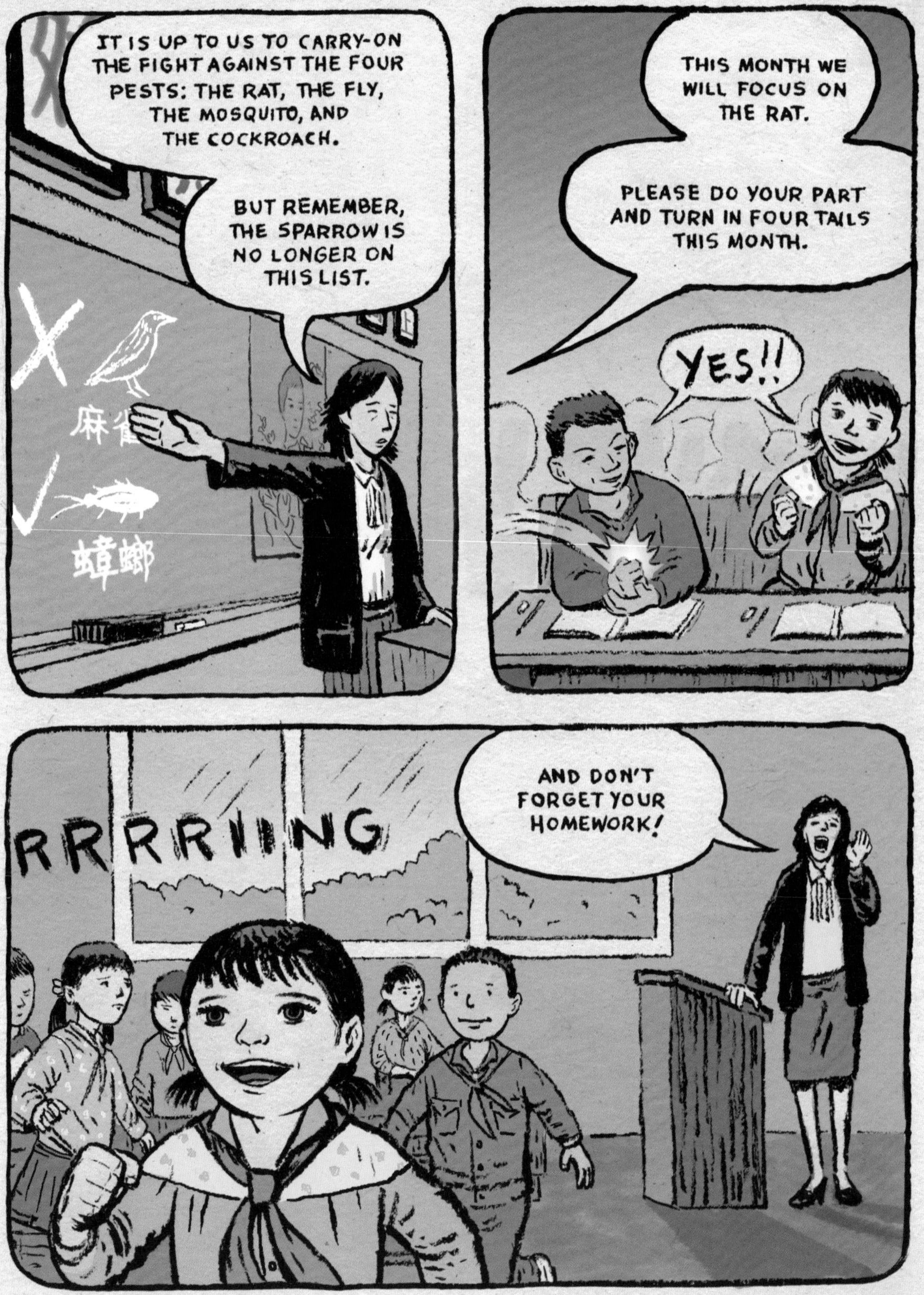

IT IS UP TO US TO CARRY-ON THE FIGHT AGAINST THE FOUR PESTS: THE RAT, THE FLY, THE MOSQUITO, AND THE COCKROACH.
BUT REMEMBER, THE SPARROW IS NO LONGER ON THIS LIST.
麻雀
蟑螂
THIS MONTH WE WILL FOCUS ON THE RAT.
PLEASE DO YOUR PART AND TURN IN FOUR TAILS THIS MONTH.
YES!!
RRRRIIING
AND DON'T FORGET YOUR HOMEWORK!

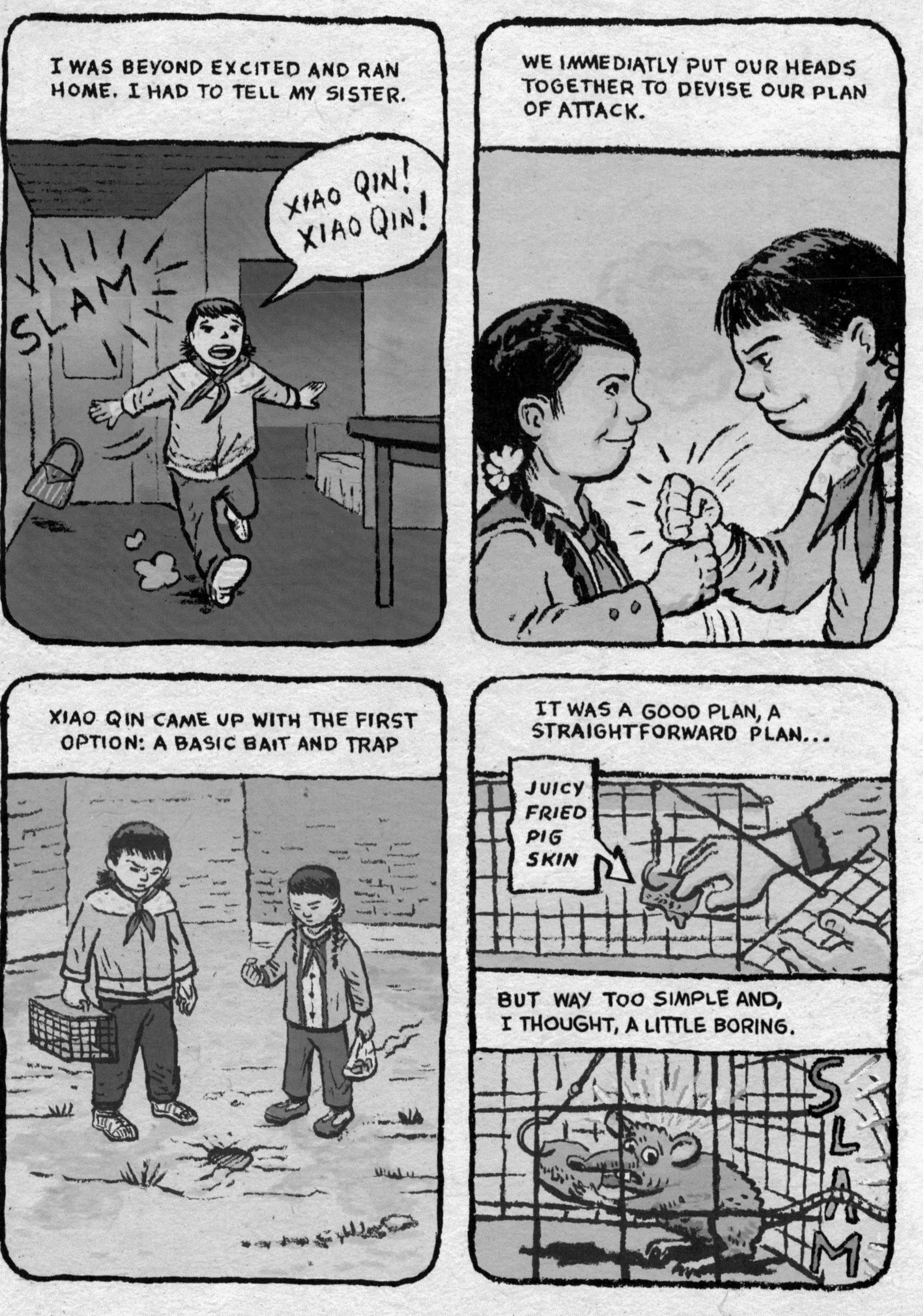
I WAS BEYOND EXCITED AND RAN HOME. I HAD TO TELL MY SISTER.
XIAO QIN! XIAO QIN!
SLAM
WE IMMEDIATLY PUT OUR HEADS TOGETHER TO DEVISE OUR PLAN OF ATTACK.
XIAO QIN CAME UP WITH THE FIRST OPTION: A BASIC BAIT AND TRAP
IT WAS A GOOD PLAN, A STRAIGHTFORWARD PLAN...
JUICY FRIED PIG SKIN
BUT WAY TOO SIMPLE AND, I THOUGHT, A LITTLE BORING.
SLAM

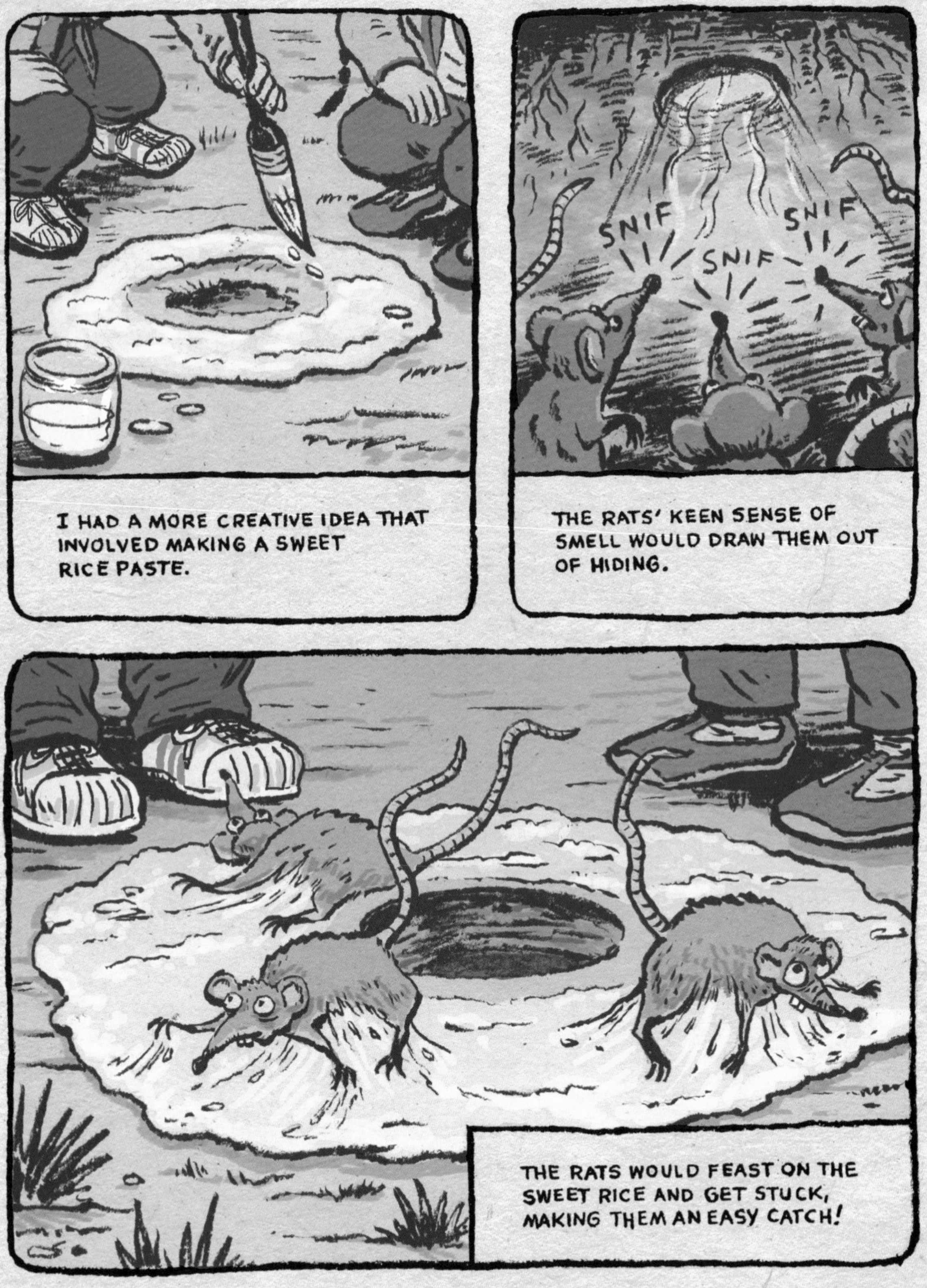
I HAD A MORE CREATIVE IDEA THAT INVOLVED MAKING A SWEET RICE PASTE.
SNIF
SNIF
SNIF
THE RATS' KEEN SENSE OF SMELL WOULD DRAW THEM OUT OF HIDING.
THE RATS WOULD FEAST ON THE SWEET RICE AND GET STUCK, MAKING THEM AN EASY CATCH!

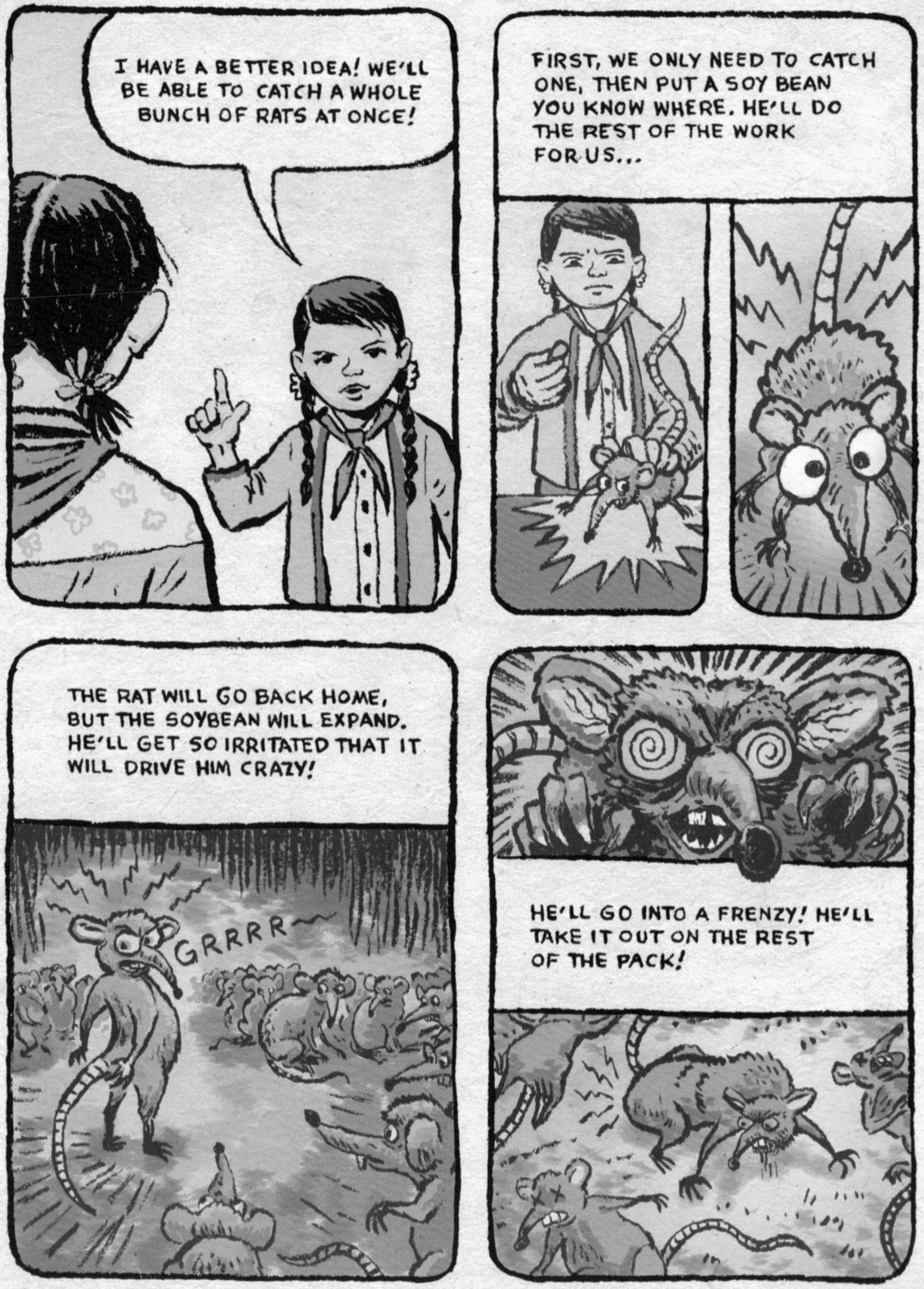
I HAVE A BETTER IDEA! WE'LL BE ABLE TO CATCH A WHOLE BUNCH OF RATS AT ONCE!
FIRST, WE ONLY NEED TO CATCH ONE, THEN PUT A SOY BEAN YOU KNOW WHERE. HE'LL DO THE REST OF THE WORK FOR US...
THE RAT WILL GO BACK HOME, BUT THE SOYBEAN WILL EXPAND. HE'LL GET SO IRRITATED THAT IT WILL DRIVE HIM CRAZY!
GRRRR
HE'LL GO INTO A FRENZY! HE'LL TAKE IT OUT ON THE REST OF THE PACK!

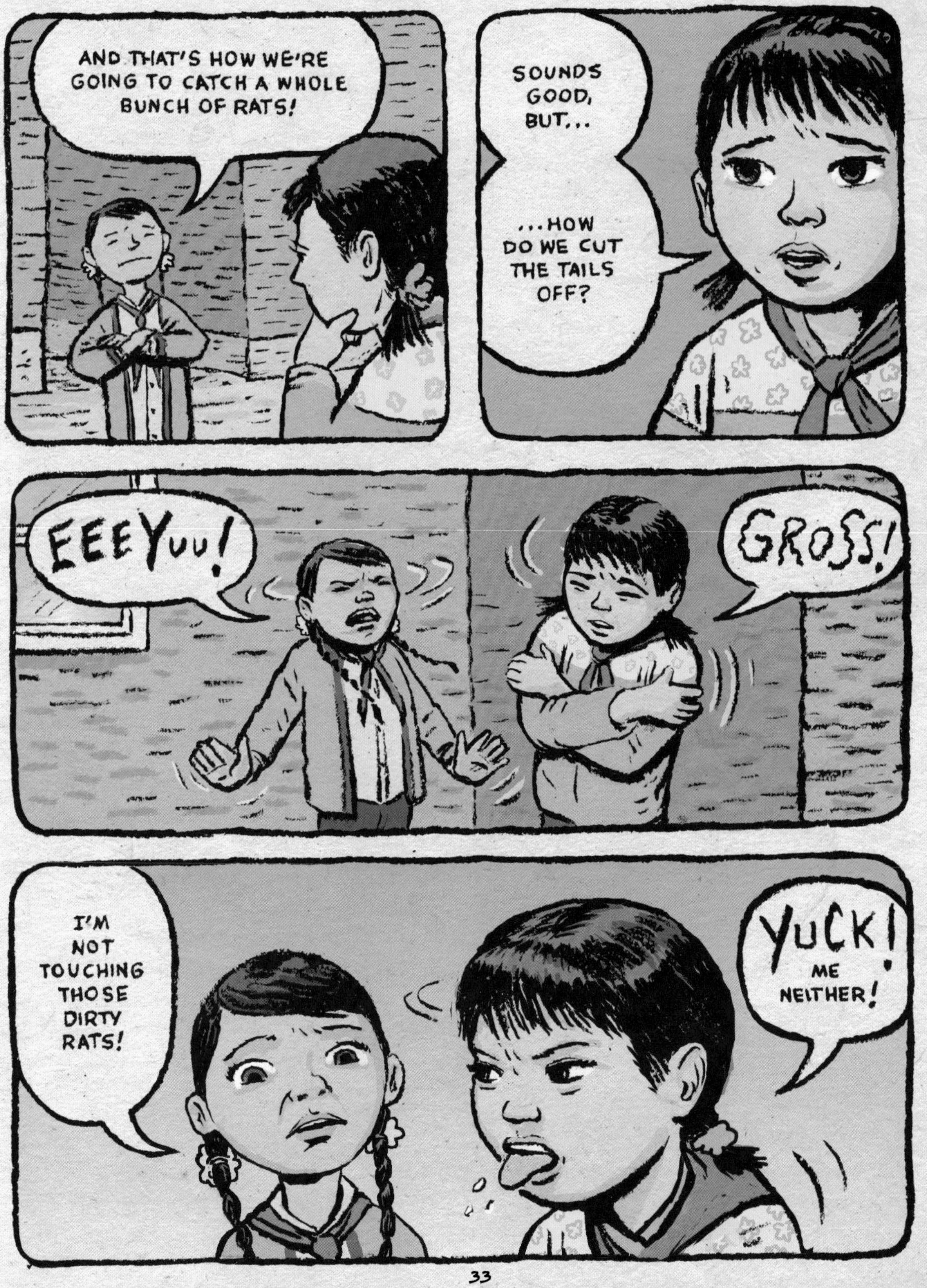
AND THAT'S HOW WE'RE GOING TO CATCH A WHOLE BUNCH OF RATS!
SOUNDS GOOD, BUT...
...HOW DO WE CUT THE TAILS OFF?
EEEYuu!
GROSS!
I'M NOT TOUCHING THOSE DIRTY RATS!
YuCK!
ME NEITHER!

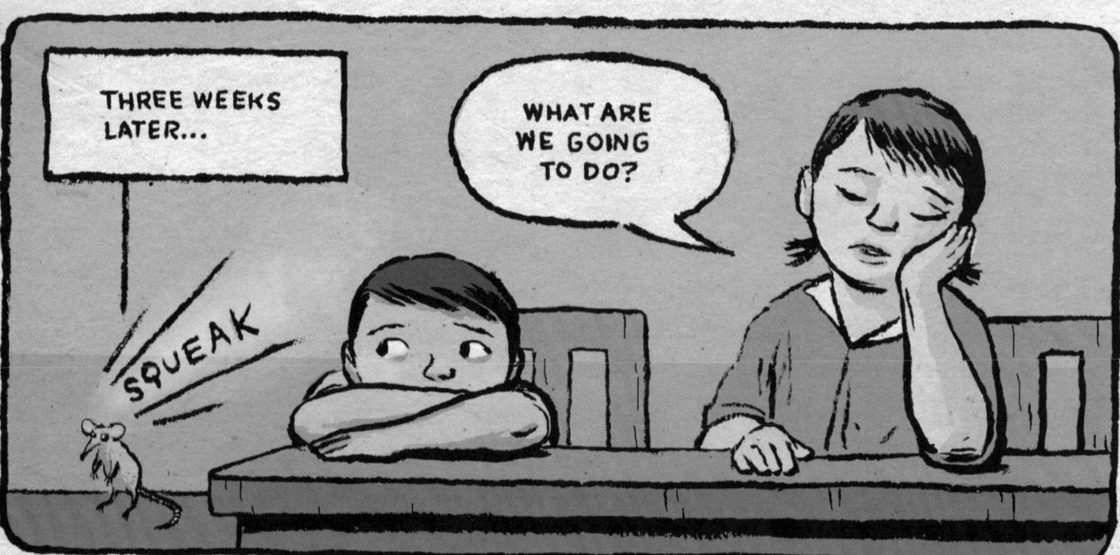
THREE WEEKS LATER...
WHAT ARE WE GOING TO DO?
SQUEAK

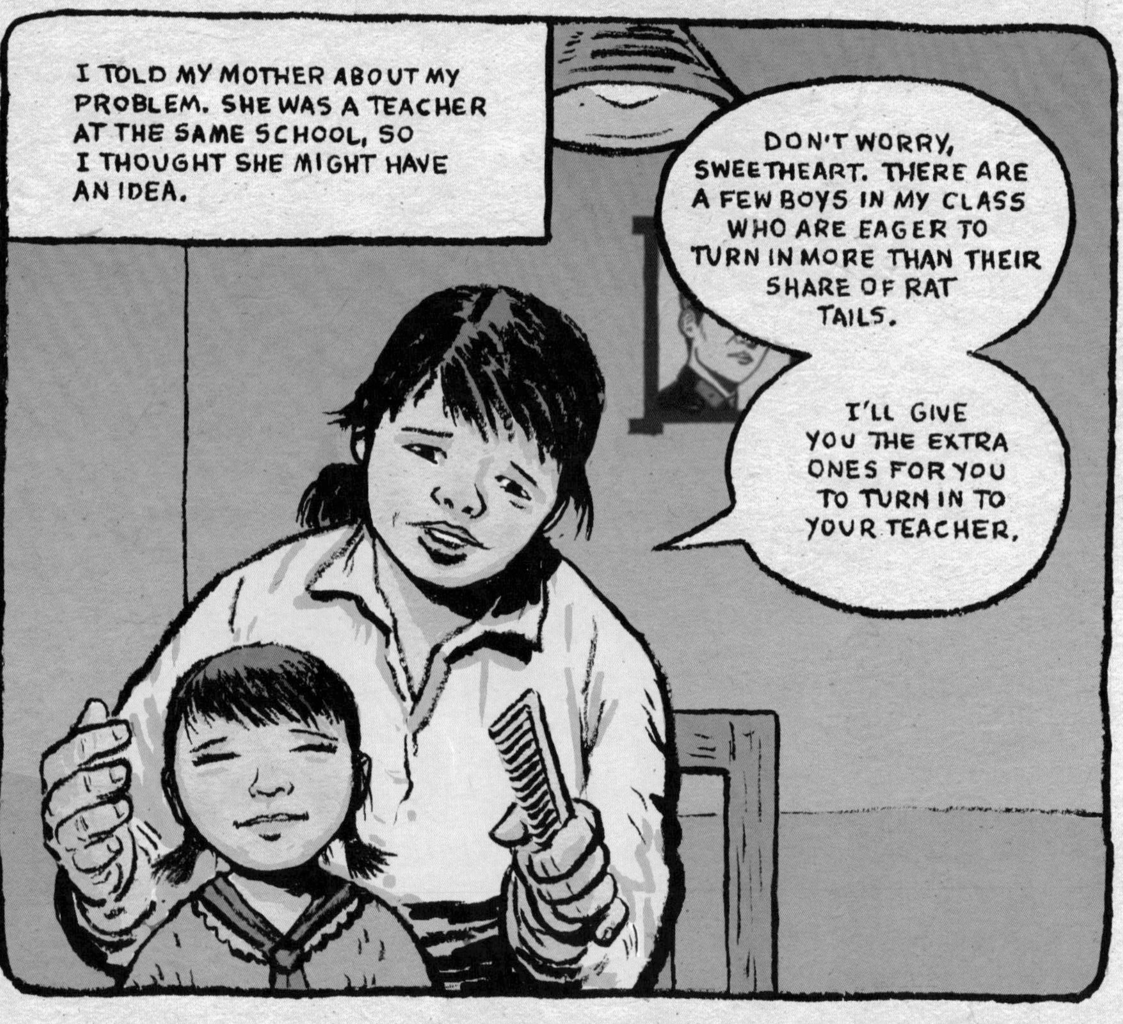
I TOLD MY MOTHER ABOUT MY PROBLEM. SHE WAS A TEACHER AT THE SAME SCHOOL, SO I THOUGHT SHE MIGHT HAVE AN IDEA.
DON'T WORRY, SWEETHEART. THERE ARE A FEW BOYS IN MY CLASS WHO ARE EAGER TO TURN IN MORE THAN THEIR SHARE OF RAT TAILS.
I'LL GIVE YOU THE EXTRA ONES FOR YOU TO TURN IN TO YOUR TEACHER.

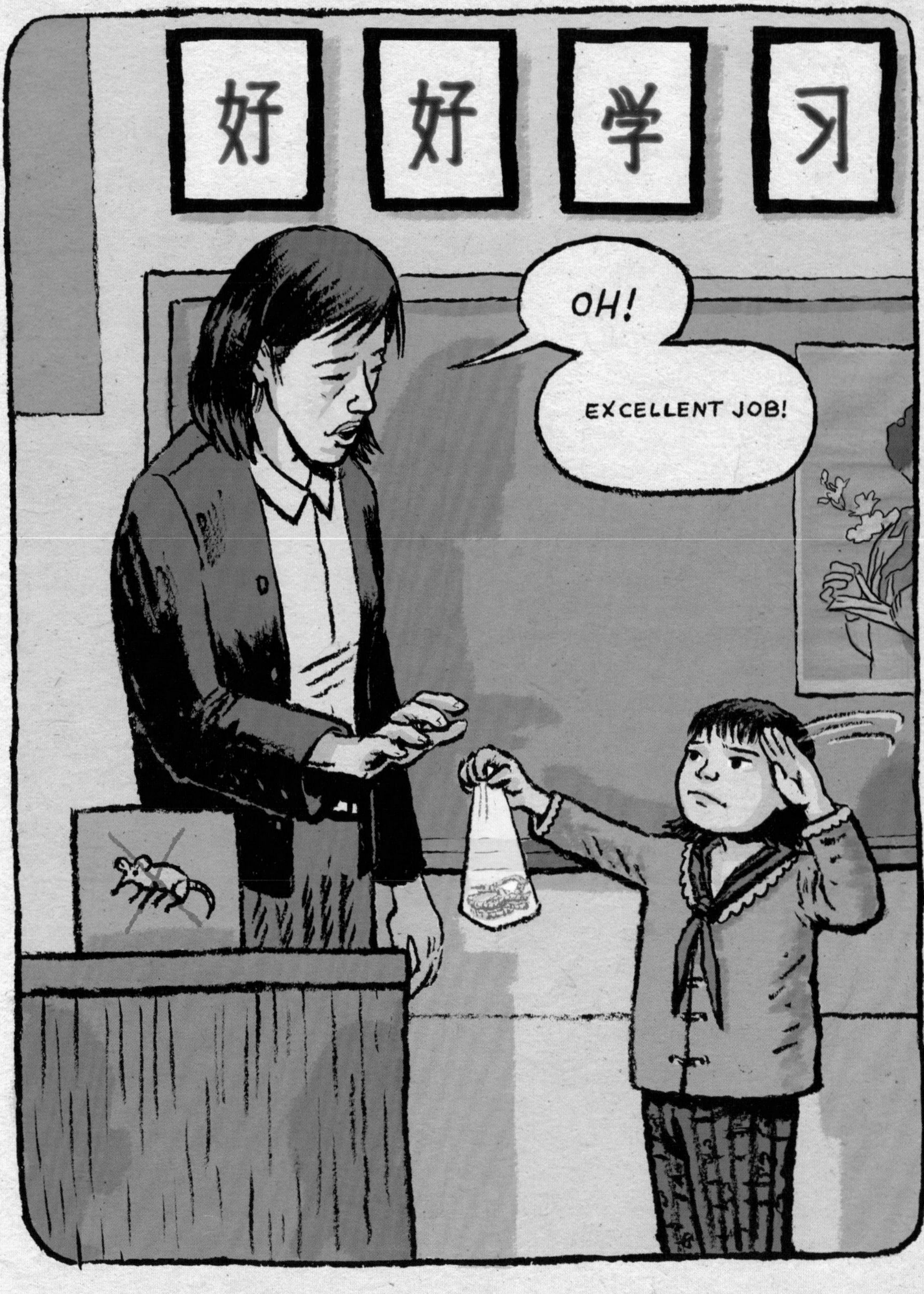
好好学习
OH!
EXCELLENT JOB!

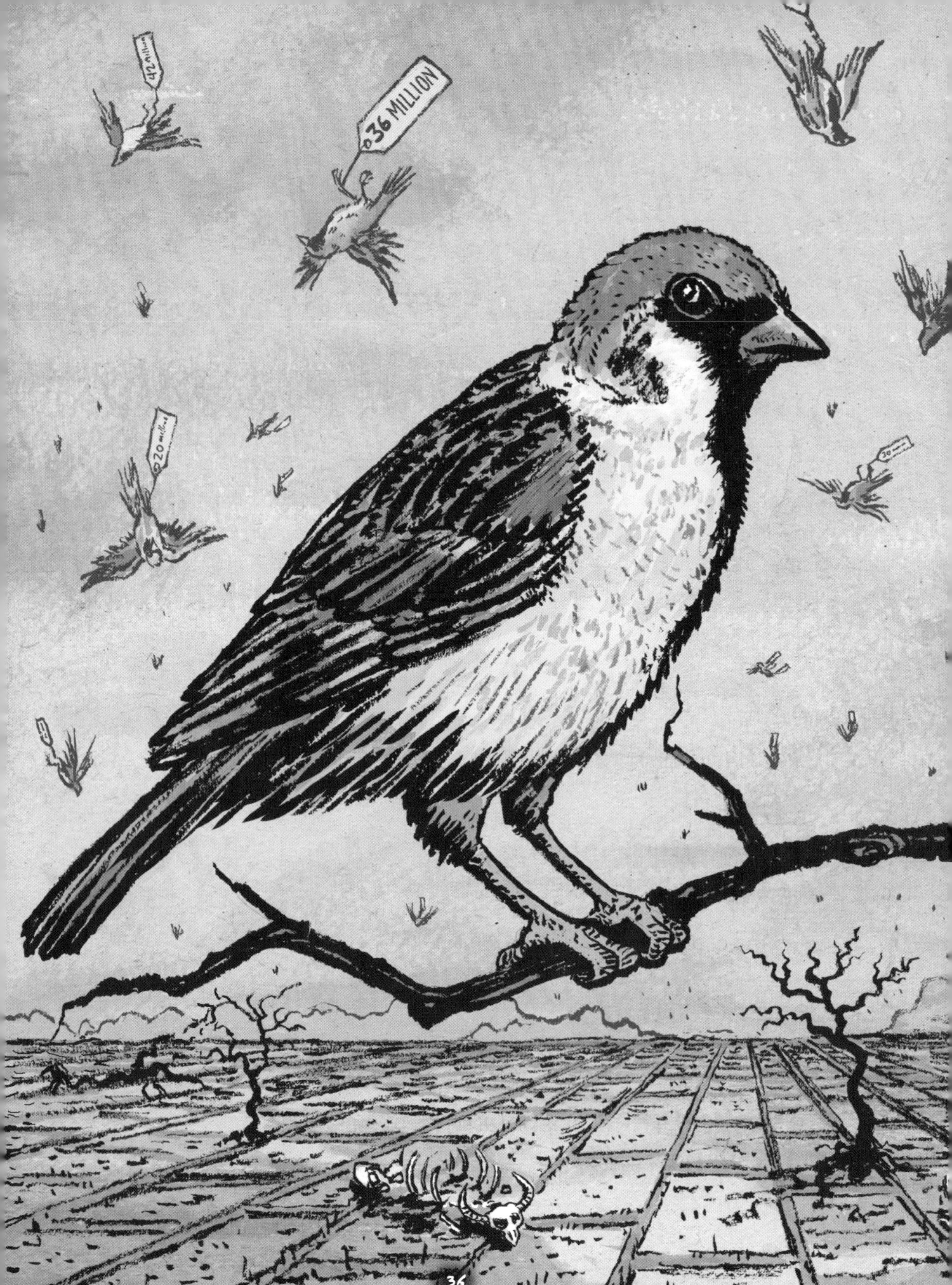
42 million
36 MILLION
20

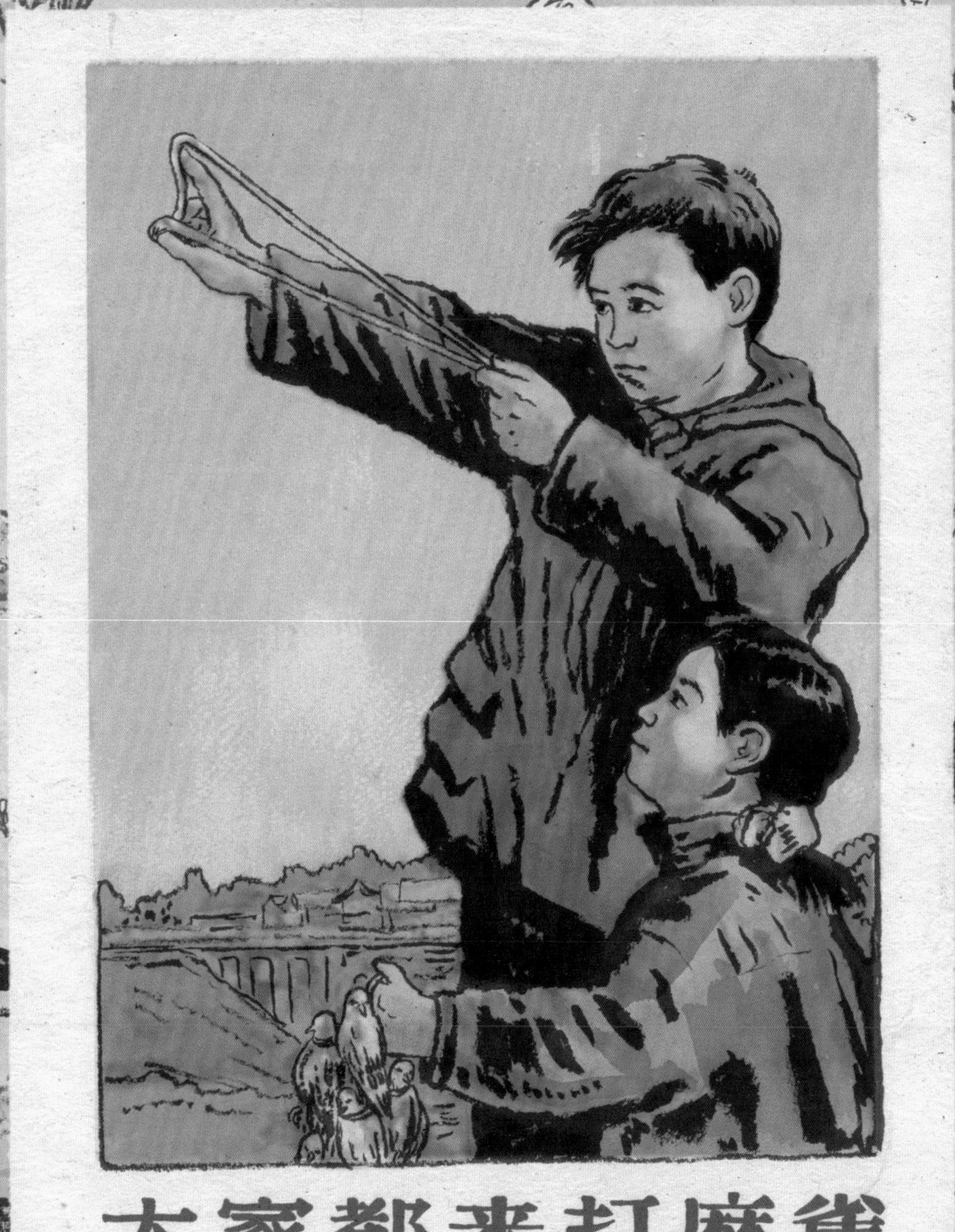
大家都来打麻雀

SPARROWS WERE ORIGINALLY ONE OF THE FOUR PESTS BECAUSE THEY EAT GRAINS FROM CROPS. WHEN MY PARENTS WERE YOUNG, MAO ENCOURAGED PEOPLE TO KILL AS MANY BIRDS AS THEY COULD. BUT SPARROWS EAT MORE INSECTS THAN GRAINS. WITH NO BIRDS TO KEEP THEM UNDER CONTROL, CROP-EATING INSECTS SUCH AS LOCUSTS MULTIPLIED. THE ORIGINAL PROBLEM BECAME A DISASTER THAT HELPED CAUSE THE GREAT CHINESE FAMINE. WHEN ALMOST ALL THE SPARROWS WERE GONE, COCKROACHES TOOK THEIR PLACE AS ONE OF THE FOUR PESTS.

"Don't Waste Your Food—Children Are Starving in China"

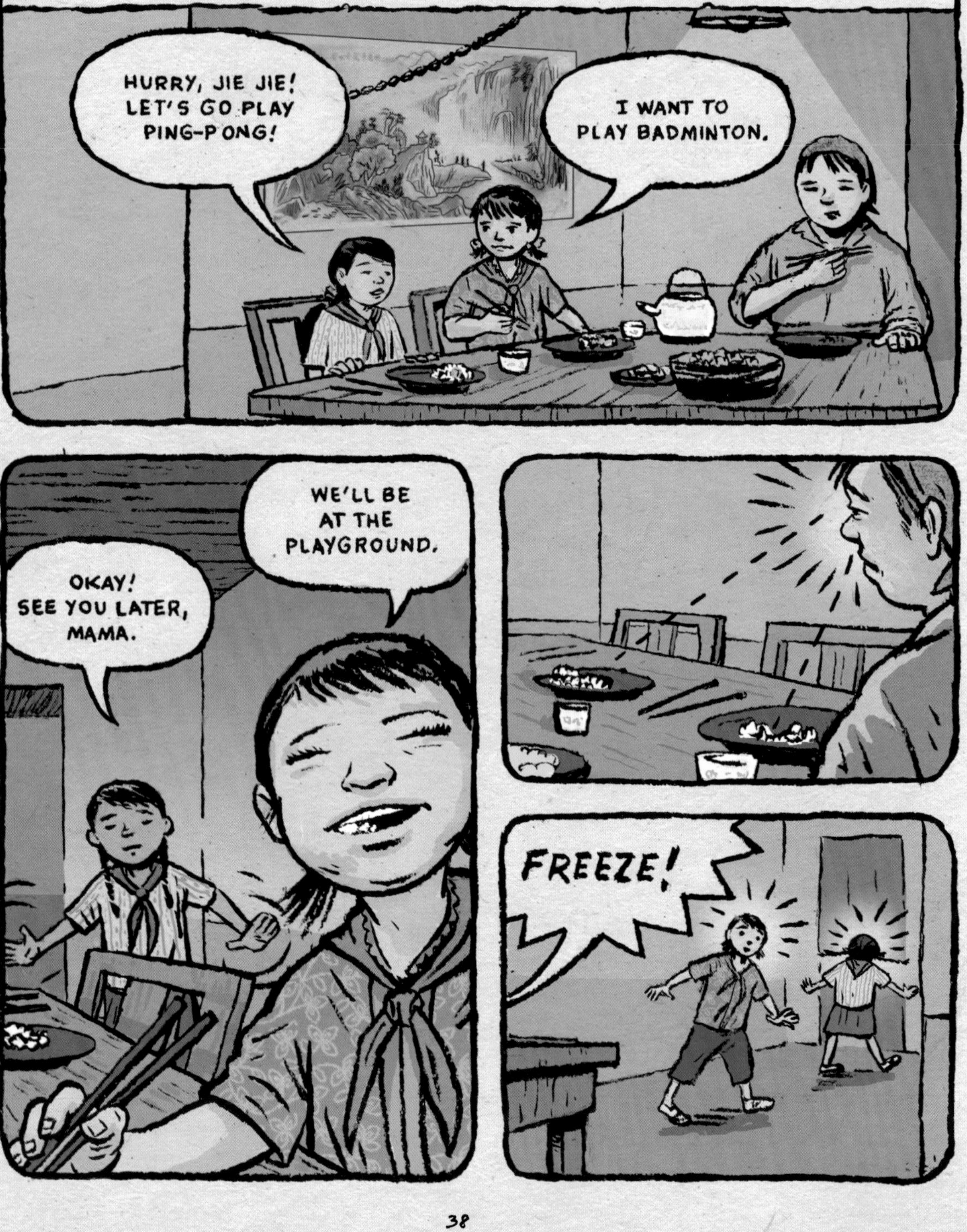
HURRY, JIE JIE! LET'S GO PLAY PING-PONG!
I WANT TO PLAY BADMINTON.
OKAY! SEE YOU LATER, MAMA.
WE'LL BE AT THE PLAYGROUND.
FREEZE!

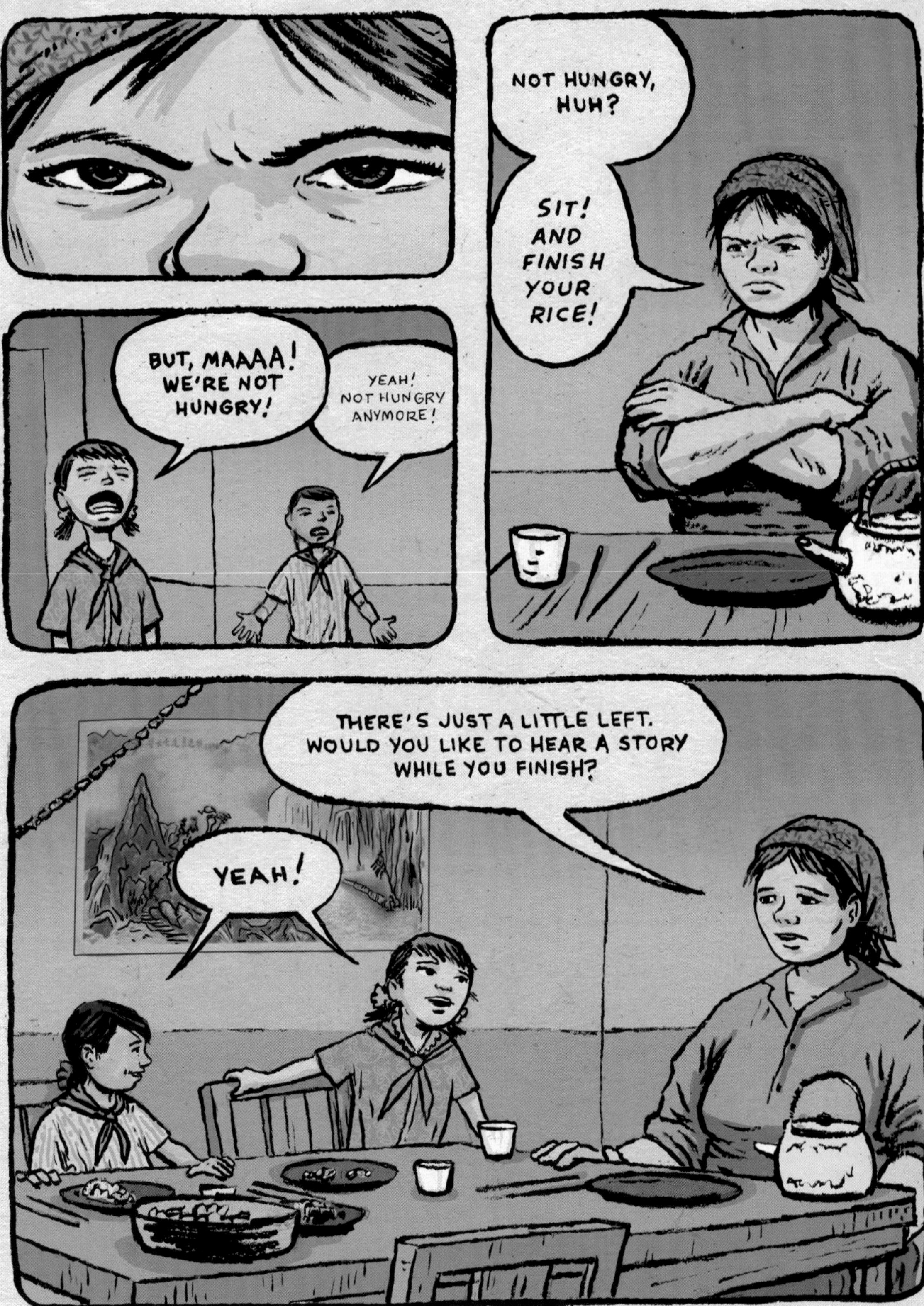
NOT HUNGRY, HUH?
SIT! AND FINISH YOUR RICE!
BUT, MAAAA! WE'RE NOT HUNGRY!
YEAH! NOT HUNGRY ANYMORE!
THERE'S JUST A LITTLE LEFT. WOULD YOU LIKE TO HEAR A STORY WHILE YOU FINISH?
YEAH!

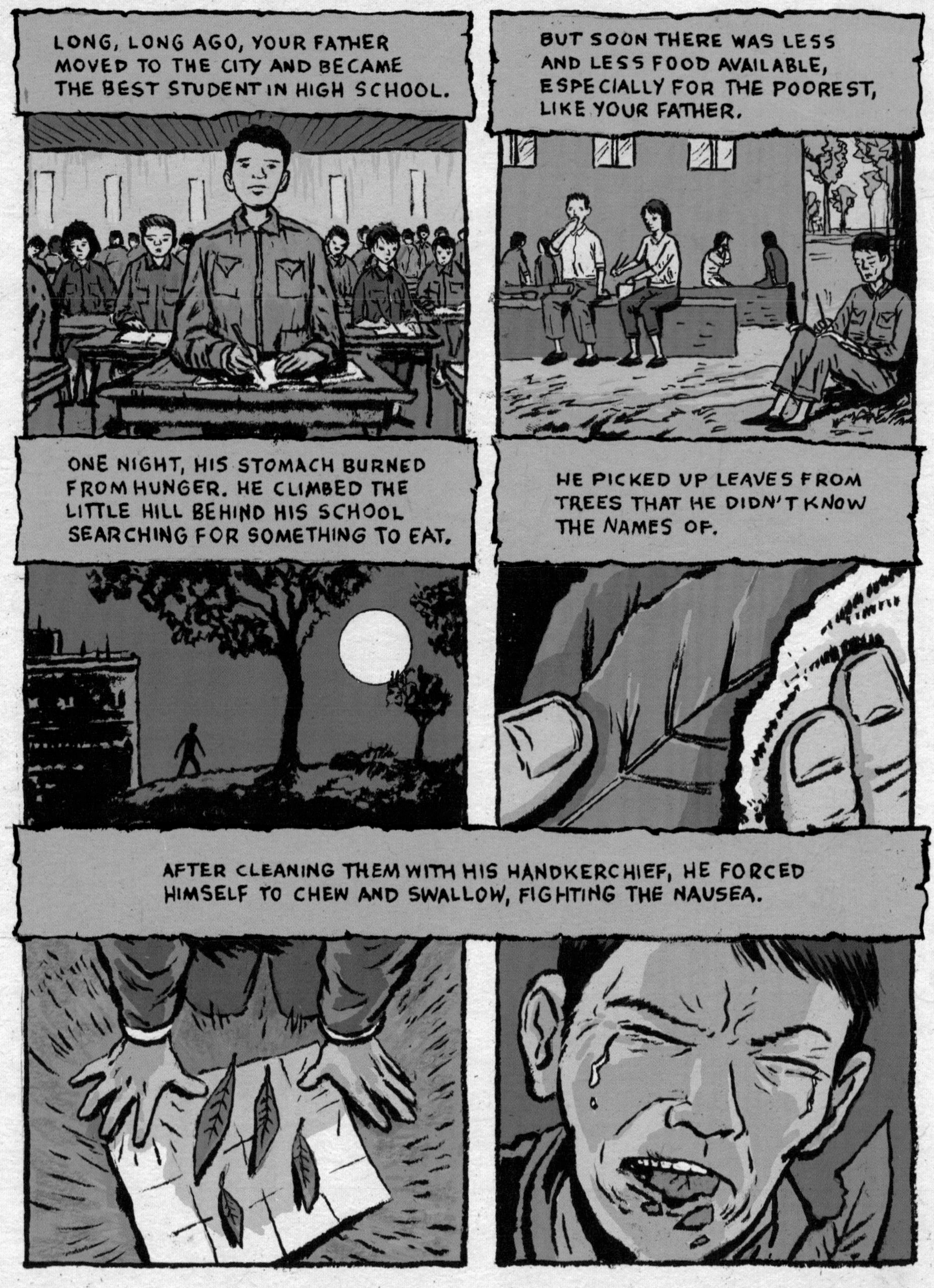
LONG, LONG AGO, YOUR FATHER MOVED TO THE CITY AND BECAME THE BEST STUDENT IN HIGH SCHOOL.
BUT SOON THERE WAS LESS AND LESS FOOD AVAILABLE, ESPECIALLY FOR THE POOREST, LIKE YOUR FATHER.
ONE NIGHT, HIS STOMACH BURNED FROM HUNGER. HE CLIMBED THE LITTLE HILL BEHIND HIS SCHOOL SEARCHING FOR SOMETHING TO EAT.
HE PICKED UP LEAVES FROM TREES THAT HE DIDN'T KNOW THE NAMES OF.
AFTER CLEANING THEM WITH HIS HANDKERCHIEF, HE FORCED HIMSELF TO CHEW AND SWALLOW, FIGHTING THE NAUSEA.

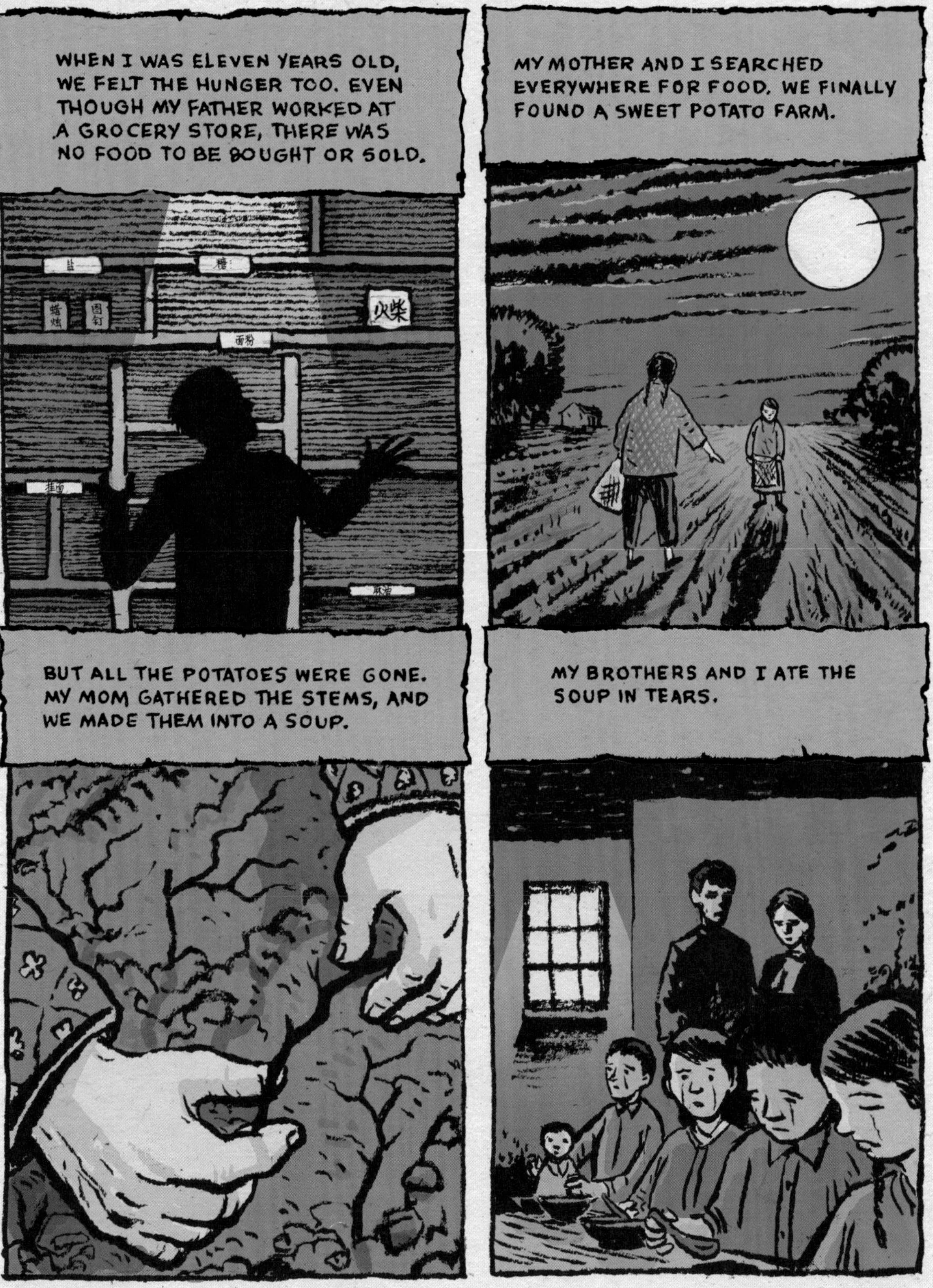
WHEN I WAS ELEVEN YEARS OLD, WE FELT THE HUNGER TOO. EVEN THOUGH MY FATHER WORKED AT A GROCERY STORE, THERE WAS NO FOOD TO BE BOUGHT OR SOLD.
糖
火柴
面粉
MY MOTHER AND I SEARCHED EVERYWHERE FOR FOOD. WE FINALLY FOUND A SWEET POTATO FARM.
BUT ALL THE POTATOES WERE GONE. MY MOM GATHERED THE STEMS, AND WE MADE THEM INTO A SOUP.
MY BROTHERS AND I ATE THE SOUP IN TEARS.

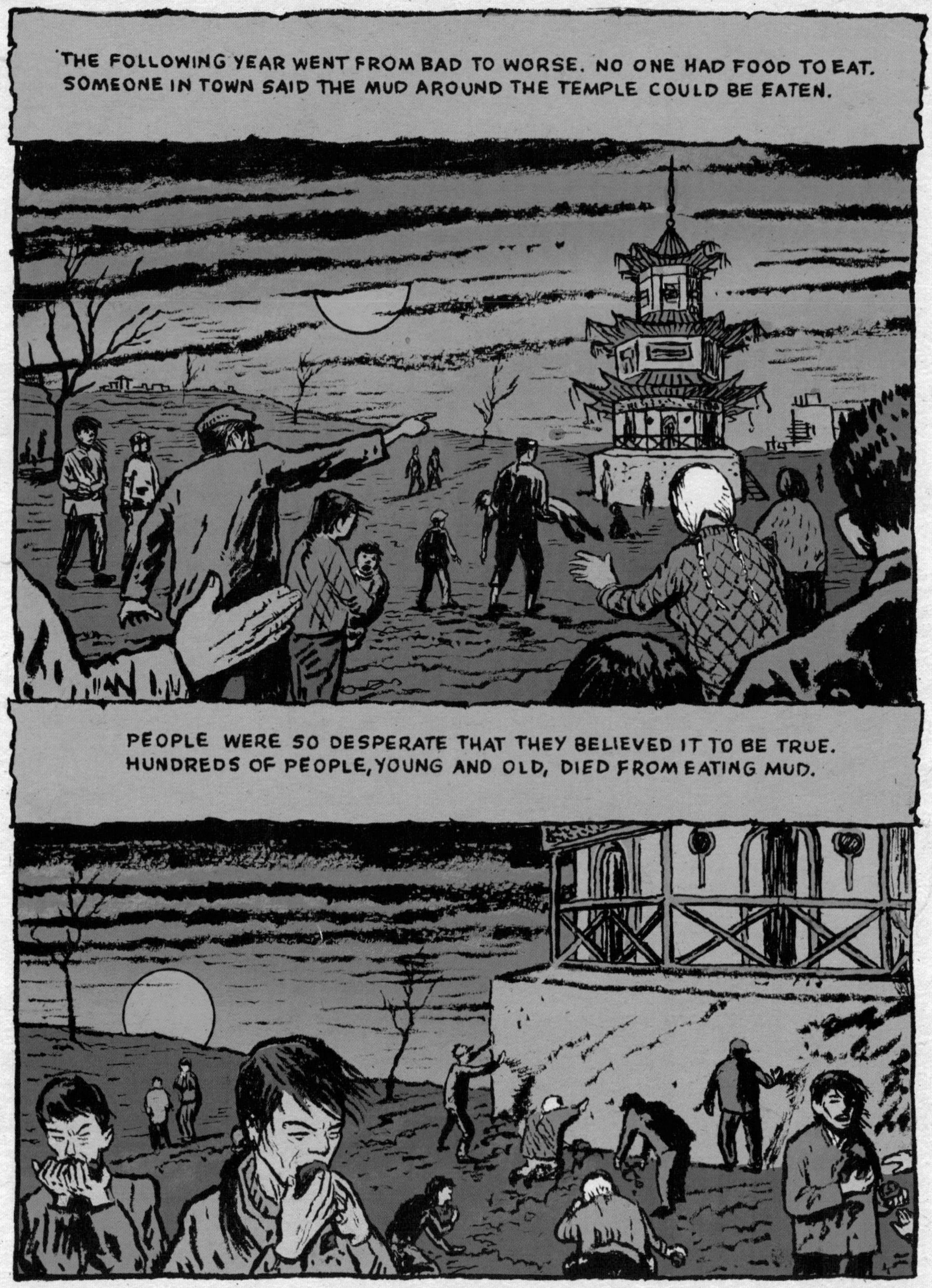
THE FOLLOWING YEAR WENT FROM BAD TO WORSE. NO ONE HAD FOOD TO EAT. SOMEONE IN TOWN SAID THE MUD AROUND THE TEMPLE COULD BE EATEN.
PEOPLE WERE SO DESPERATE THAT THEY BELIEVED IT TO BE TRUE. HUNDREDS OF PEOPLE, YOUNG AND OLD, DIED FROM EATING MUD.

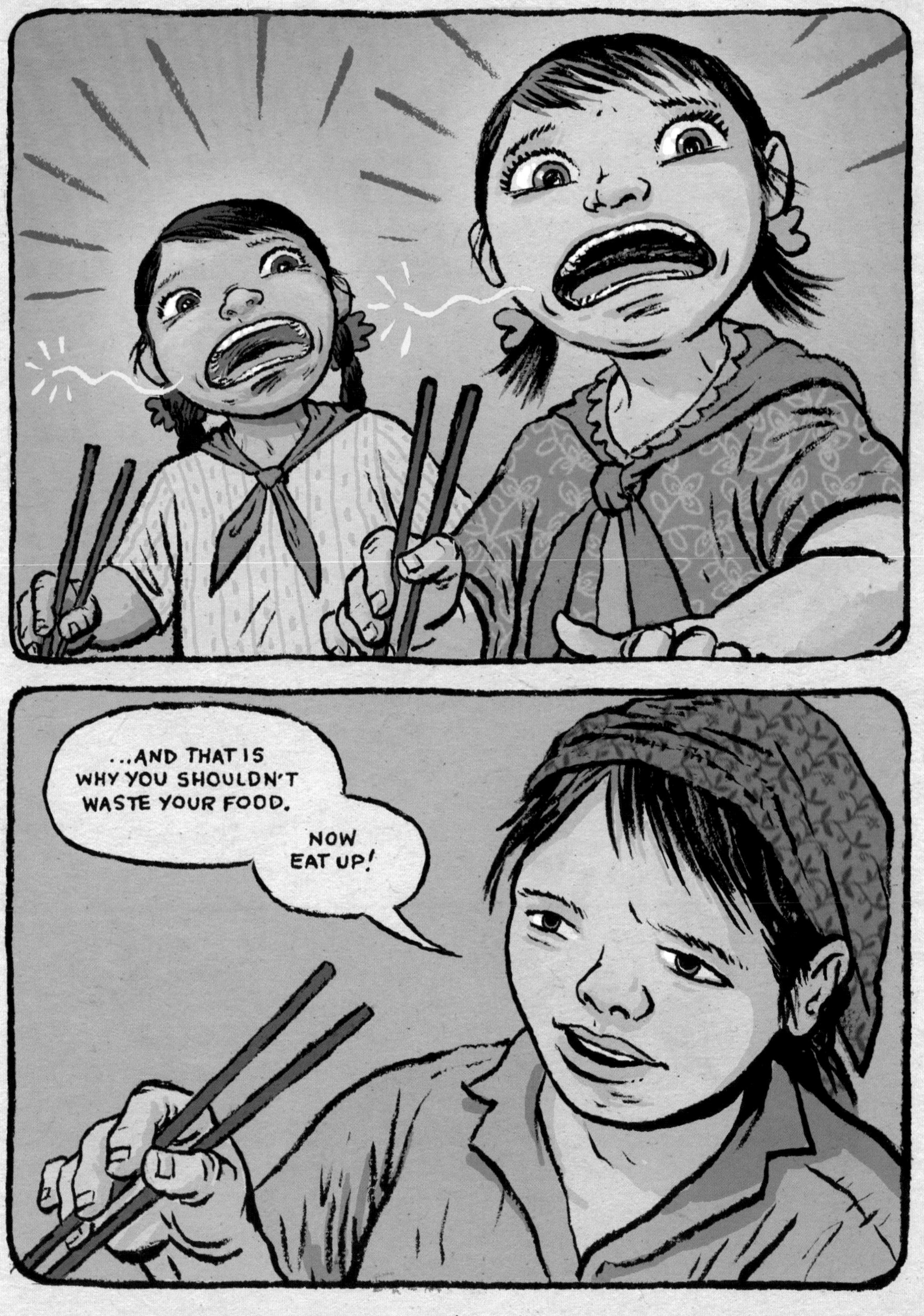
...AND THAT IS WHY YOU SHOULDN'T WASTE YOUR FOOD.
NOW EAT UP!

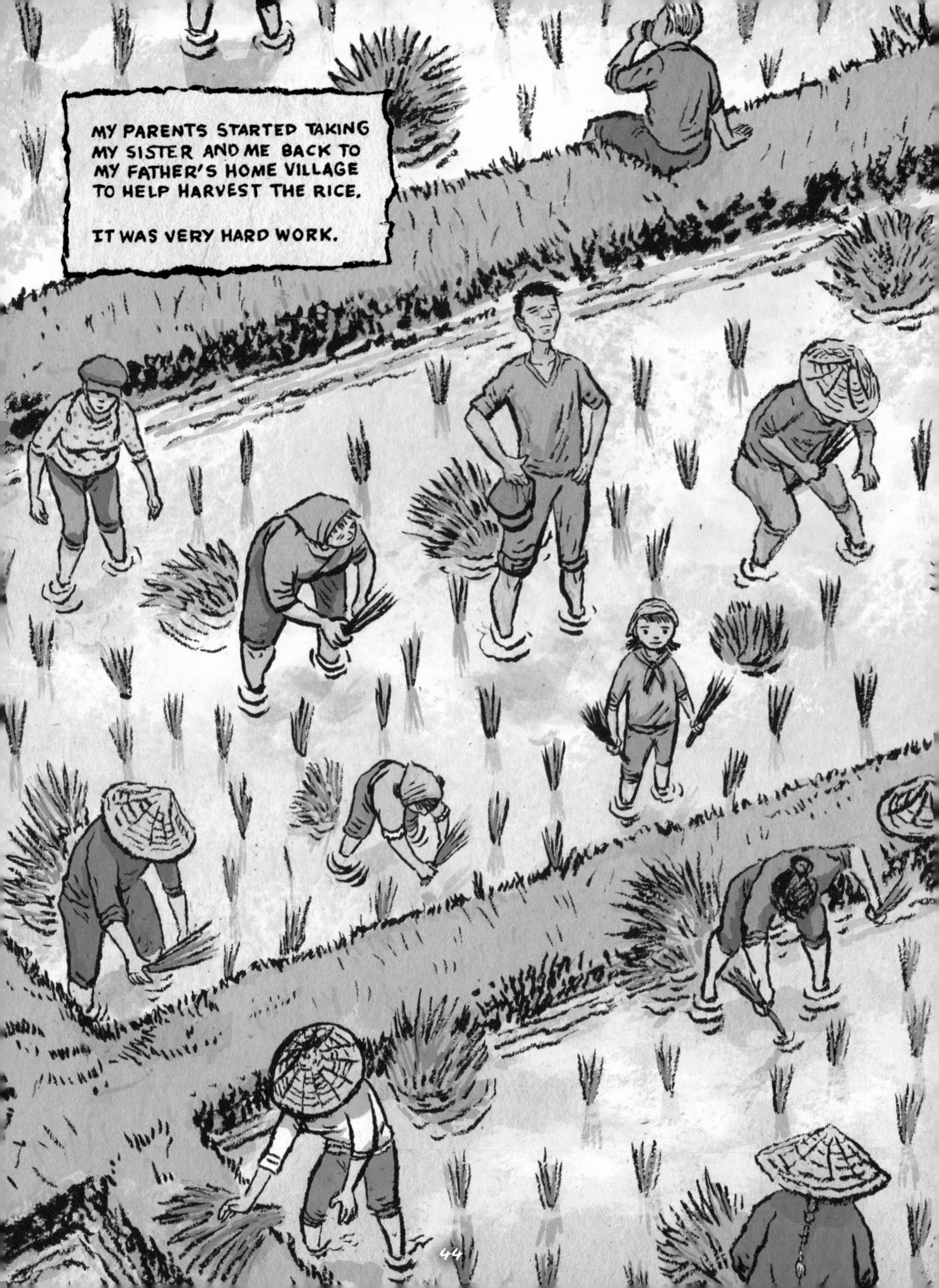
MY PARENTS STARTED TAKING MY SISTER AND ME BACK TO MY FATHER'S HOME VILLAGE TO HELP HARVEST THE RICE.
IT WAS VERY HARD WORK.

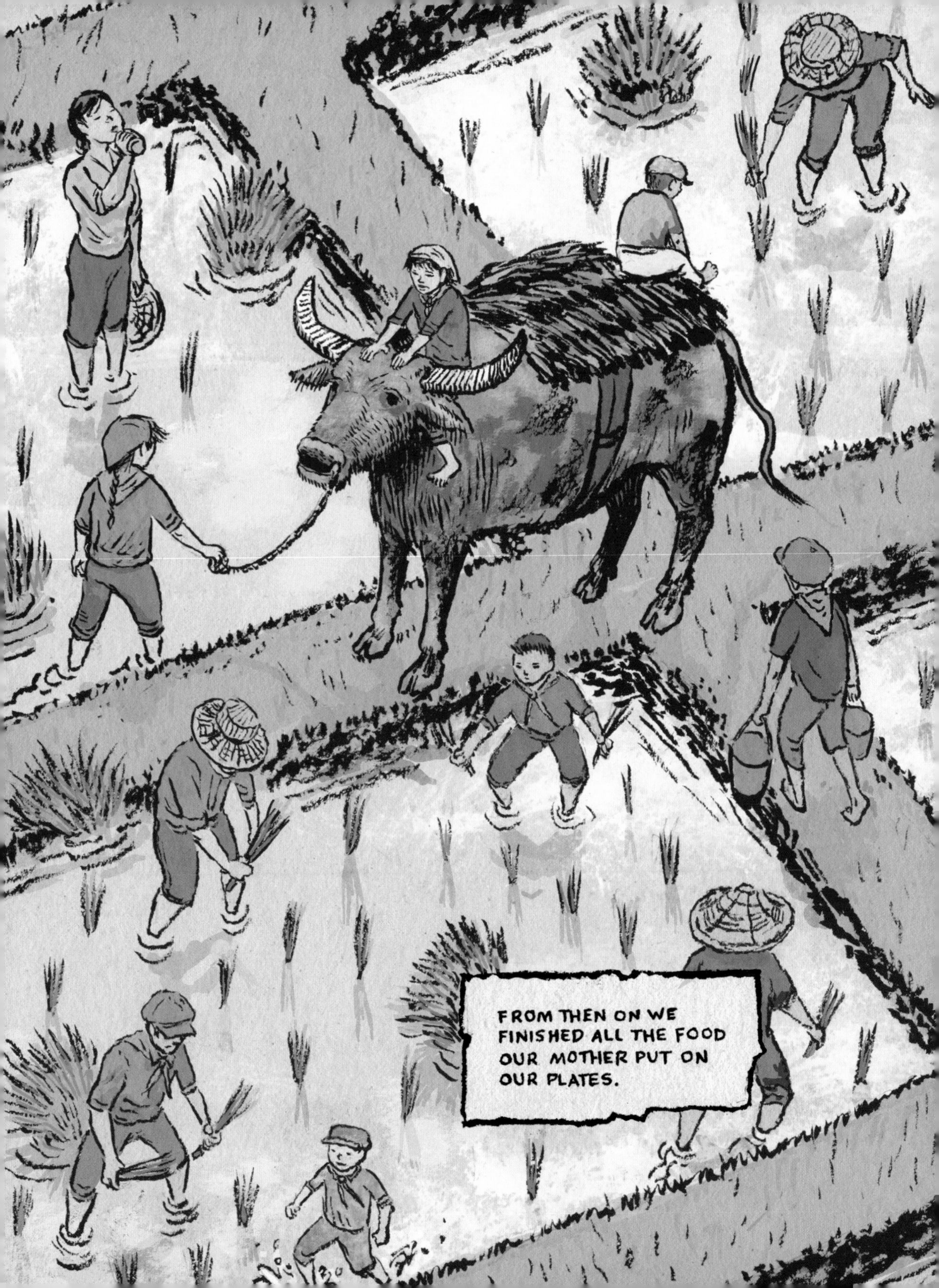
FROM THEN ON WE FINISHED ALL THE FOOD OUR MOTHER PUT ON OUR PLATES.

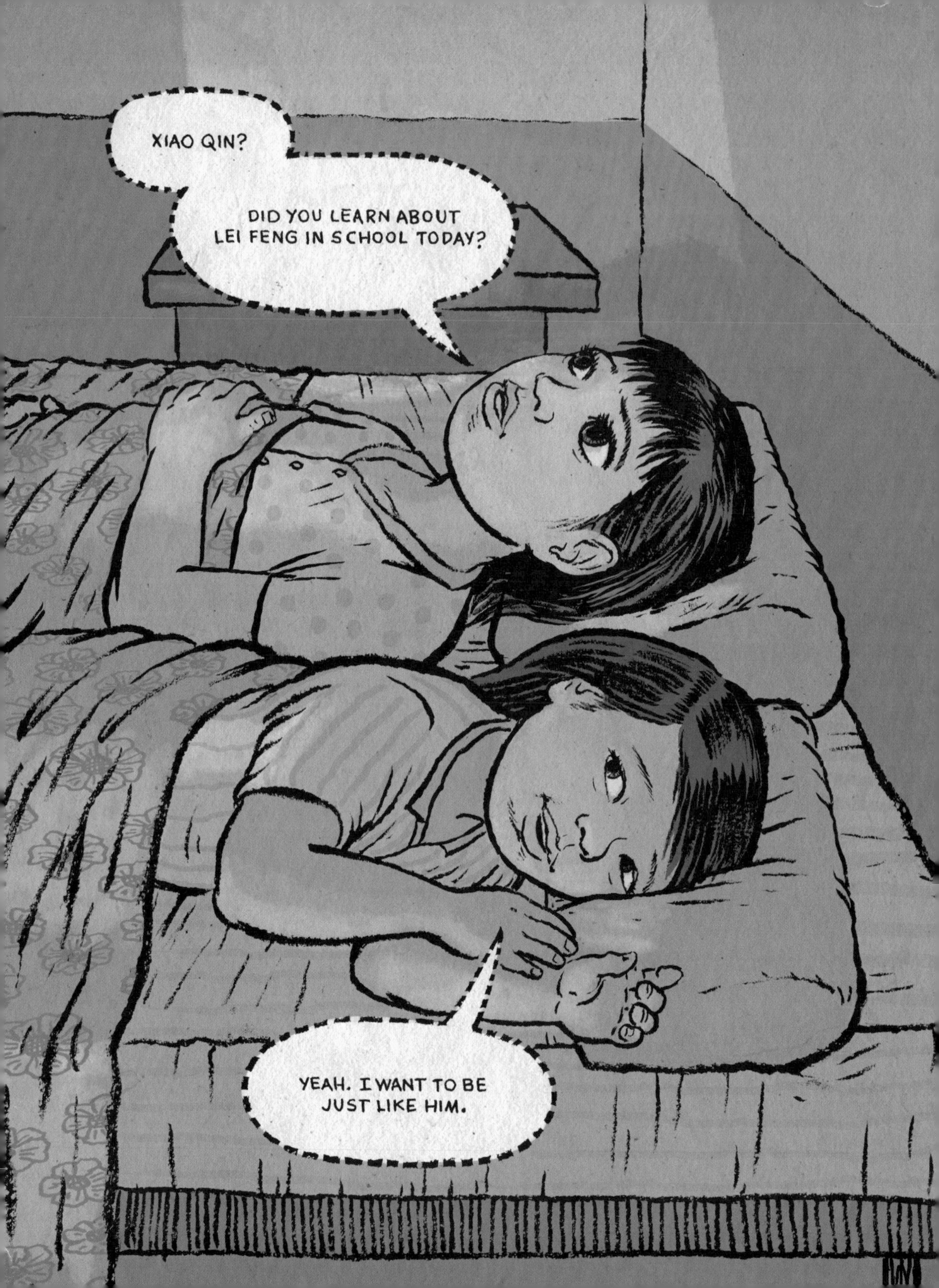
XIAO QIN?
DID YOU LEARN ABOUT LEI FENG IN SCHOOL TODAY?
YEAH. I WANT TO BE JUST LIKE HIM.

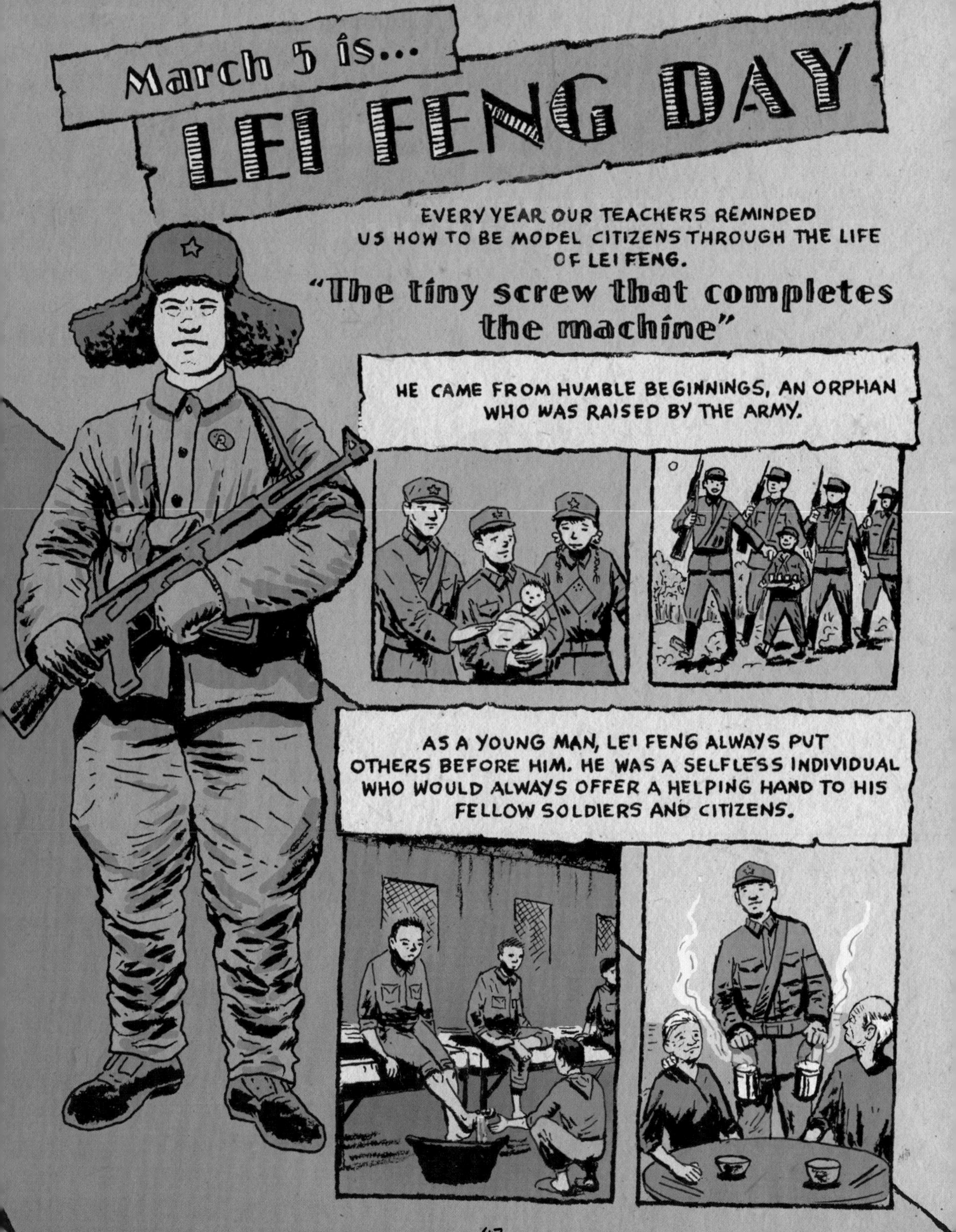
March 5 is...
LEI FENG DAY
EVERY YEAR OUR TEACHERS REMINDED US HOW TO BE MODEL CITIZENS THROUGH THE LIFE OF LEI FENG.
"The tiny screw that completes the machine"
HE CAME FROM HUMBLE BEGINNINGS, AN ORPHAN WHO WAS RAISED BY THE ARMY.
AS A YOUNG MAN, LEI FENG ALWAYS PUT OTHERS BEFORE HIM. HE WAS A SELFLESS INDIVIDUAL WHO WOULD ALWAYS OFFER A HELPING HAND TO HIS FELLOW SOLDIERS AND CITIZENS.

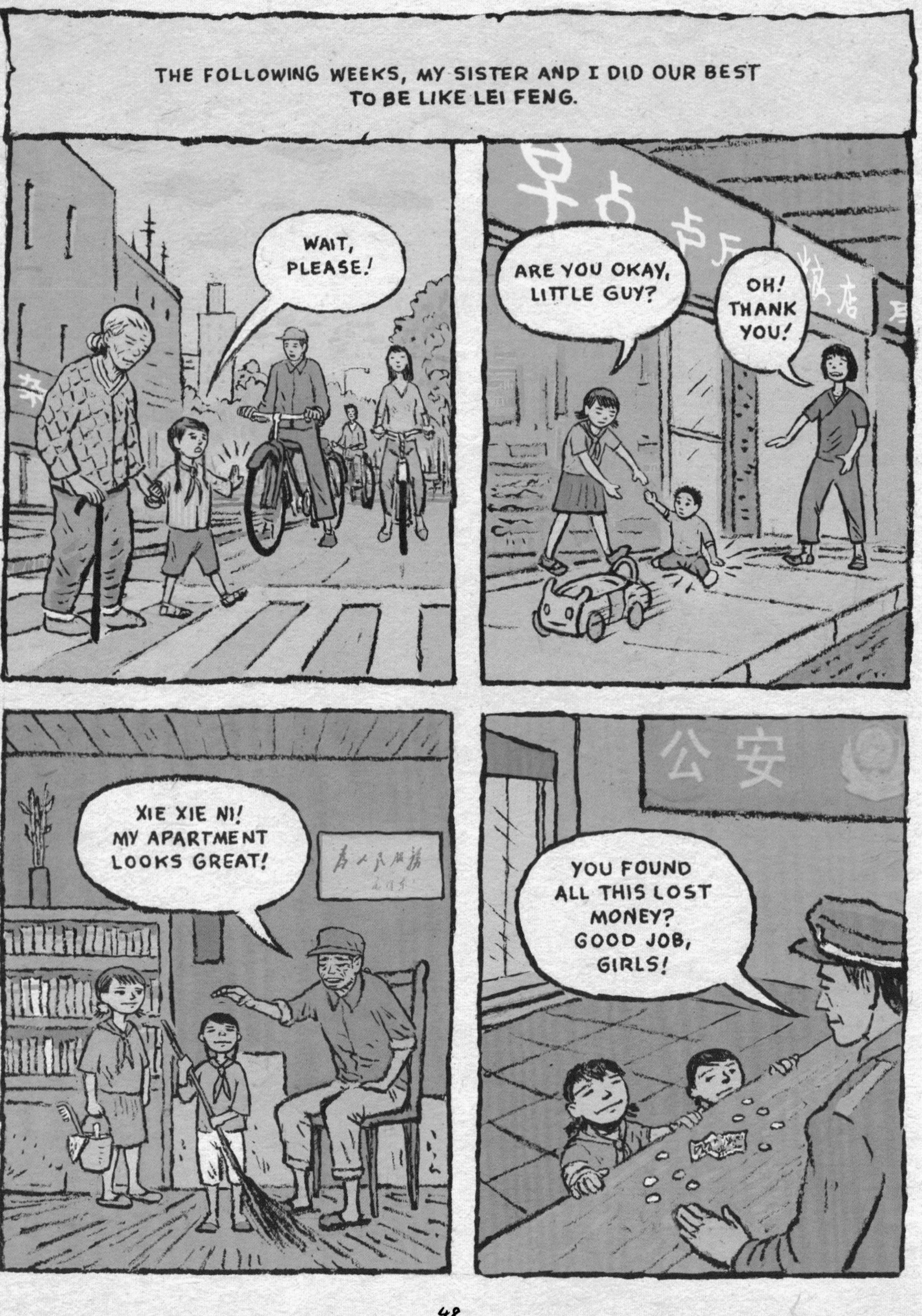
THE FOLLOWING WEEKS, MY SISTER AND I DID OUR BEST TO BE LIKE LEI FENG.
WAIT, PLEASE!
ARE YOU OKAY, LITTLE GUY?
OH! THANK YOU!
XIE XIE NI! MY APARTMENT LOOKS GREAT!
公安
YOU FOUND ALL THIS LOST MONEY? GOOD JOB, GIRLS!

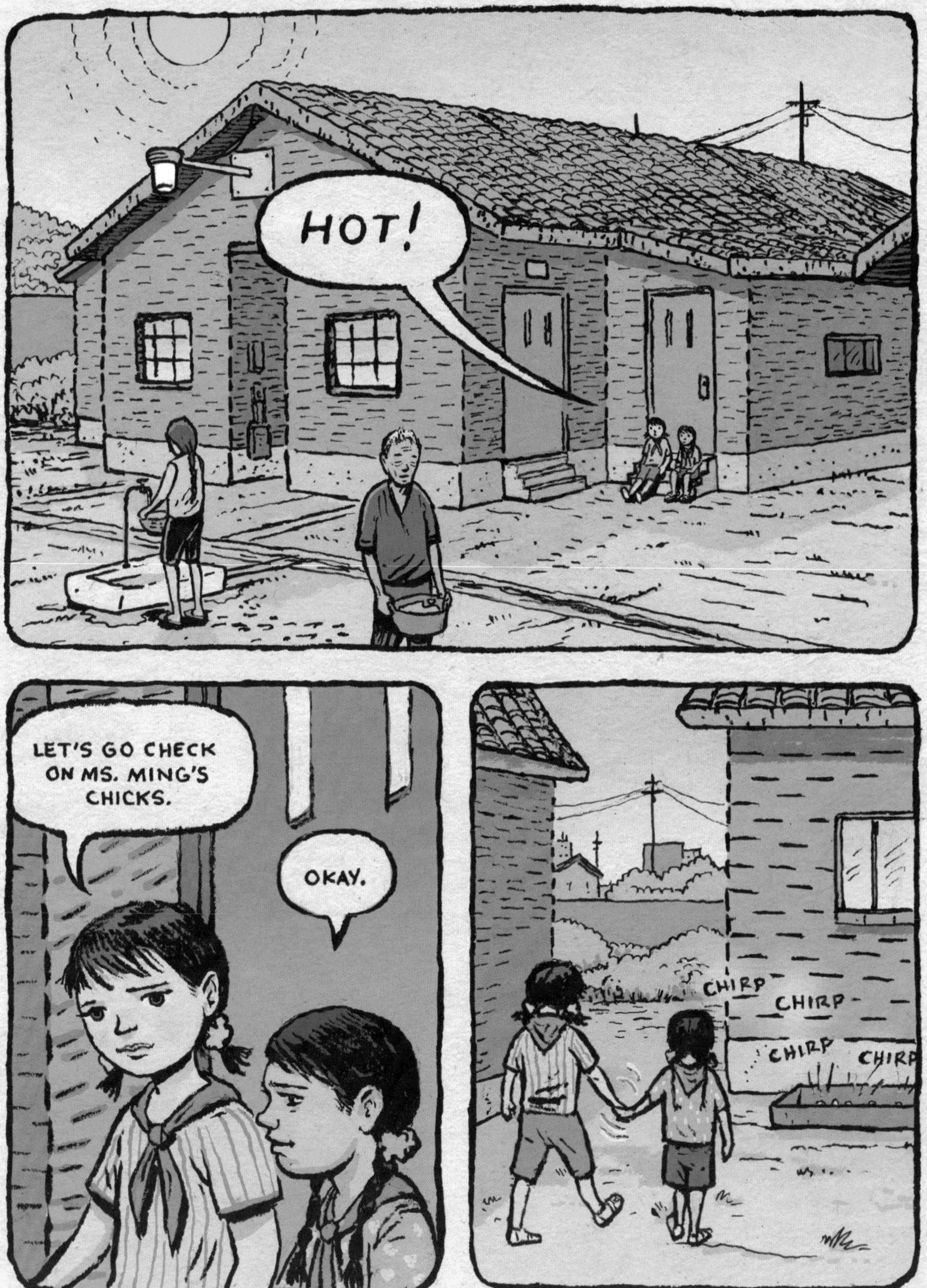
HOT!
LET'S GO CHECK ON MS. MING'S CHICKS.
OKAY.
CHIRP
CHIRP
CHIRP
CHIRP

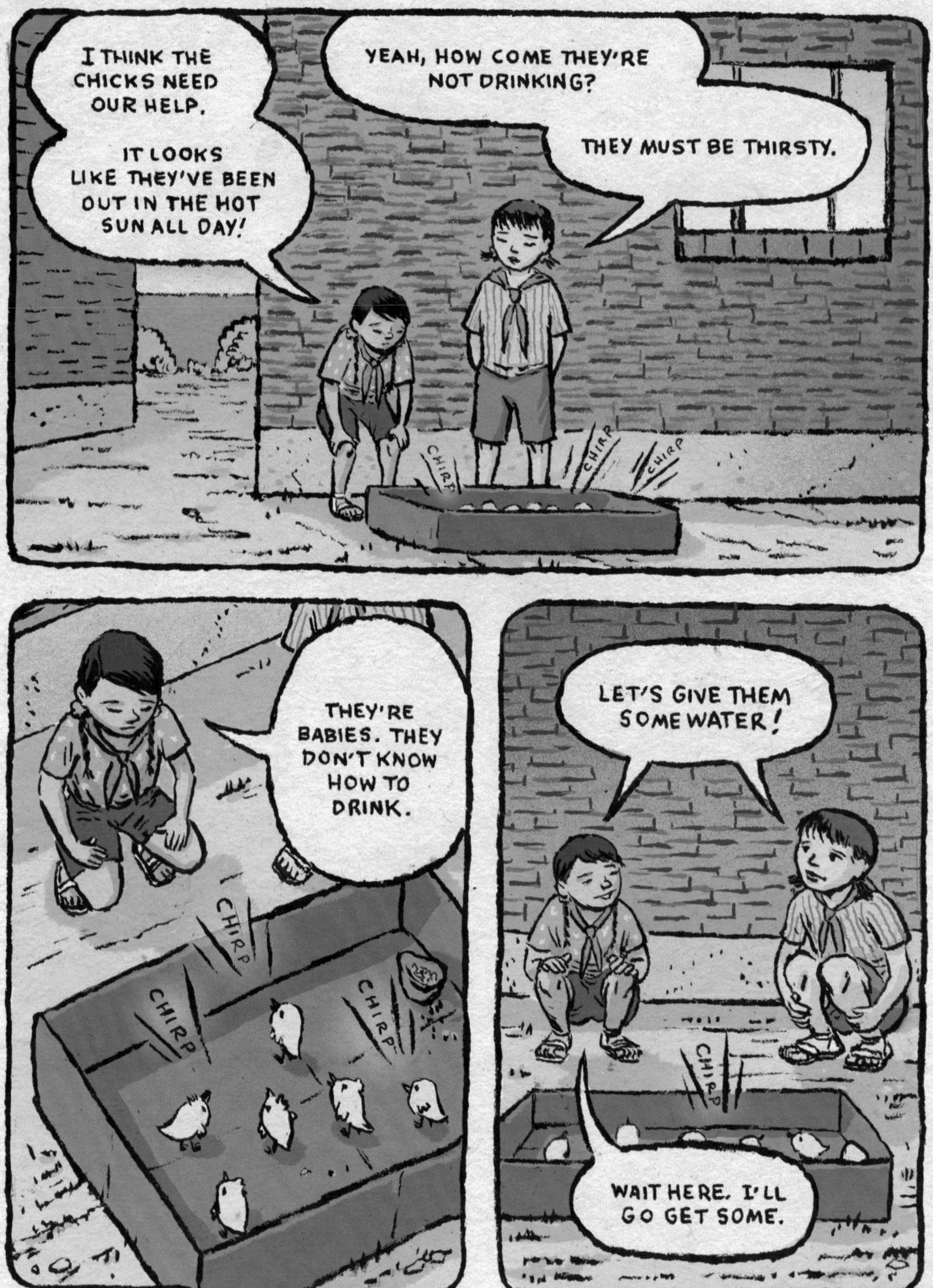
I THINK THE CHICKS NEED OUR HELP.
IT LOOKS LIKE THEY'VE BEEN OUT IN THE HOT SUN ALL DAY!
YEAH, HOW COME THEY'RE NOT DRINKING?
THEY MUST BE THIRSTY.
CHIRP
CHIRP
CHIRP
THEY'RE BABIES. THEY DON'T KNOW HOW TO DRINK.
CHIRP
CHIRP
CHIRP
LET'S GIVE THEM SOME WATER!
CHIRP
WAIT HERE. I'LL GO GET SOME.

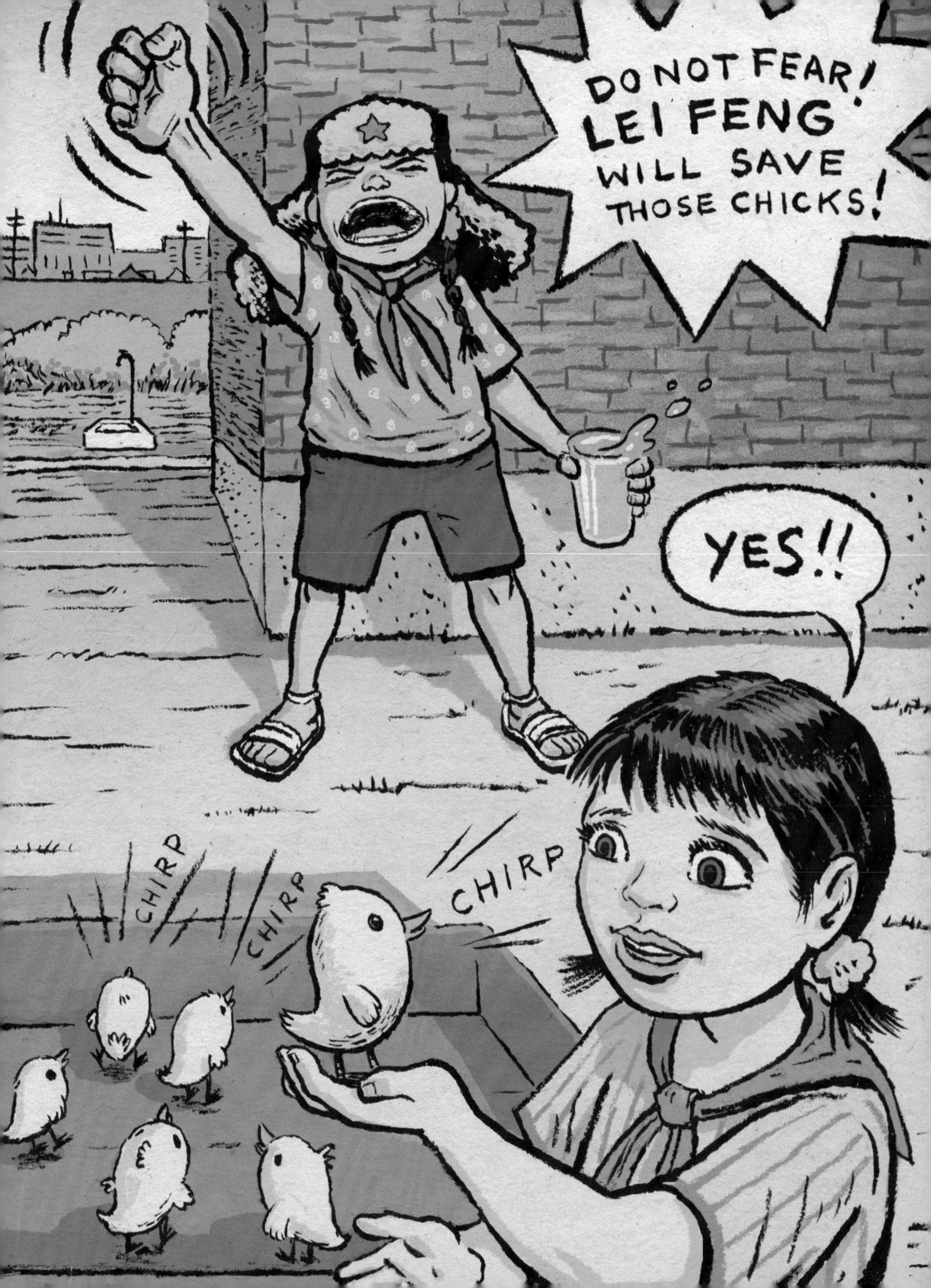
DO NOT FEAR!
LEI FENG
WILL SAVE
THOSE CHICKS!
YES!!
CHIRP
CHIRP
CHIRP

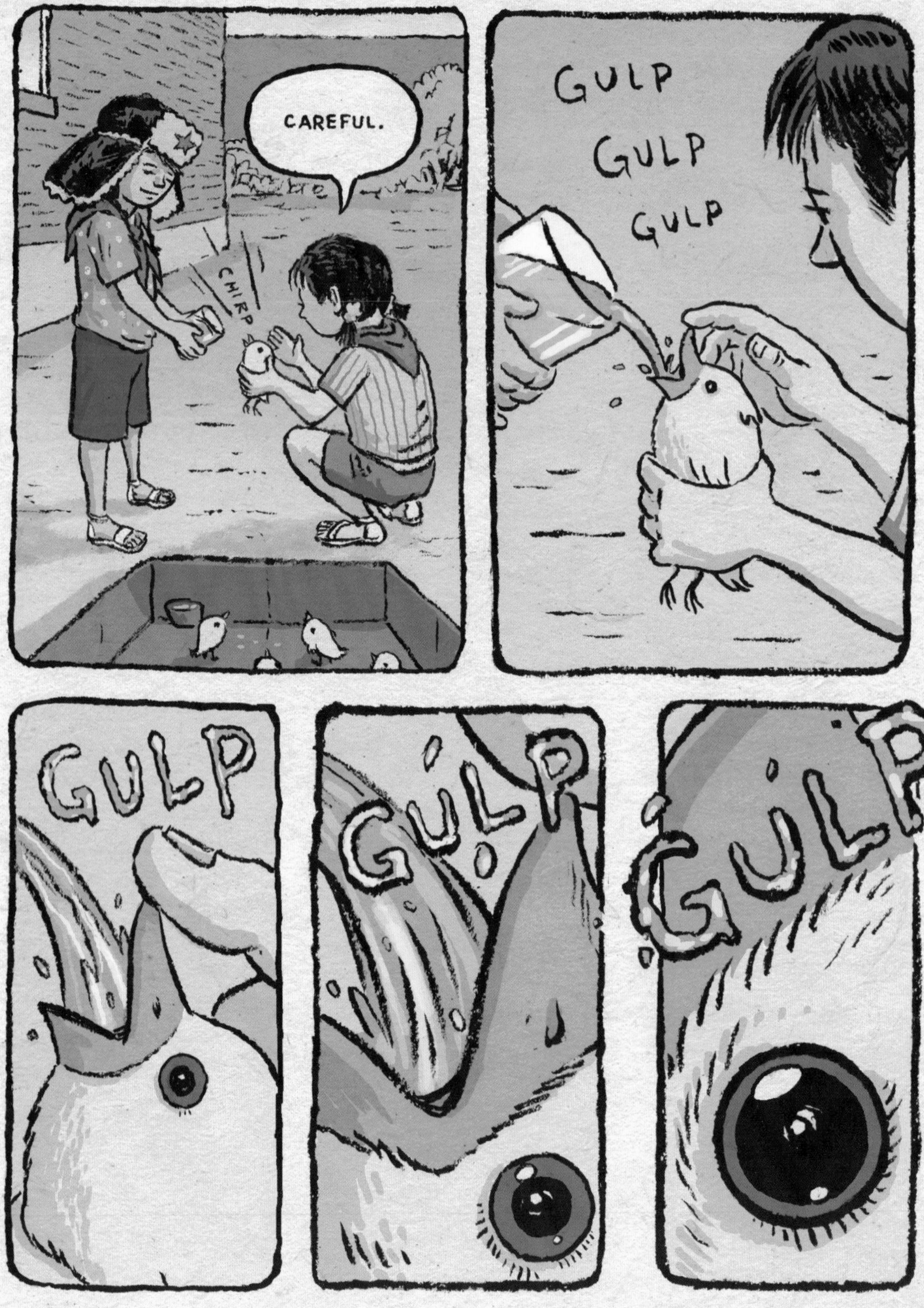
CAREFUL.
CHIRP
GULP
GULP
GULP
GULP
GULP
GULP

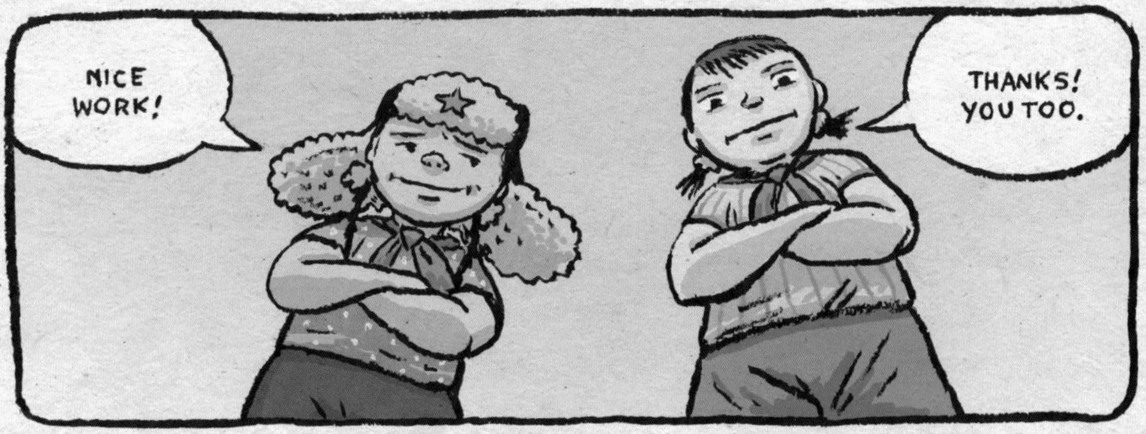
NICE WORK!
THANKS! YOU TOO.

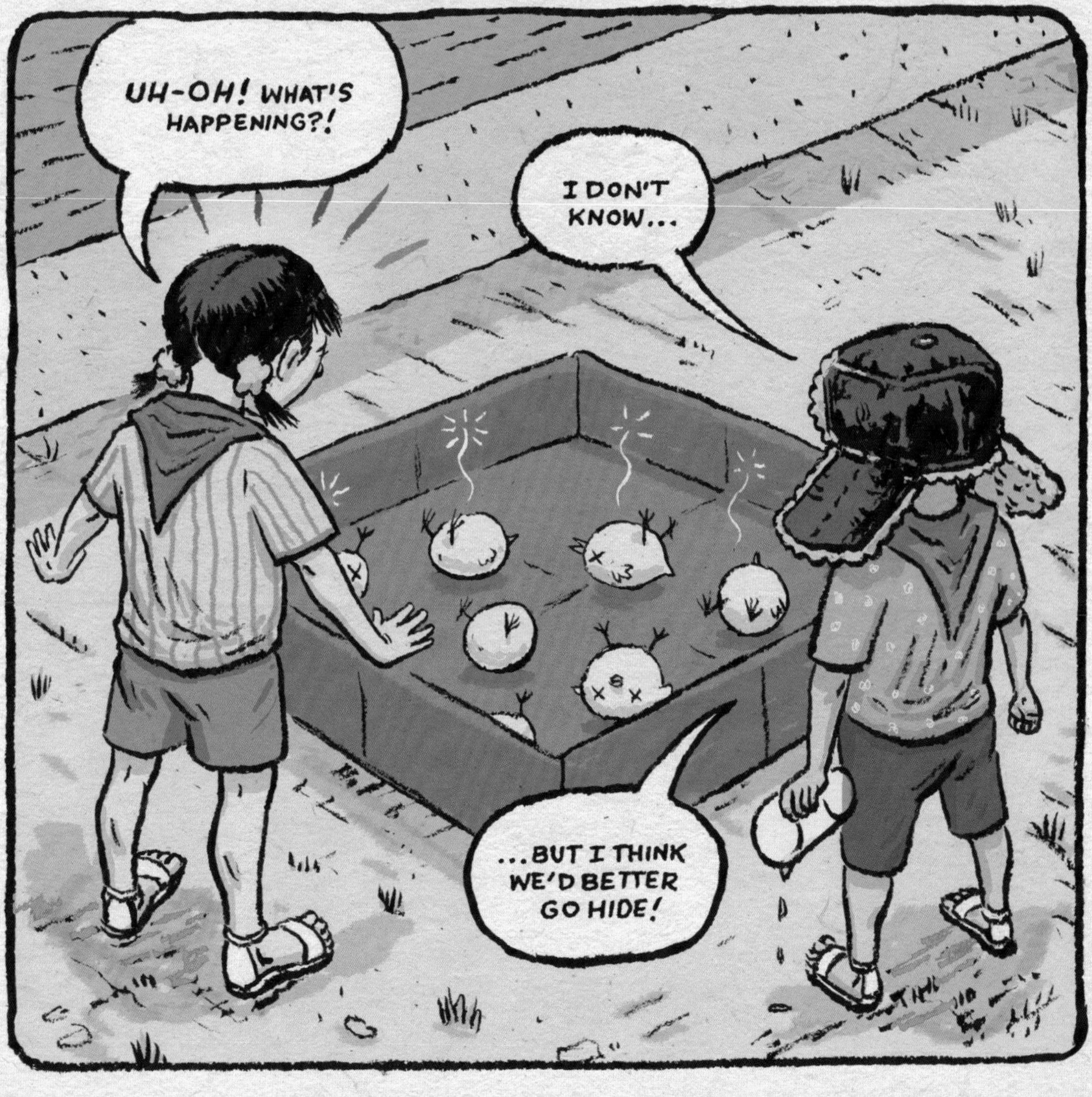
UH-OH! WHAT'S HAPPENING?!
I DON'T KNOW...
...BUT I THINK WE'D BETTER GO HIDE!

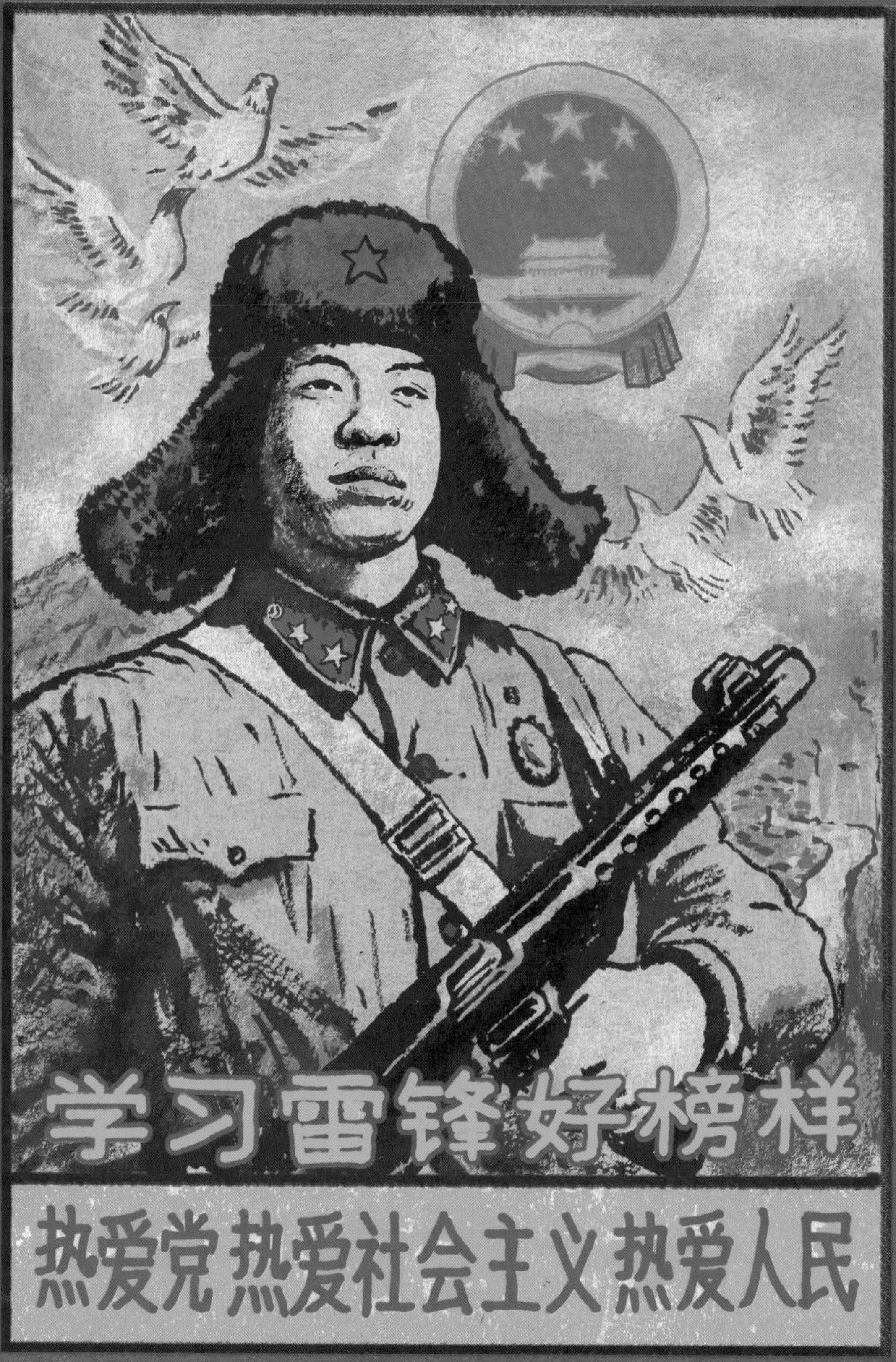
学习雷锋好榜样
热爱党 热爱社会主义 热爱人民

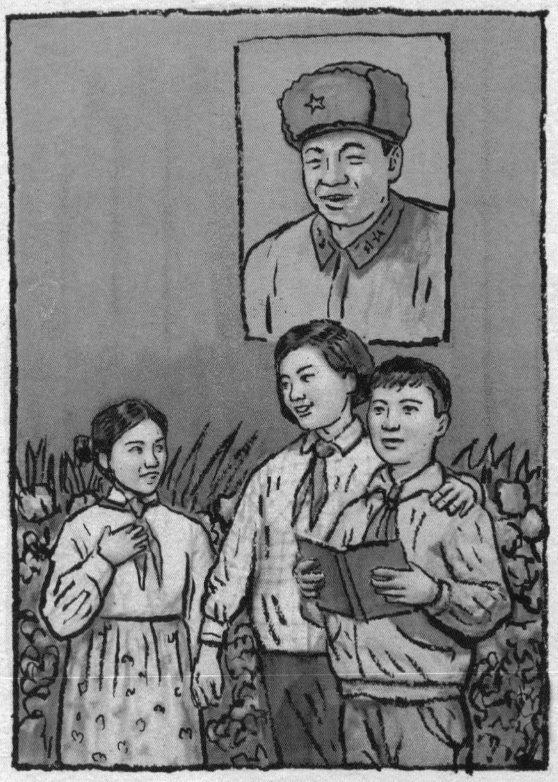

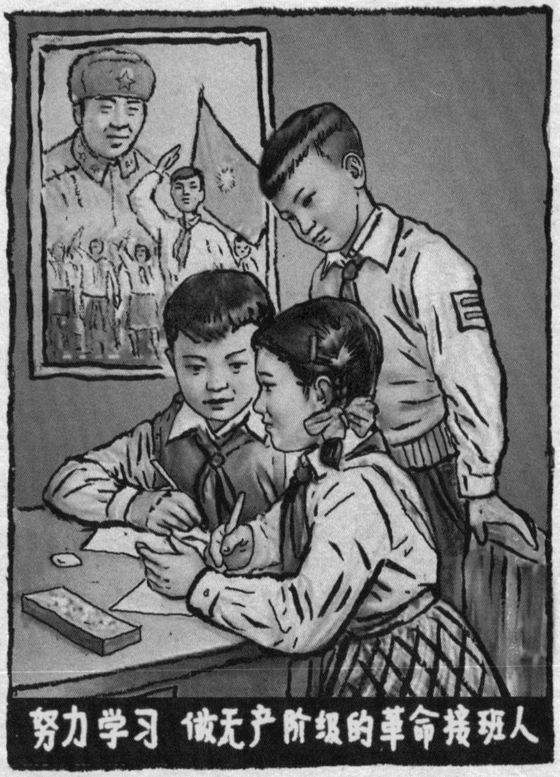
努力学习 做无产阶级的革命接班人

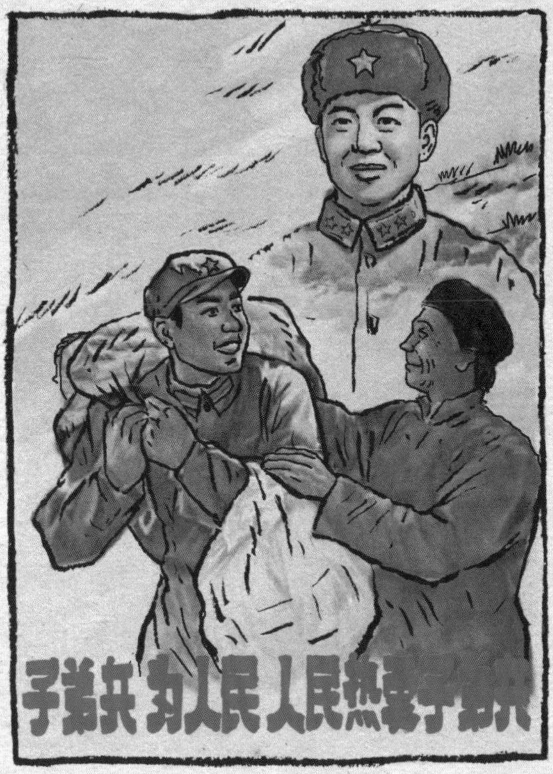
子弟兵 为人民 人民热爱子弟兵

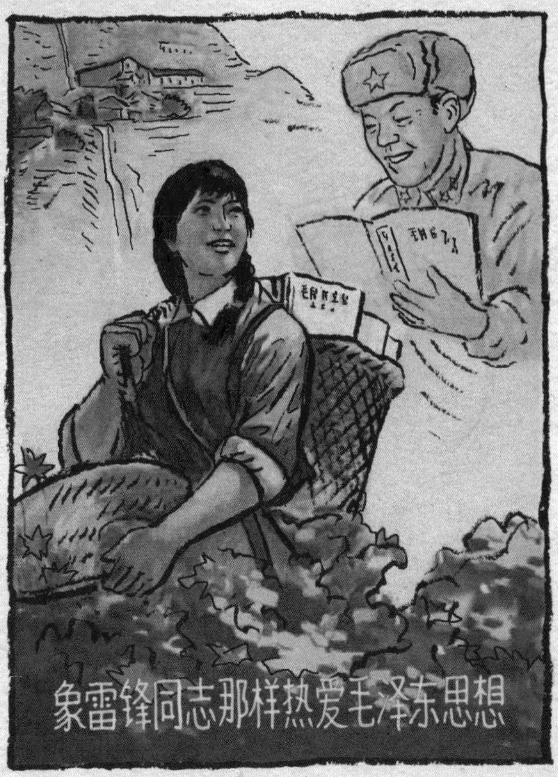
象雷锋同志那样热爱毛泽东思想

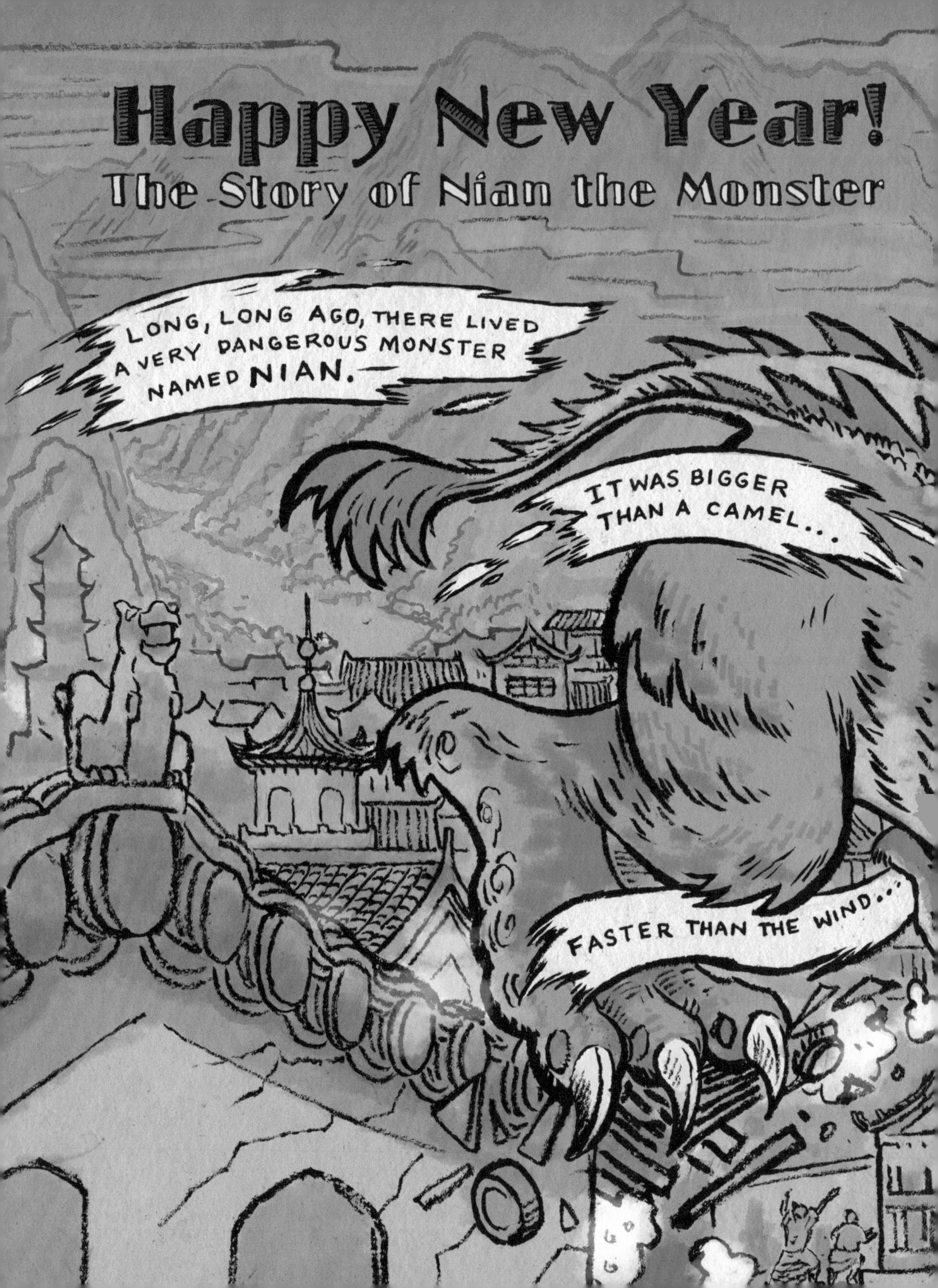
Happy New Year!
The Story of Nian the Monster
LONG, LONG AGO, THERE LIVED A VERY DANGEROUS MONSTER NAMED NIAN.
IT WAS BIGGER THAN A CAMEL...
FASTER THAN THE WIND...

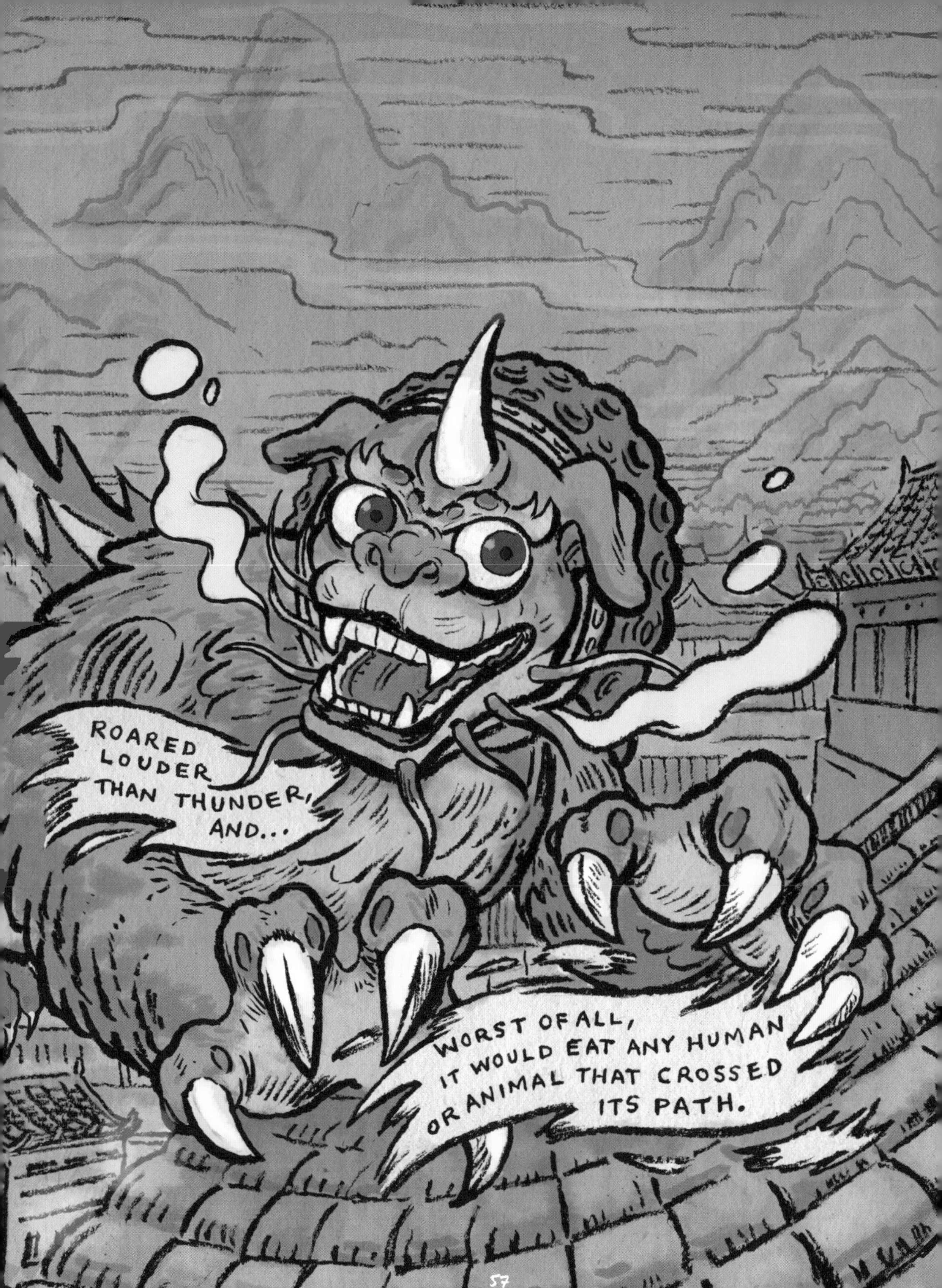
ROARED LOUDER THAN THUNDER, AND...
WORST OF ALL, IT WOULD EAT ANY HUMAN OR ANIMAL THAT CROSSED ITS PATH.

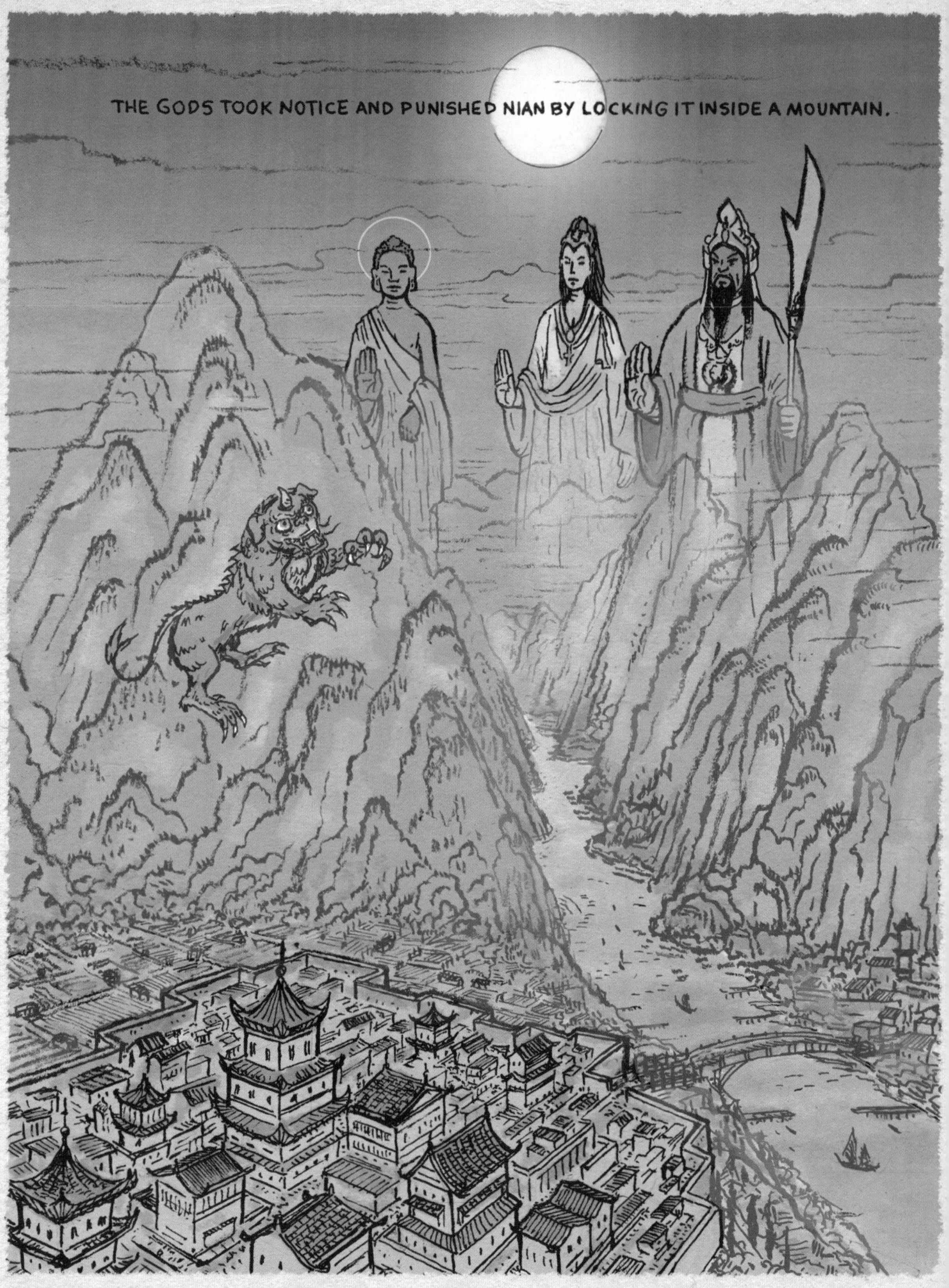
THE GODS TOOK NOTICE AND PUNISHED NIAN BY LOCKING IT INSIDE A MOUNTAIN.

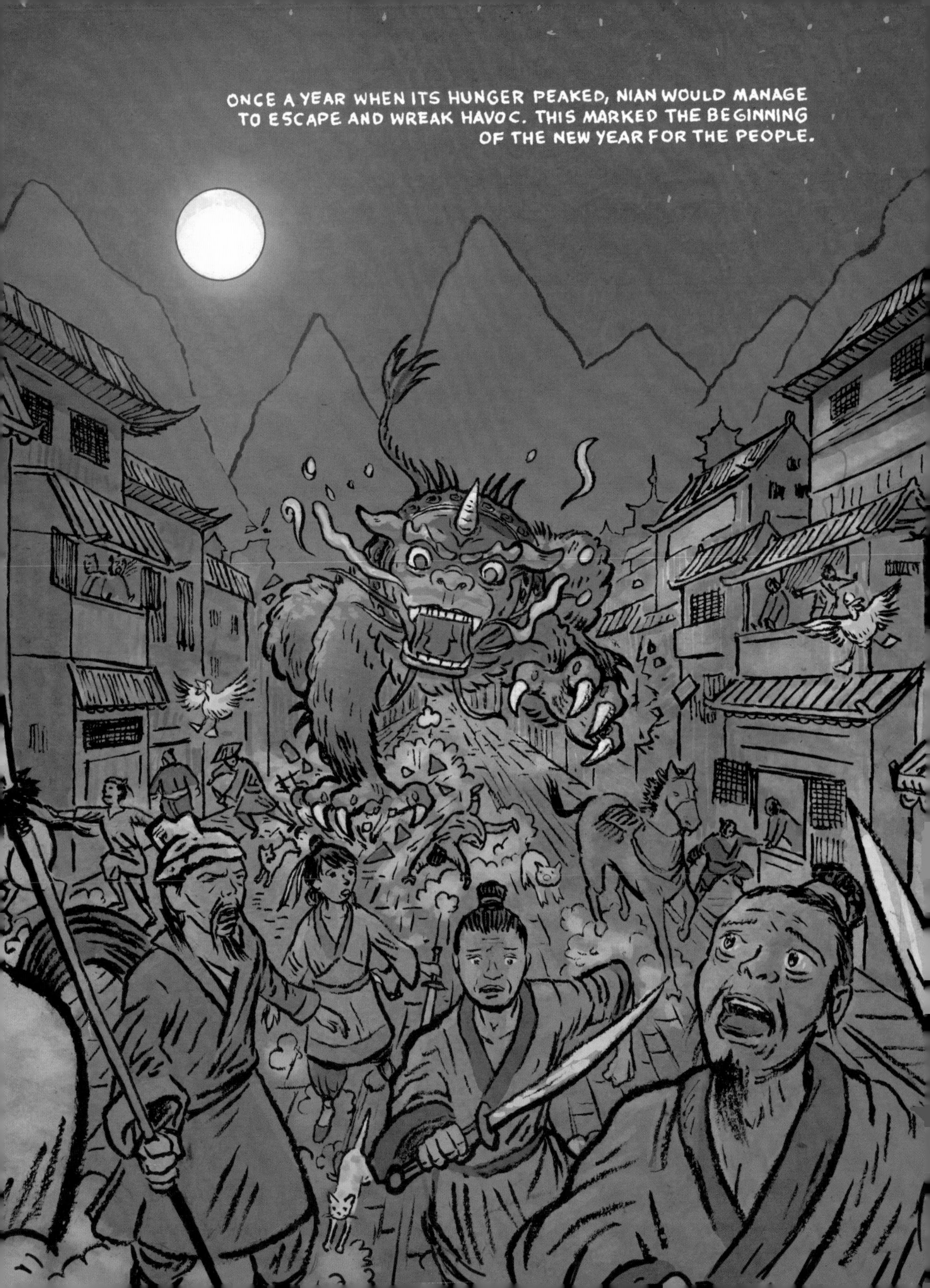
ONCE A YEAR WHEN ITS HUNGER PEAKED, NIAN WOULD MANAGE TO ESCAPE AND WREAK HAVOC. THIS MARKED THE BEGINNING OF THE NEW YEAR FOR THE PEOPLE.

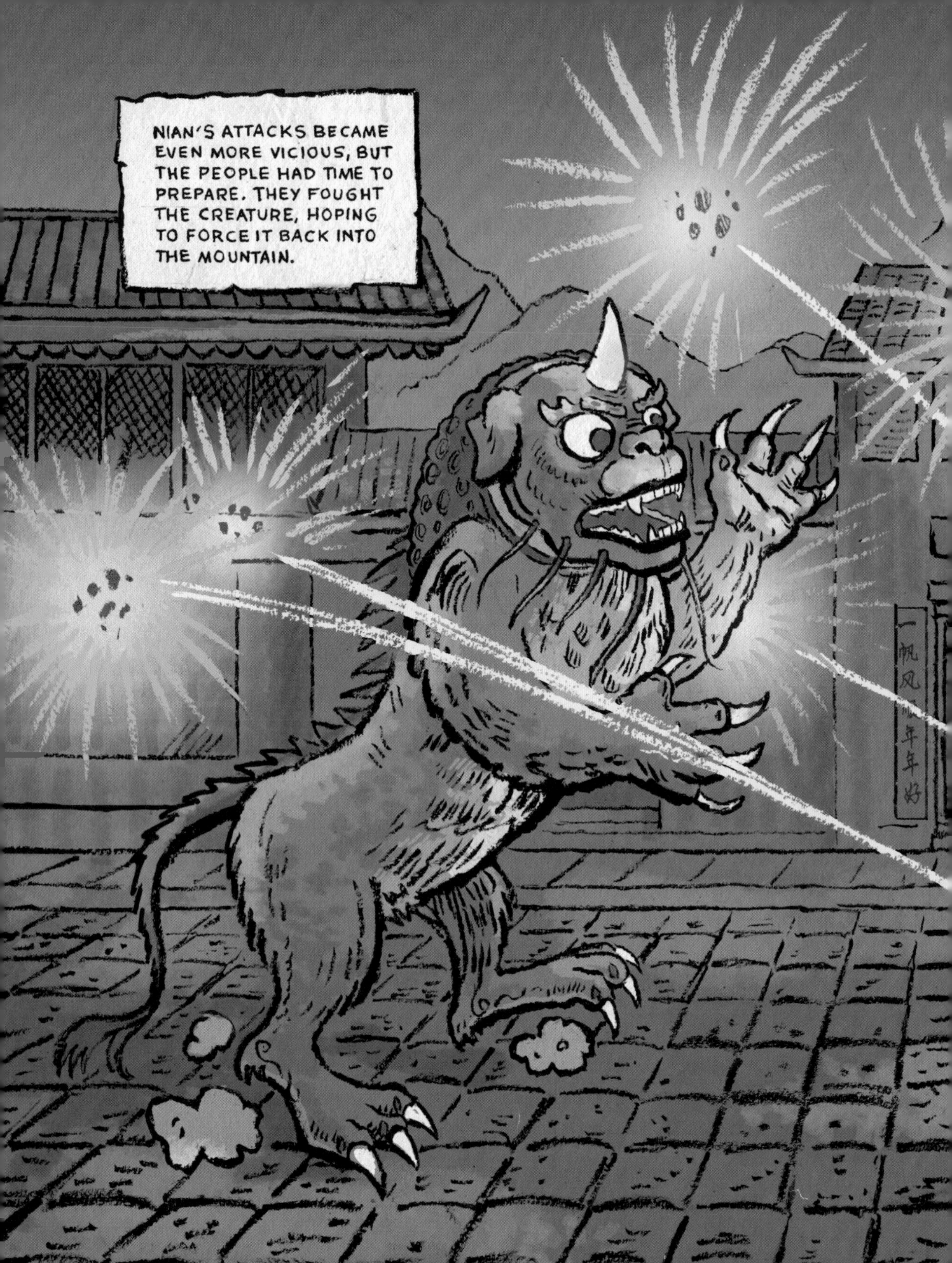
NIAN'S ATTACKS BECAME EVEN MORE VICIOUS, BUT THE PEOPLE HAD TIME TO PREPARE. THEY FOUGHT THE CREATURE, HOPING TO FORCE IT BACK INTO THE MOUNTAIN.
一帆风顺年年好

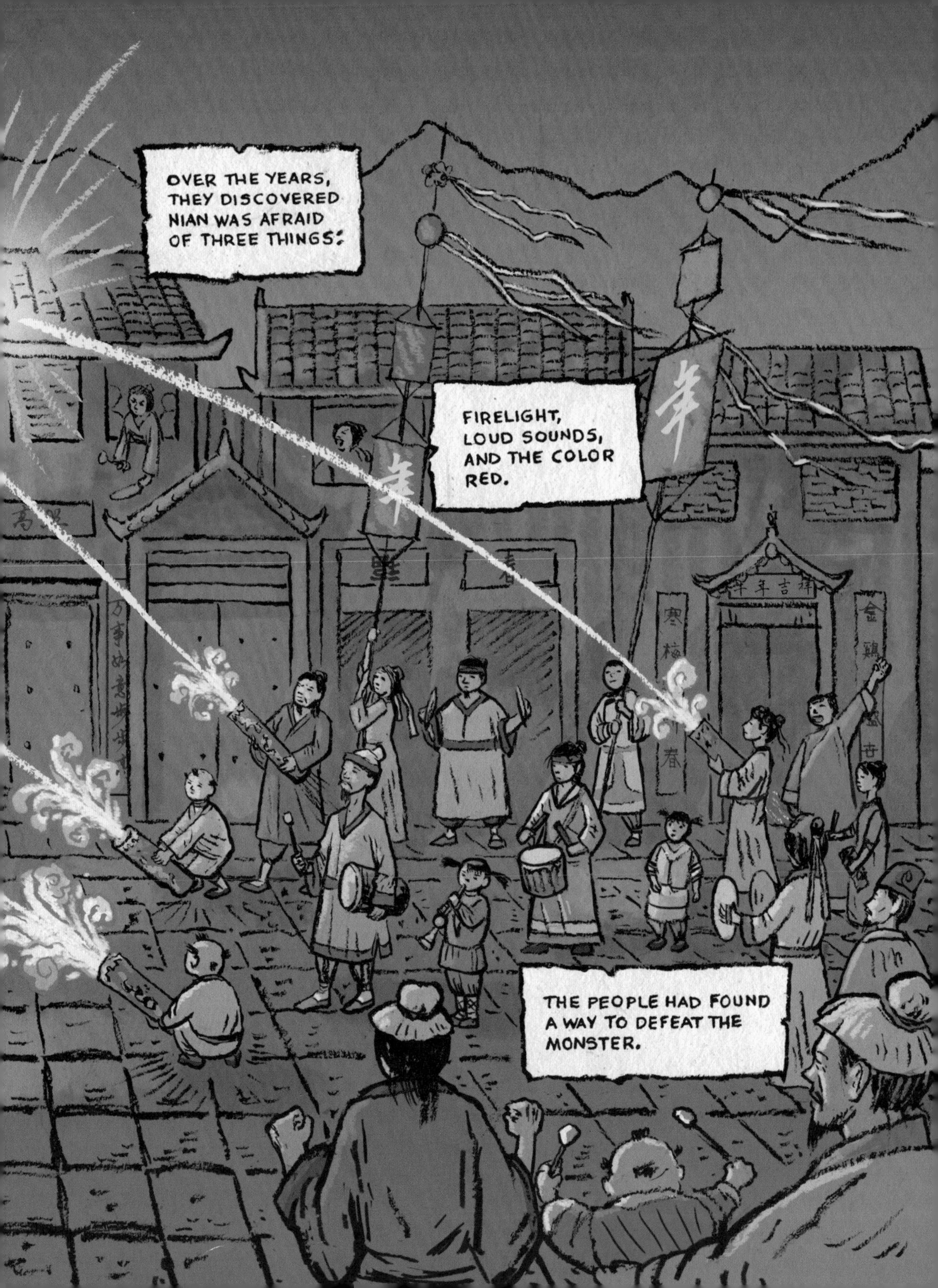
OVER THE YEARS, THEY DISCOVERED NIAN WAS AFRAID OF THREE THINGS:
FIRELIGHT, LOUD SOUNDS, AND THE COLOR RED.
THE PEOPLE HAD FOUND A WAY TO DEFEAT THE MONSTER.

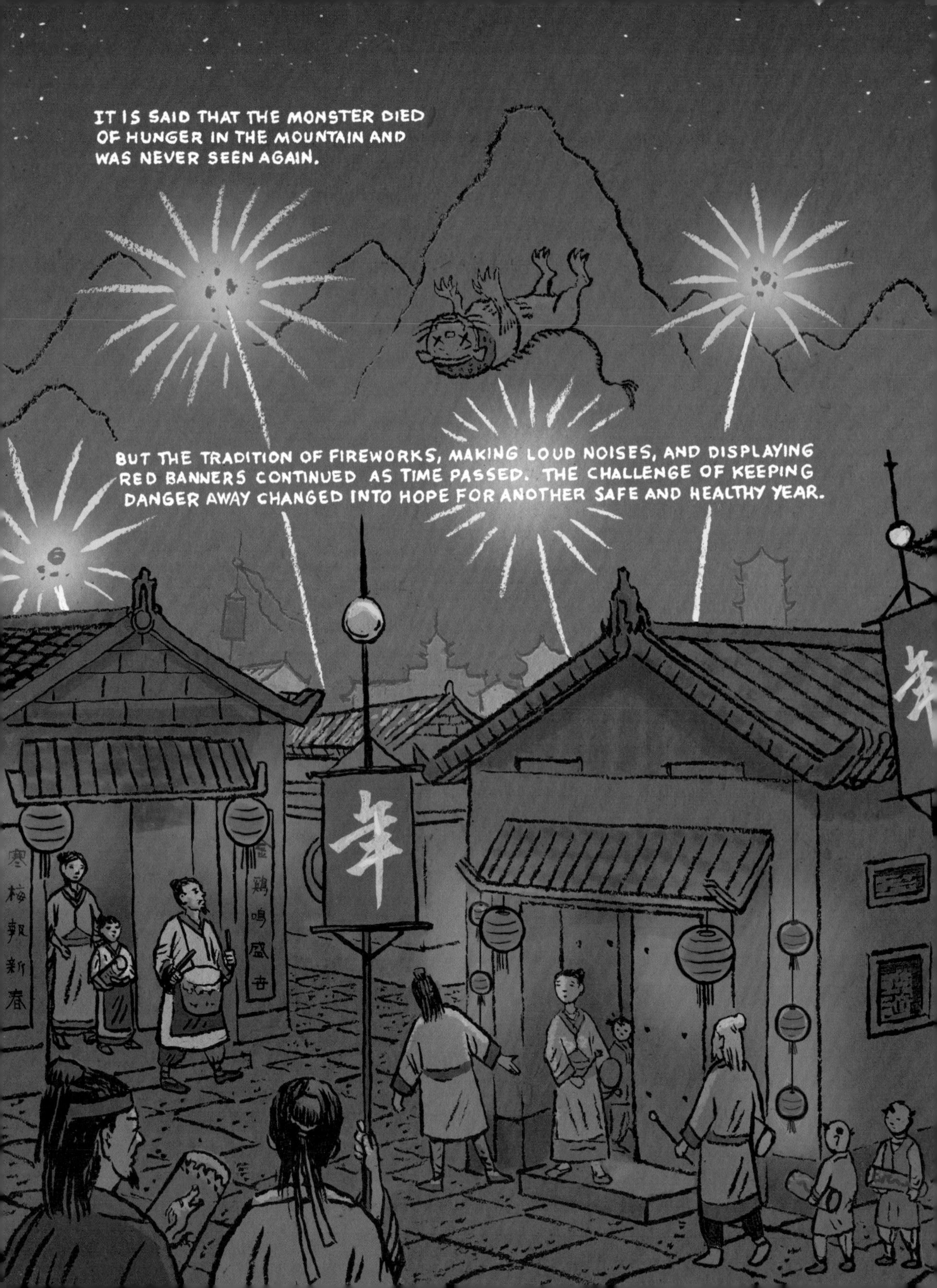
IT IS SAID THAT THE MONSTER DIED OF HUNGER IN THE MOUNTAIN AND WAS NEVER SEEN AGAIN.
BUT THE TRADITION OF FIREWORKS, MAKING LOUD NOISES, AND DISPLAYING RED BANNERS CONTINUED AS TIME PASSED. THE CHALLENGE OF KEEPING DANGER AWAY CHANGED INTO HOPE FOR ANOTHER SAFE AND HEALTHY YEAR.
寒梅報新春
金鷄鳴盛
年
年

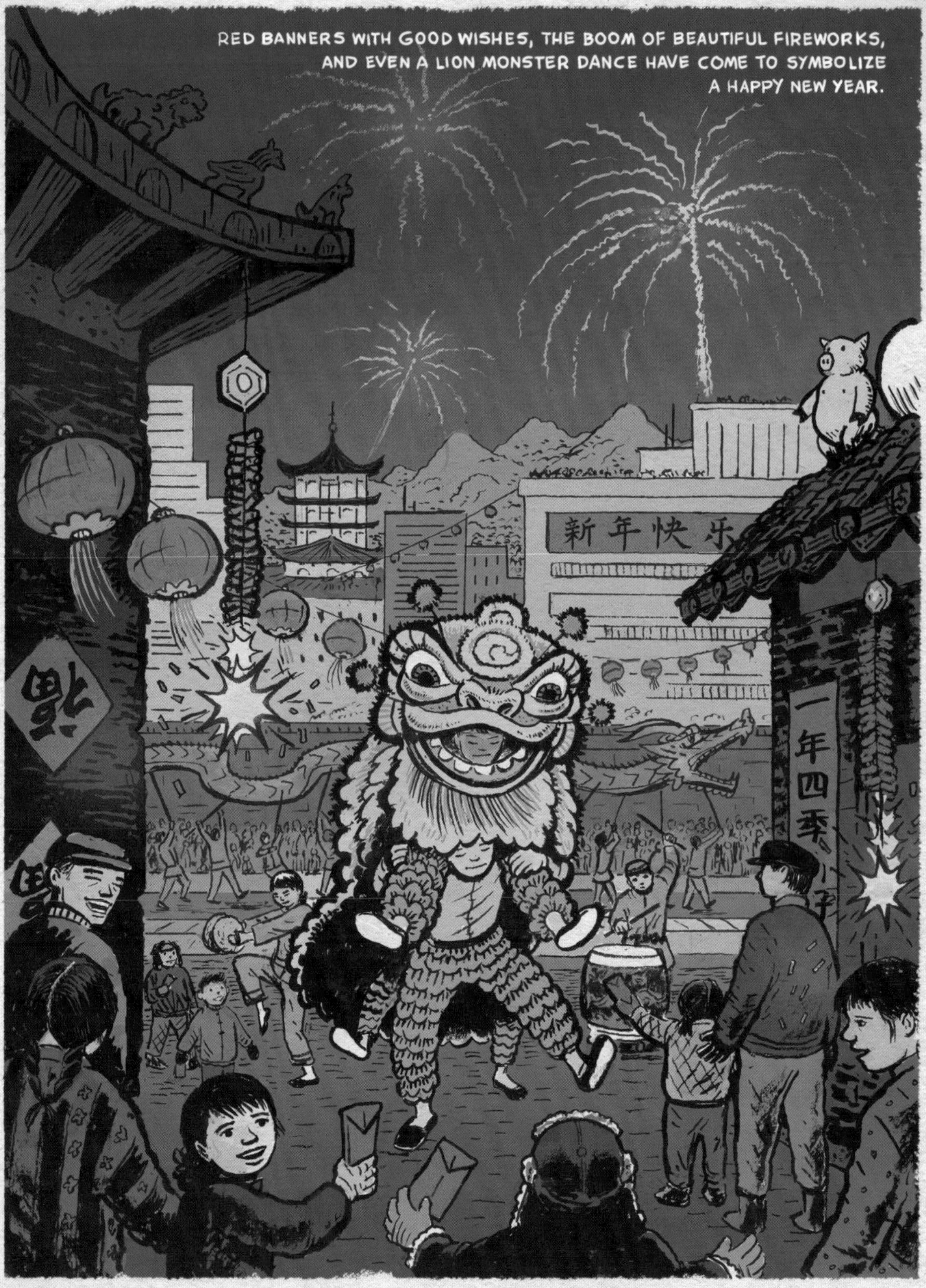
RED BANNERS WITH GOOD WISHES, THE BOOM OF BEAUTIFUL FIREWORKS, AND EVEN A LION MONSTER DANCE HAVE COME TO SYMBOLIZE A HAPPY NEW YEAR.
新年快乐
一年四季

My New Year Feast

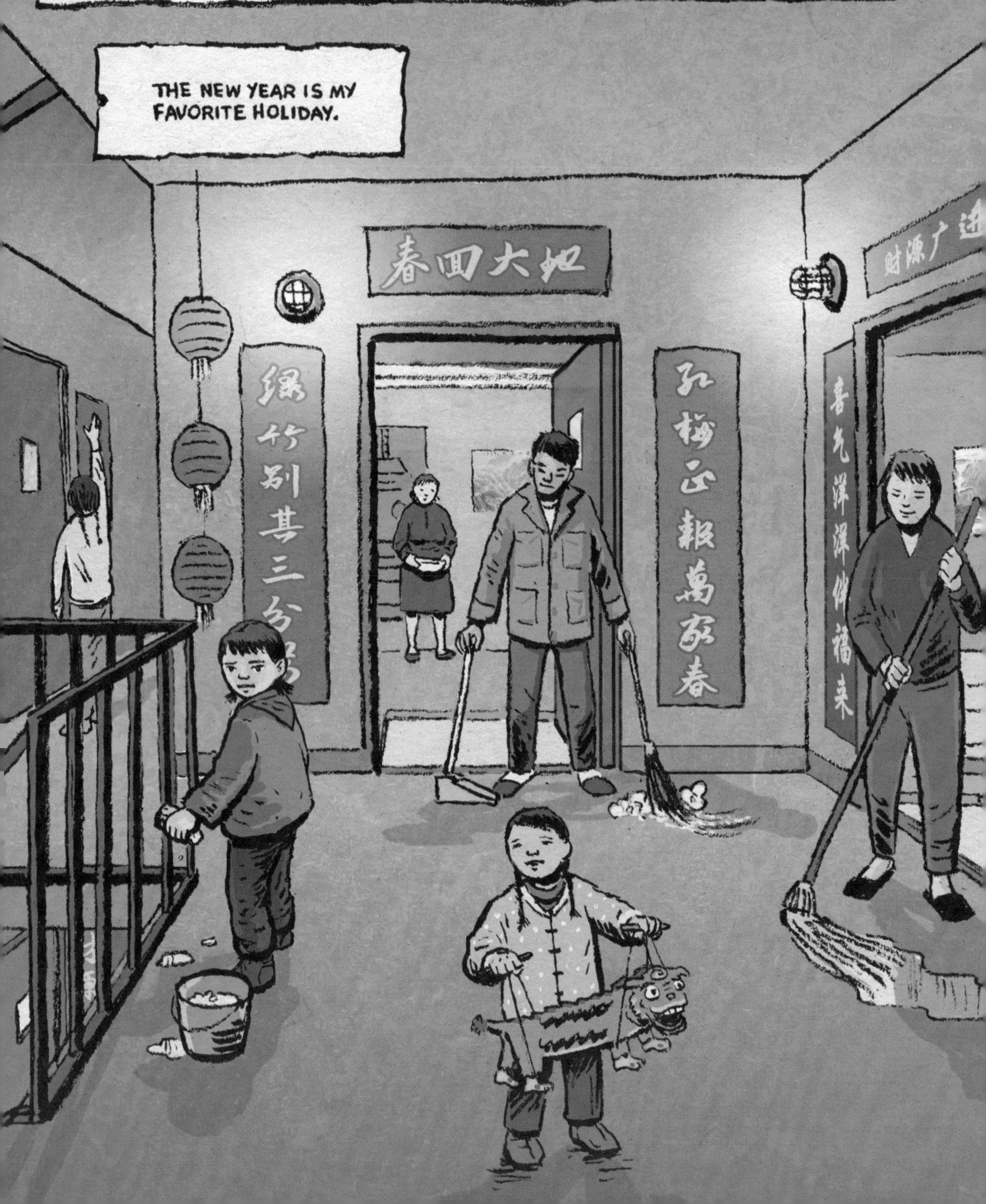

THE NEW YEAR IS MY FAVORITE HOLIDAY.
春回大地
绿竹别其三分
红梅正报萬家春
喜气洋洋伴福来
财源广进

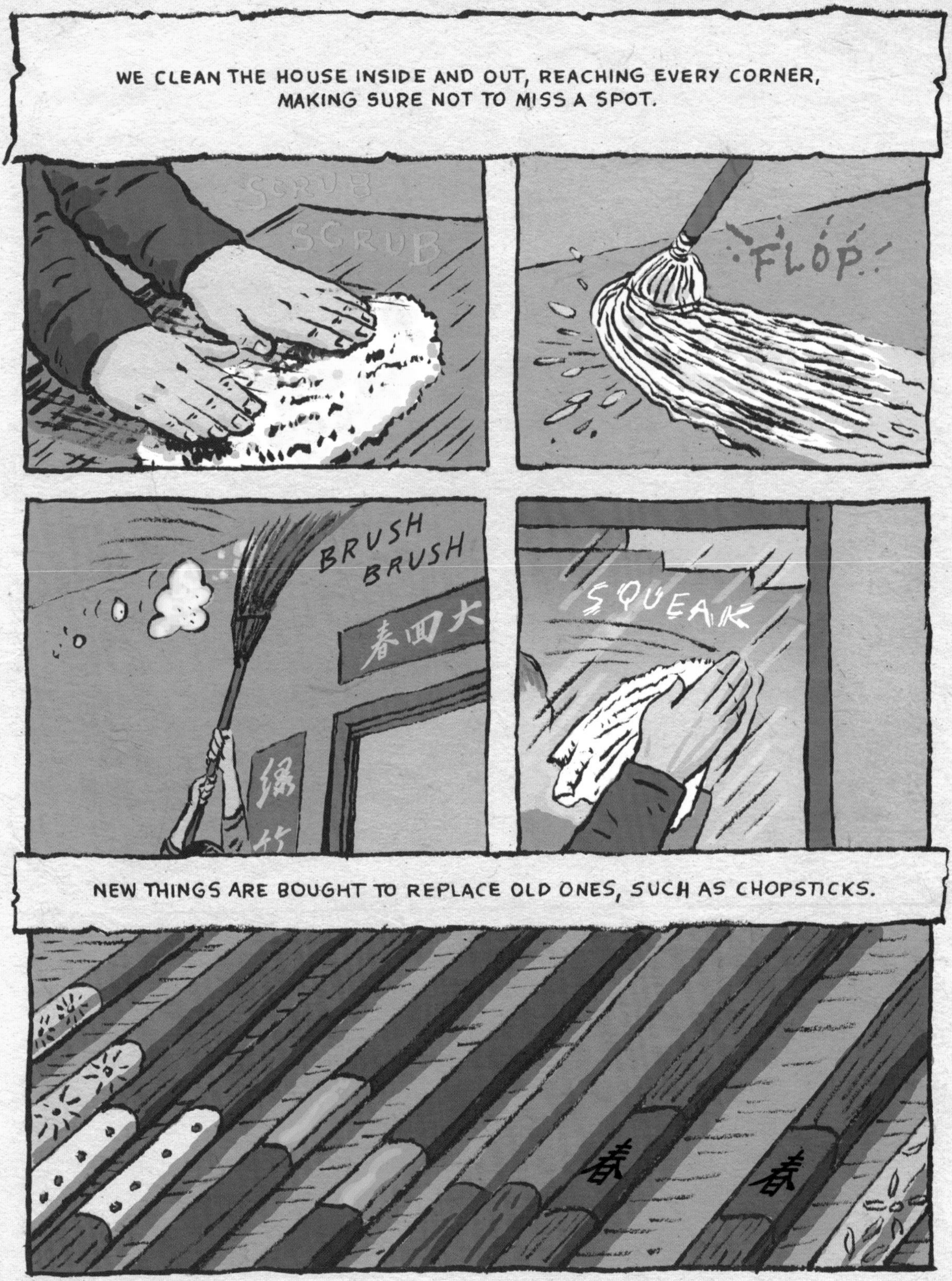
WE CLEAN THE HOUSE INSIDE AND OUT, REACHING EVERY CORNER, MAKING SURE NOT TO MISS A SPOT.
SCRUB
SCRUB
FLOP
BRUSH
BRUSH
SQUEAK
NEW THINGS ARE BOUGHT TO REPLACE OLD ONES, SUCH AS CHOPSTICKS.
春
春

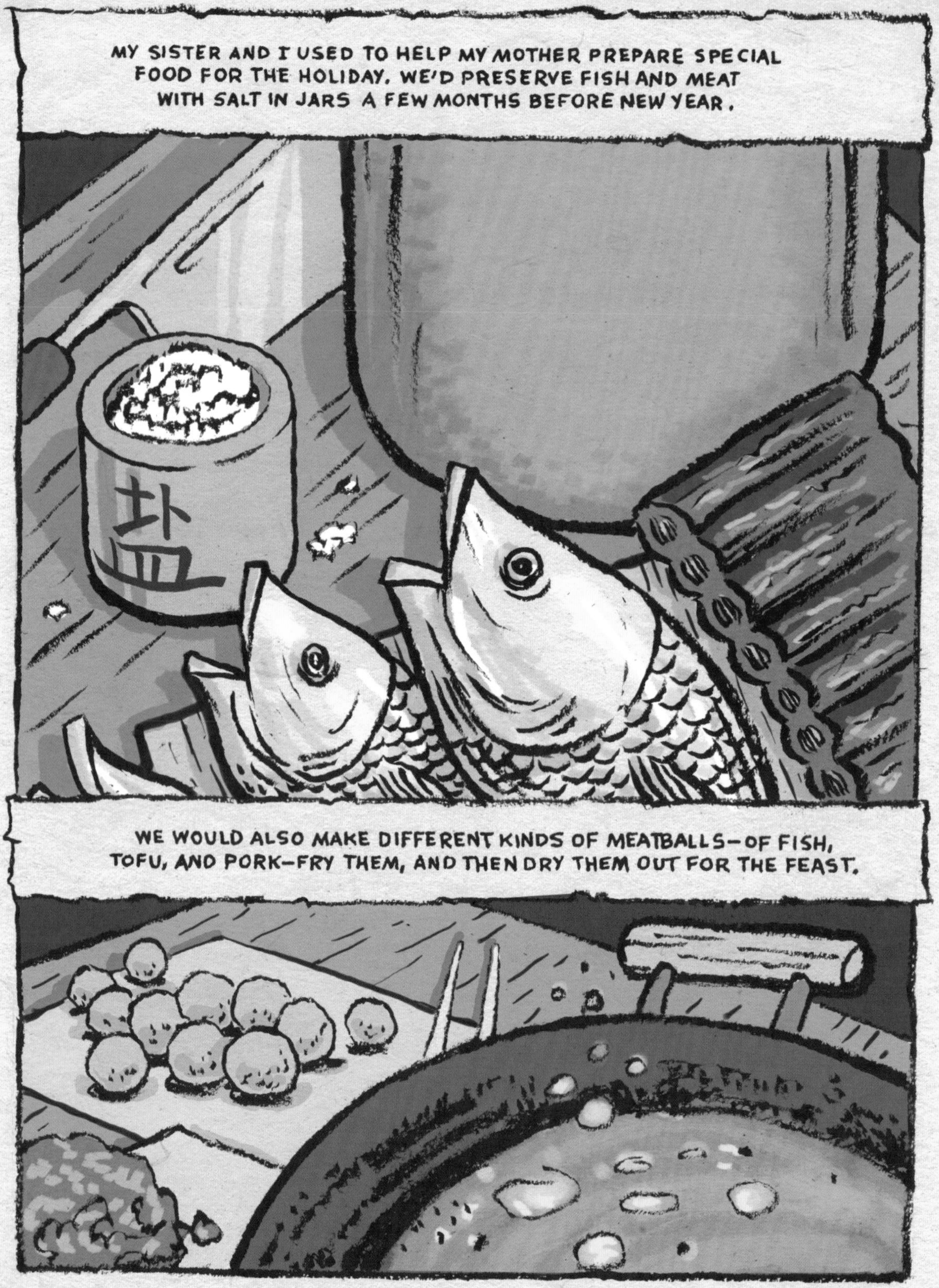
MY SISTER AND I USED TO HELP MY MOTHER PREPARE SPECIAL FOOD FOR THE HOLIDAY. WE'D PRESERVE FISH AND MEAT WITH SALT IN JARS A FEW MONTHS BEFORE NEW YEAR.
盐
WE WOULD ALSO MAKE DIFFERENT KINDS OF MEATBALLS—OF FISH, TOFU, AND PORK—FRY THEM, AND THEN DRY THEM OUT FOR THE FEAST.

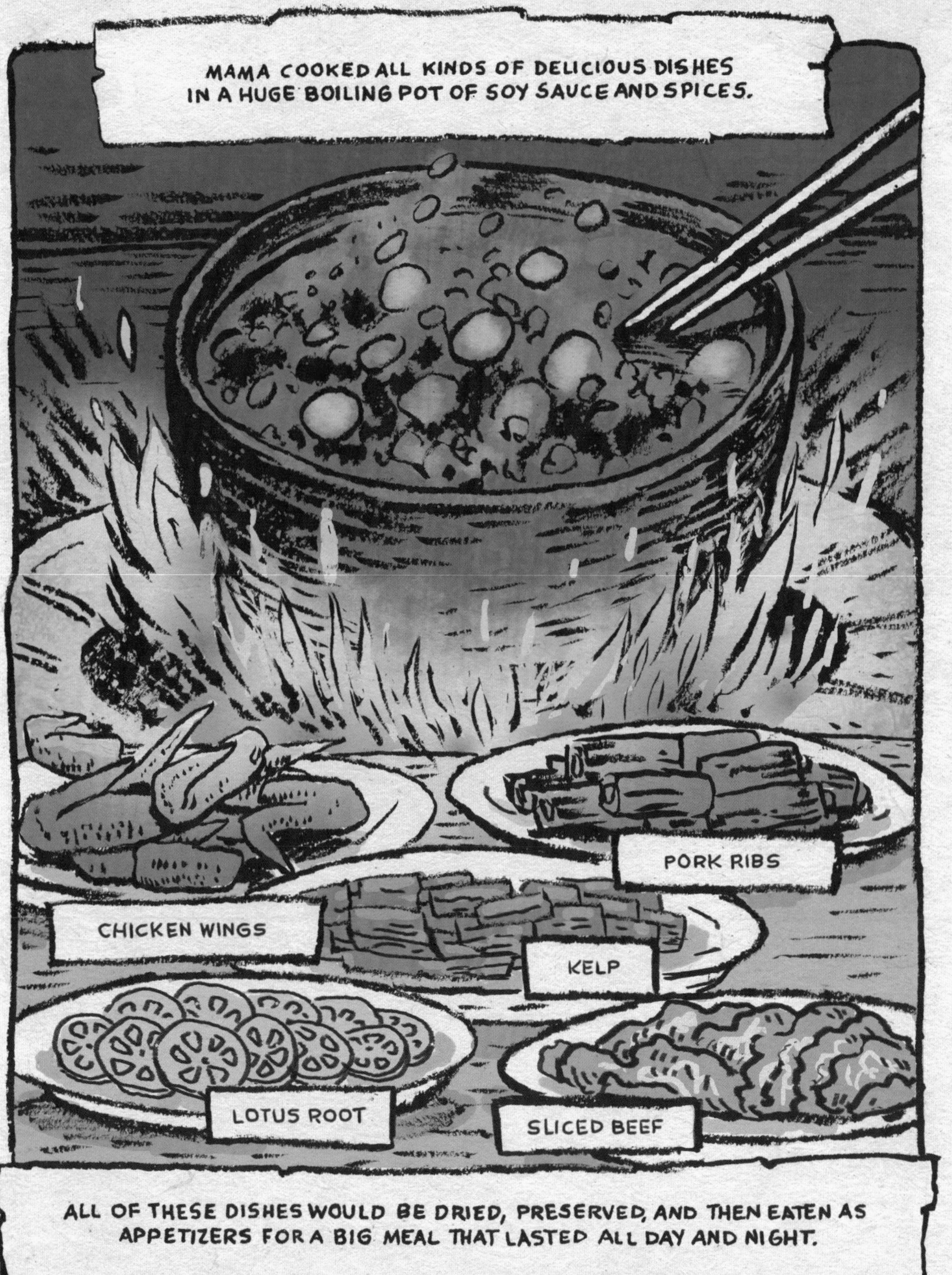
MAMA COOKED ALL KINDS OF DELICIOUS DISHES IN A HUGE BOILING POT OF SOY SAUCE AND SPICES.
PORK RIBS
CHICKEN WINGS
KELP
LOTUS ROOT
SLICED BEEF
ALL OF THESE DISHES WOULD BE DRIED, PRESERVED, AND THEN EATEN AS APPETIZERS FOR A BIG MEAL THAT LASTED ALL DAY AND NIGHT.

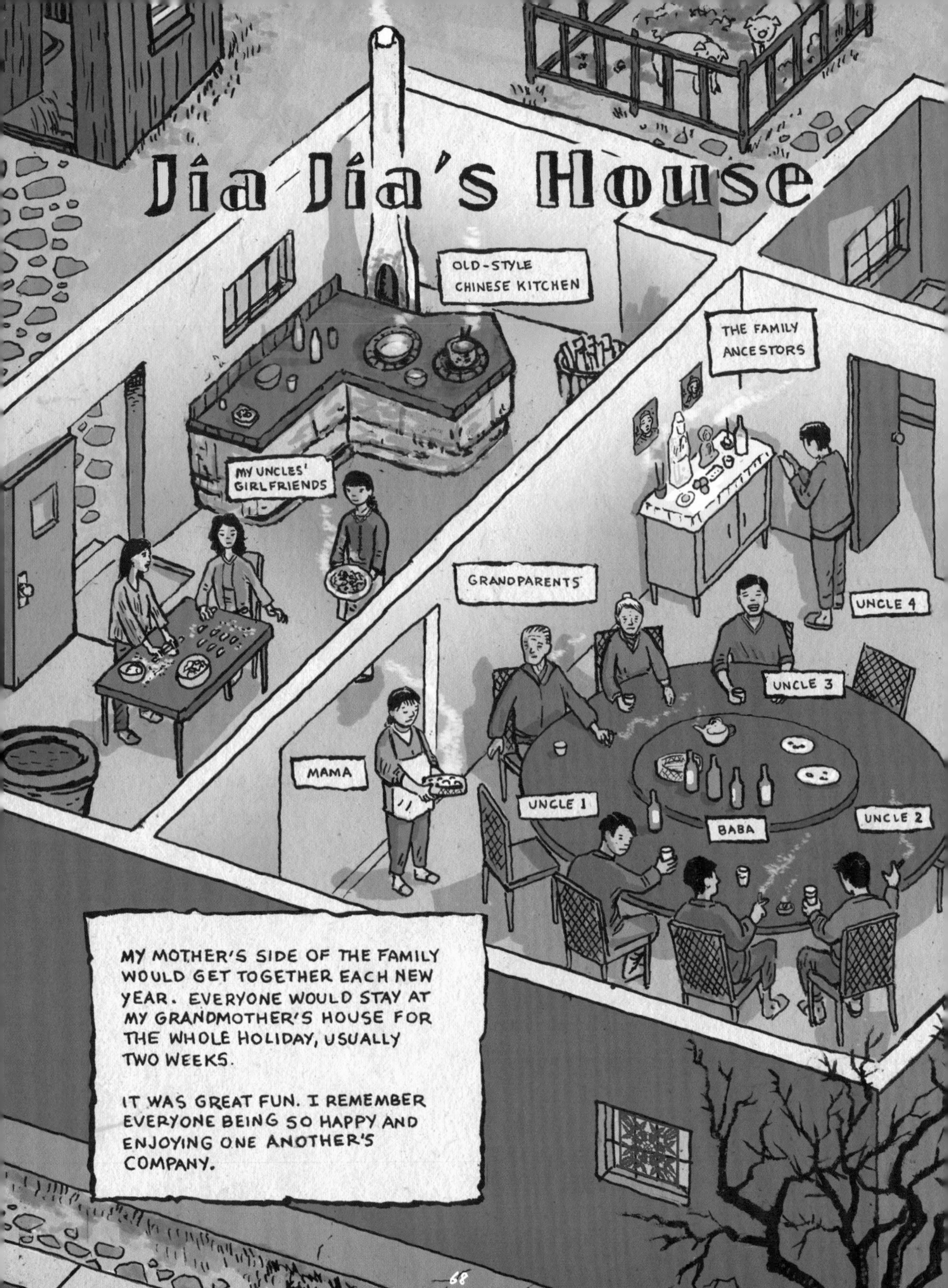

Jia Jia's House
OLD-STYLE CHINESE KITCHEN
THE FAMILY ANCESTORS
MY UNCLES' GIRLFRIENDS
GRANDPARENTS
UNCLE 4
UNCLE 3
MAMA
UNCLE 1
BABA
UNCLE 2
MY MOTHER'S SIDE OF THE FAMILY WOULD GET TOGETHER EACH NEW YEAR. EVERYONE WOULD STAY AT MY GRANDMOTHER'S HOUSE FOR THE WHOLE HOLIDAY, USUALLY TWO WEEKS.
IT WAS GREAT FUN. I REMEMBER EVERYONE BEING SO HAPPY AND ENJOYING ONE ANOTHER'S COMPANY.

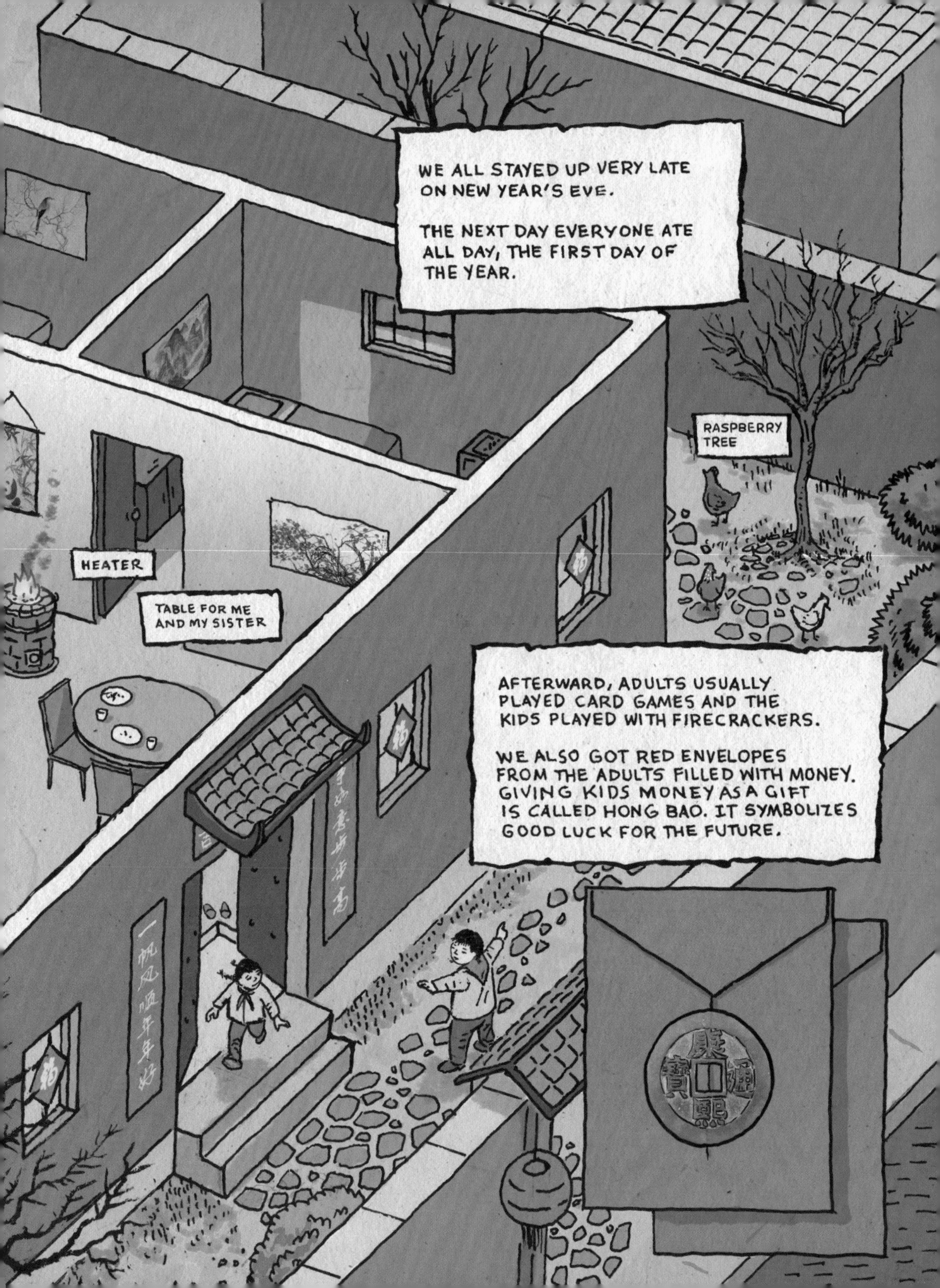
WE ALL STAYED UP VERY LATE ON NEW YEAR'S EVE.
THE NEXT DAY EVERYONE ATE ALL DAY, THE FIRST DAY OF THE YEAR.
RASPBERRY TREE
HEATER
TABLE FOR ME AND MY SISTER
AFTERWARD, ADULTS USUALLY PLAYED CARD GAMES AND THE KIDS PLAYED WITH FIRECRACKERS.
WE ALSO GOT RED ENVELOPES FROM THE ADULTS FILLED WITH MONEY. GIVING KIDS MONEY AS A GIFT IS CALLED HONG BAO. IT SYMBOLIZES GOOD LUCK FOR THE FUTURE.

Little White Duck

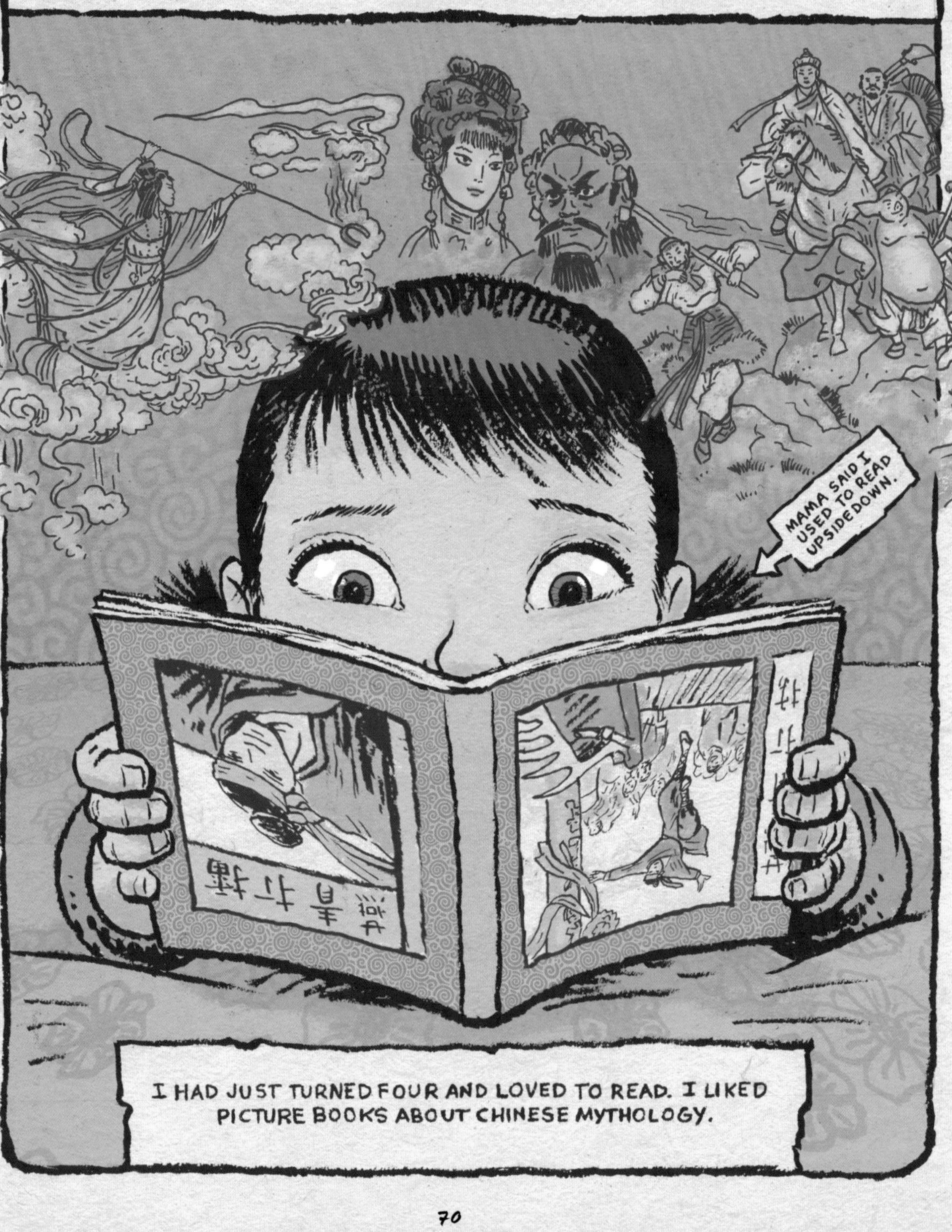
MAMA SAID I USED TO READ UPSIDE DOWN.
I HAD JUST TURNED FOUR AND LOVED TO READ. I LIKED PICTURE BOOKS ABOUT CHINESE MYTHOLOGY.

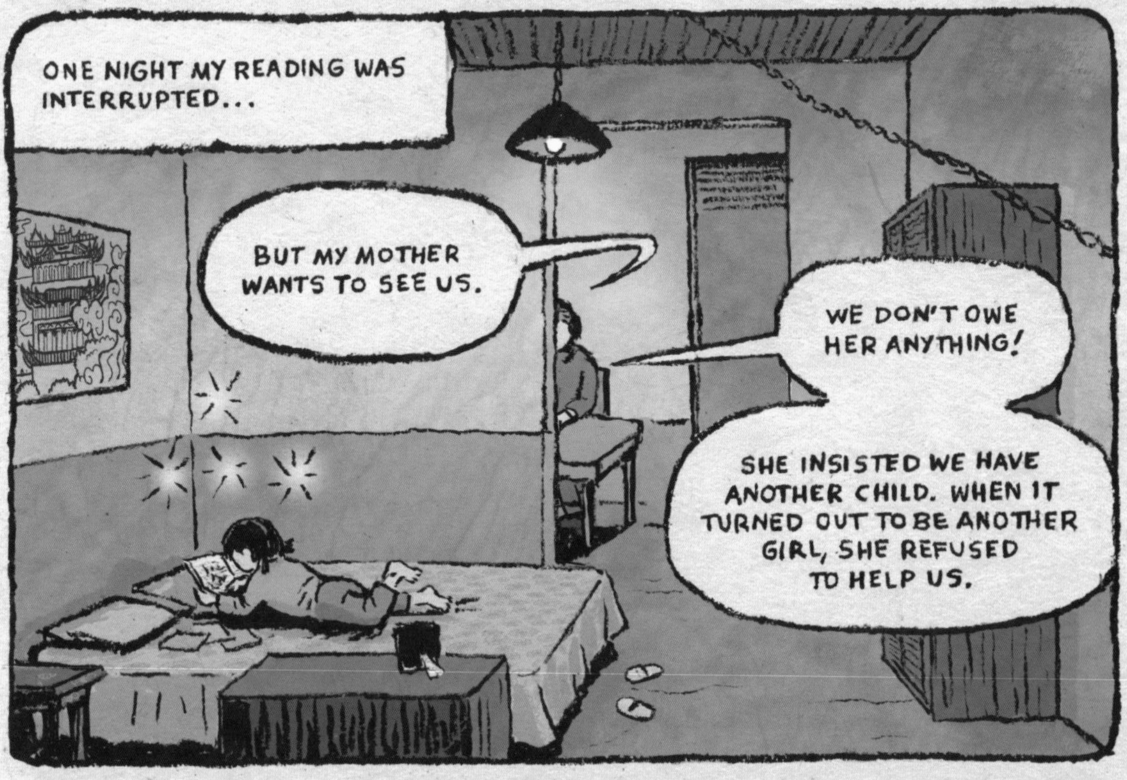
ONE NIGHT MY READING WAS INTERRUPTED...
BUT MY MOTHER WANTS TO SEE US.
WE DON'T OWE HER ANYTHING!
SHE INSISTED WE HAVE ANOTHER CHILD. WHEN IT TURNED OUT TO BE ANOTHER GIRL, SHE REFUSED TO HELP US.

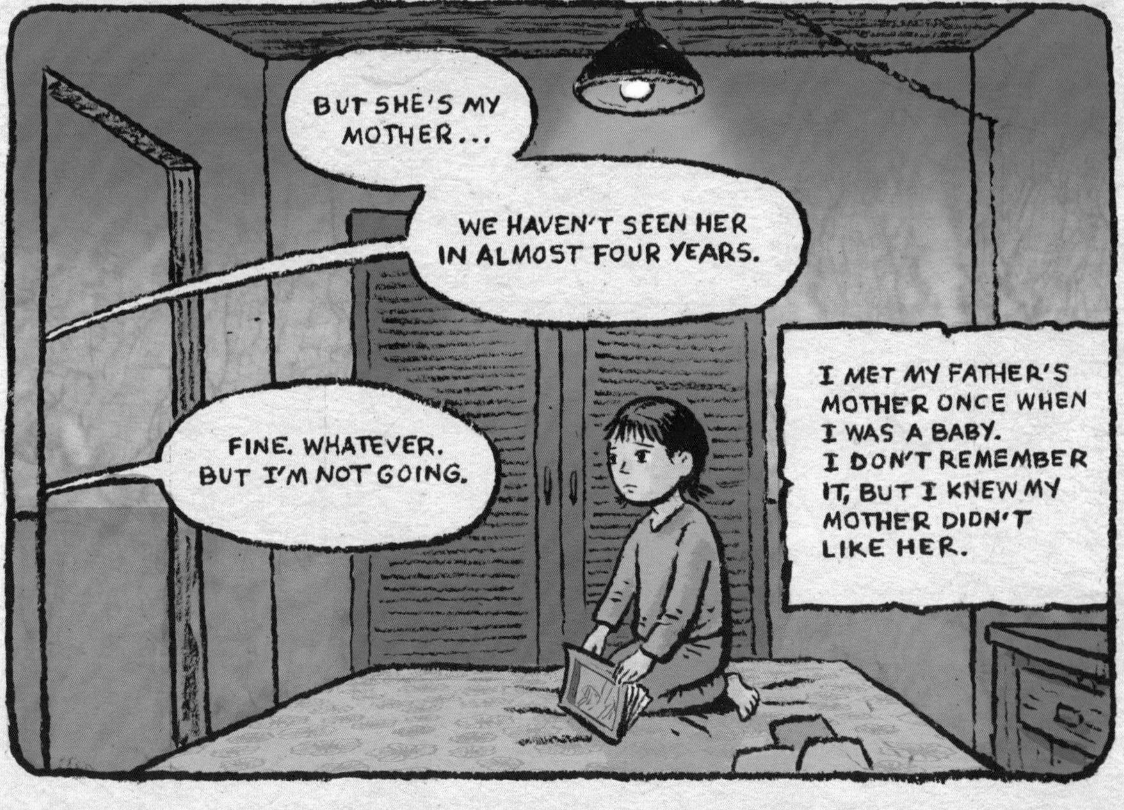
BUT SHE'S MY MOTHER...
WE HAVEN'T SEEN HER IN ALMOST FOUR YEARS.
FINE. WHATEVER. BUT I'M NOT GOING.
I MET MY FATHER'S MOTHER ONCE WHEN I WAS A BABY. I DON'T REMEMBER IT, BUT I KNEW MY MOTHER DIDN'T LIKE HER.

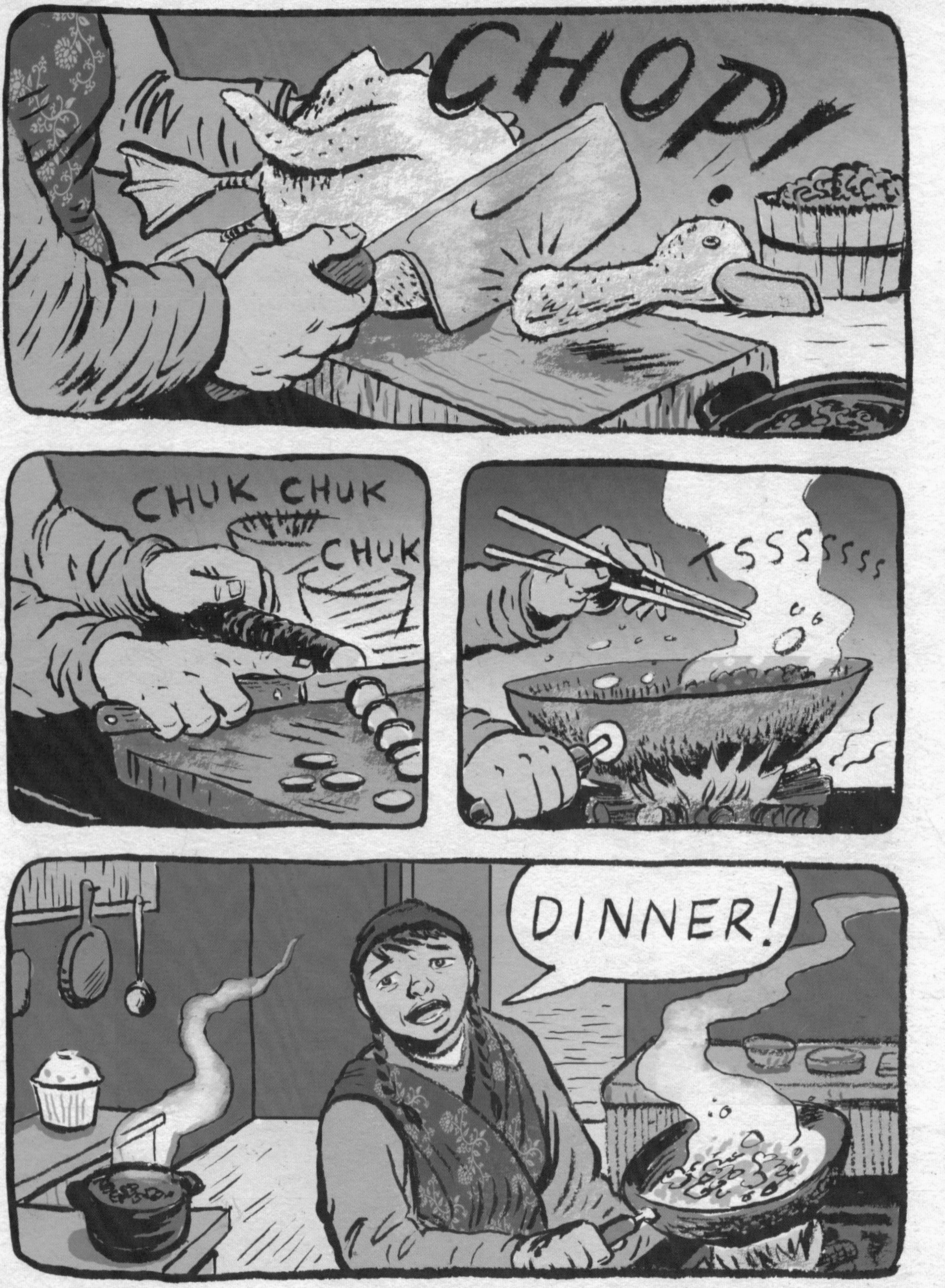
CHOP!
CHUK CHUK
CHUK
TSSSSSSS
DINNER!

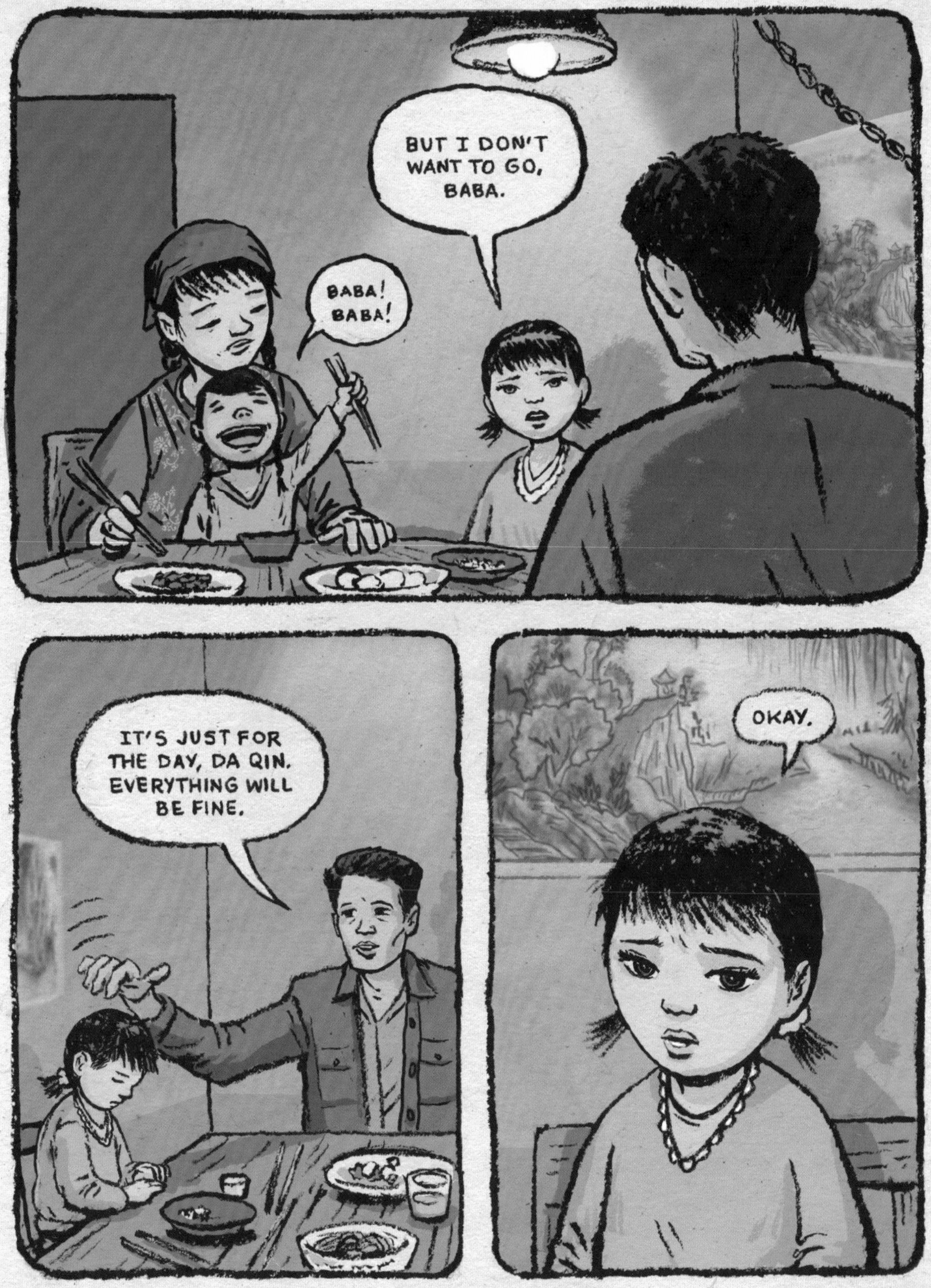
BUT I DON'T WANT TO GO, BABA.
BABA! BABA!
IT'S JUST FOR THE DAY, DA QIN. EVERYTHING WILL BE FINE.
OKAY.

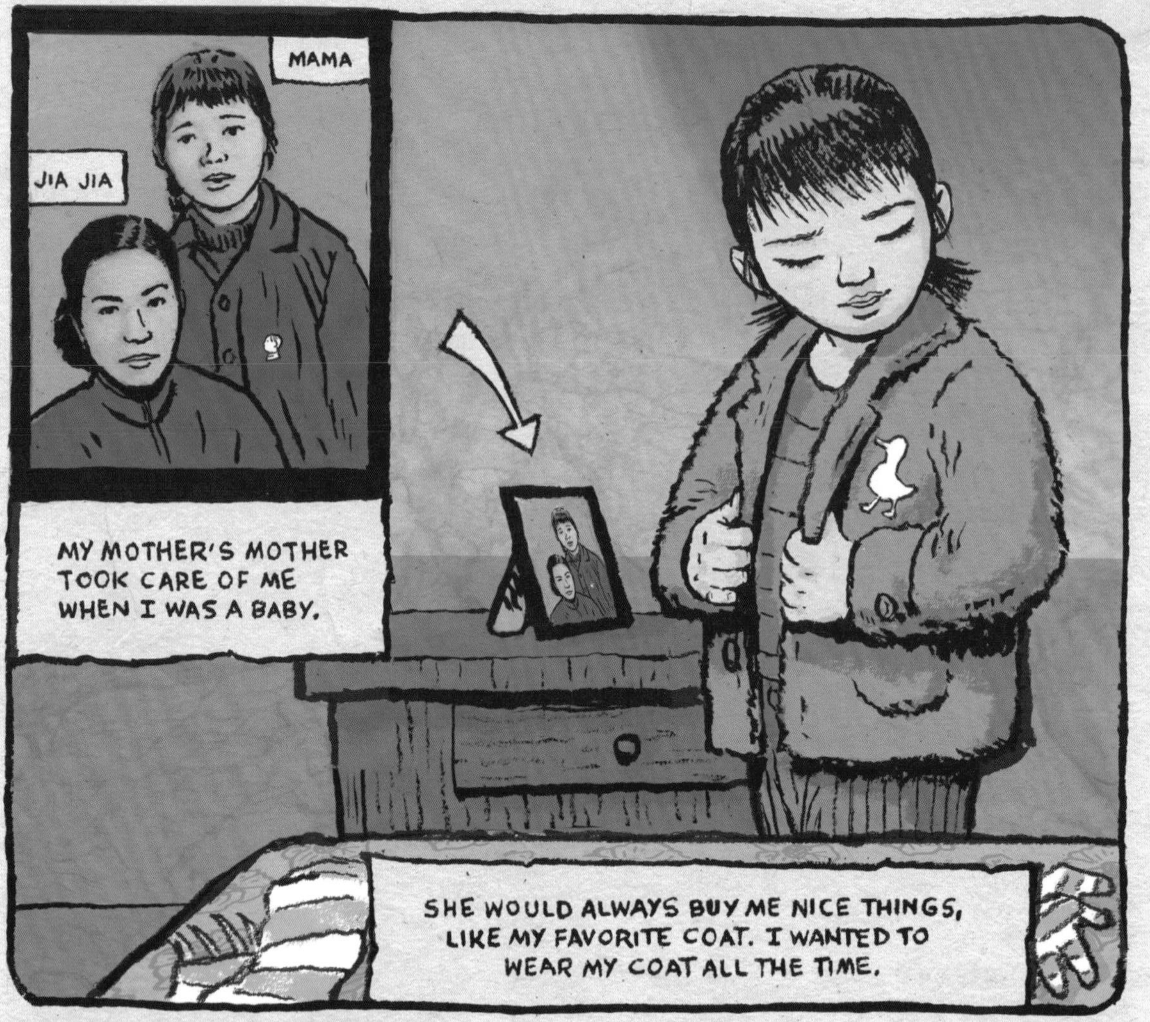
MAMA
JIA JIA
MY MOTHER'S MOTHER TOOK CARE OF ME WHEN I WAS A BABY.
SHE WOULD ALWAYS BUY ME NICE THINGS, LIKE MY FAVORITE COAT. I WANTED TO WEAR MY COAT ALL THE TIME.

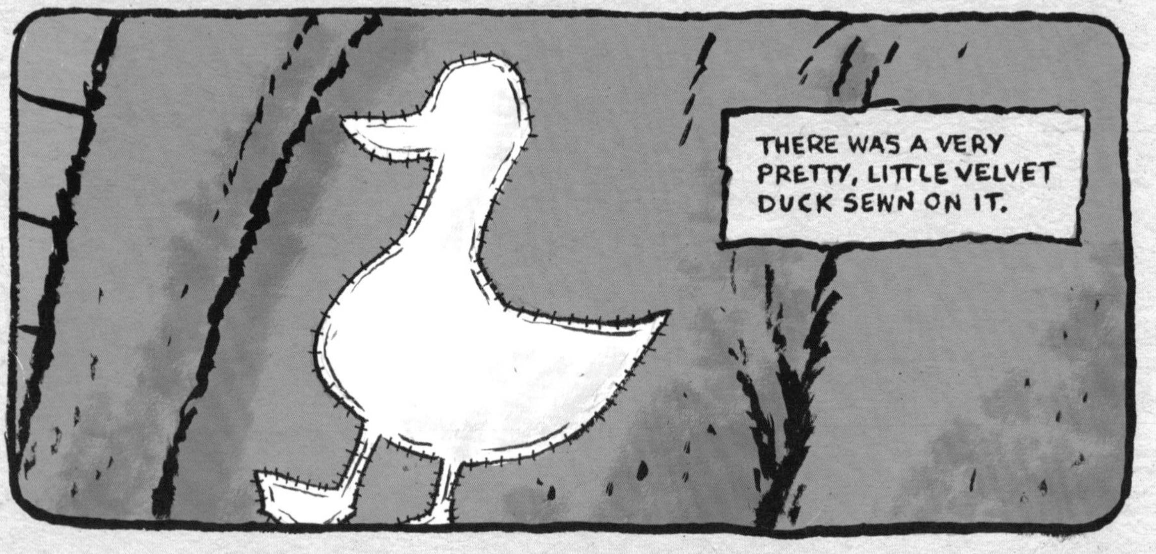
THERE WAS A VERY PRETTY, LITTLE VELVET DUCK SEWN ON IT.

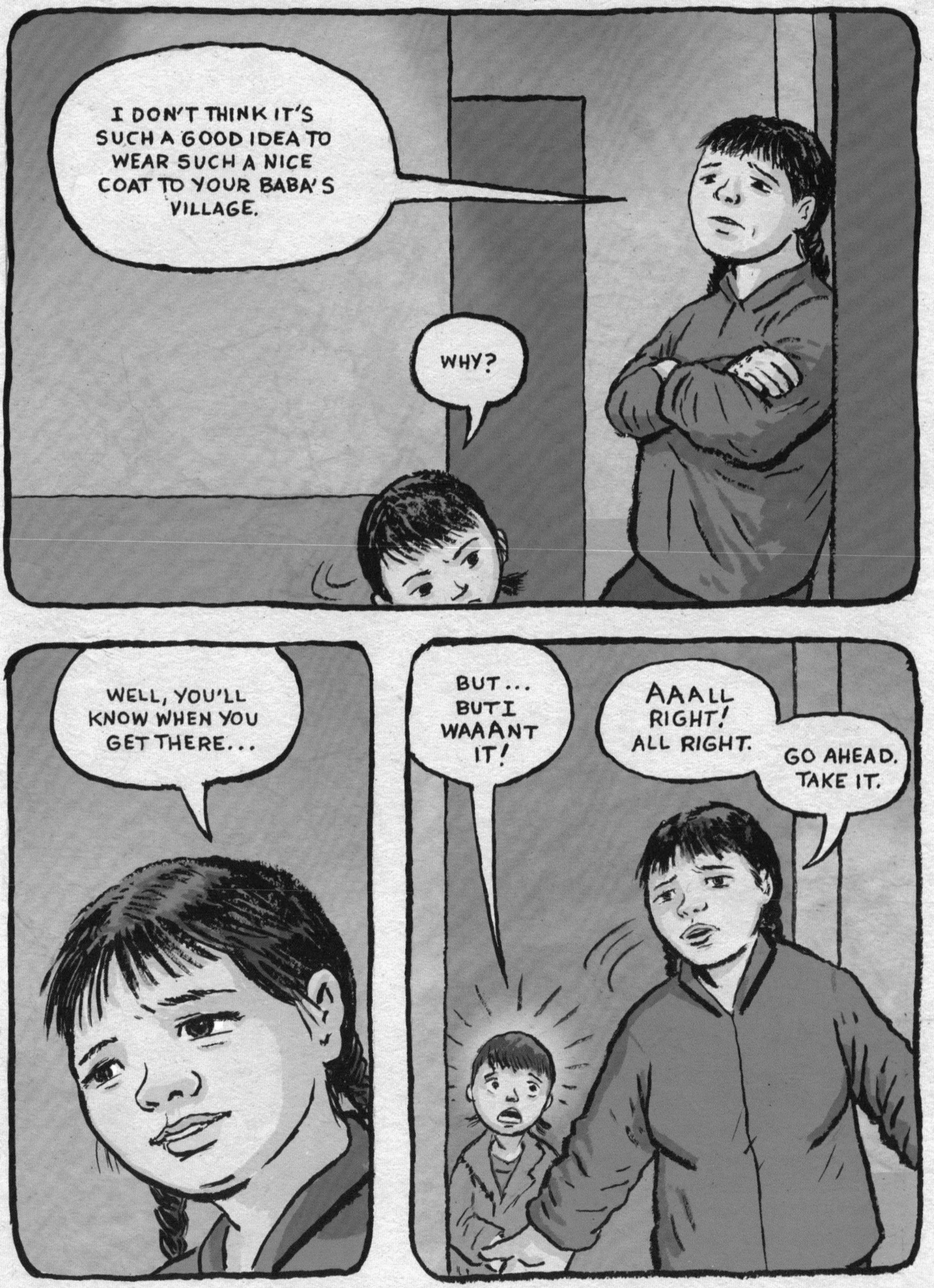

I DON'T THINK IT'S SUCH A GOOD IDEA TO WEAR SUCH A NICE COAT TO YOUR BABA'S VILLAGE.
WHY?
WELL, YOU'LL KNOW WHEN YOU GET THERE...
BUT... BUT I WAAANT IT!
AAALL RIGHT! ALL RIGHT.
GO AHEAD. TAKE IT.

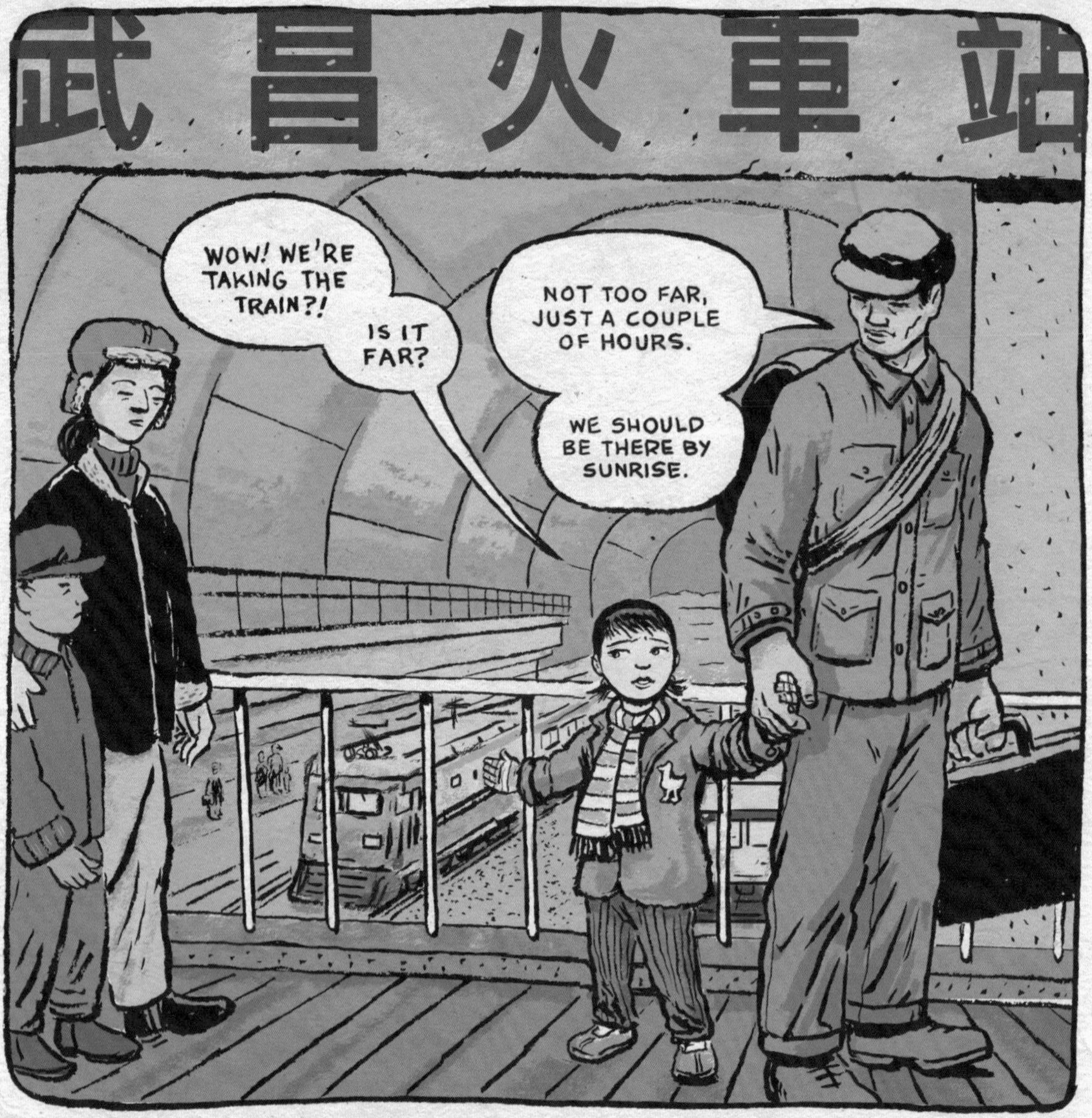
武昌火車站
WOW! WE'RE TAKING THE TRAIN?!
IS IT FAR?
NOT TOO FAR, JUST A COUPLE OF HOURS.
WE SHOULD BE THERE BY SUNRISE.

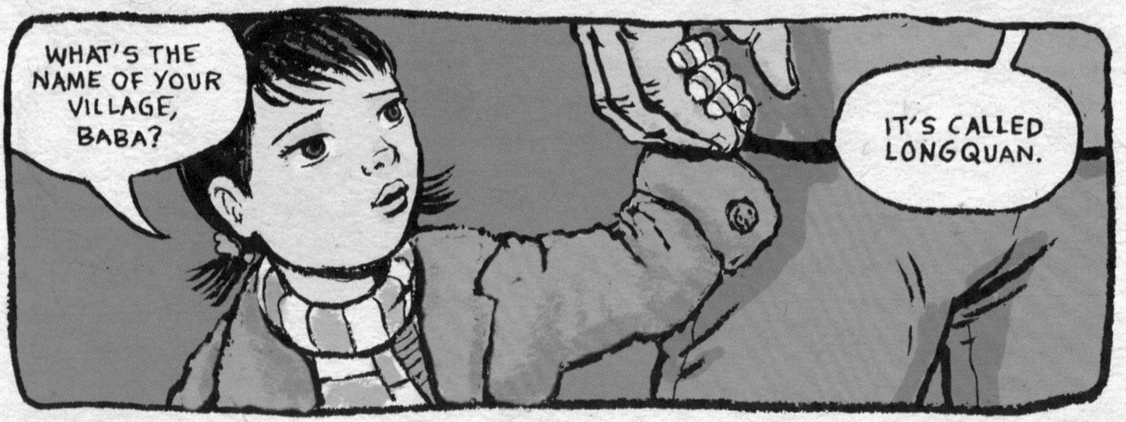
WHAT'S THE NAME OF YOUR VILLAGE, BABA?
IT'S CALLED LONGQUAN.

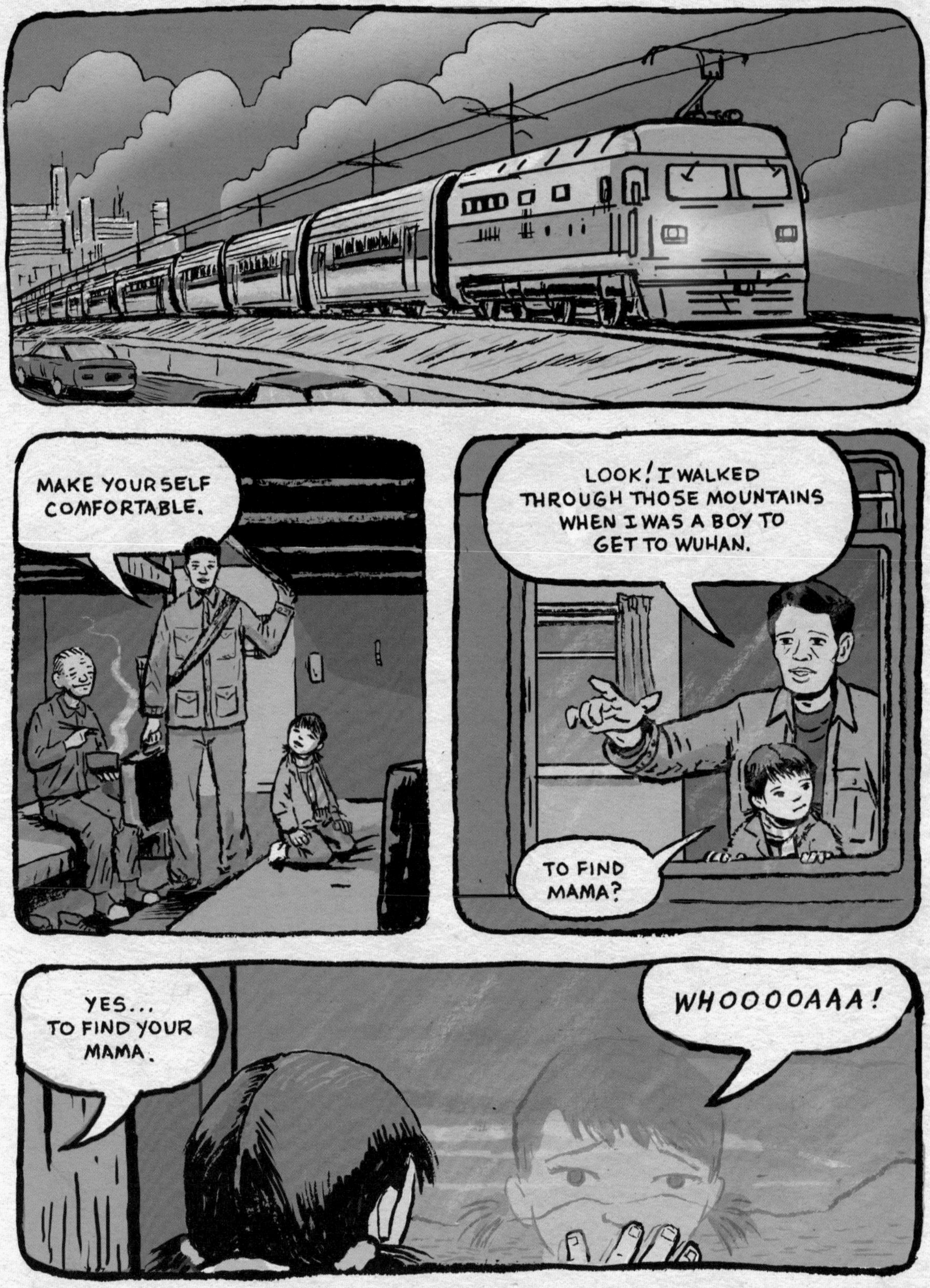

MAKE YOURSELF COMFORTABLE.
LOOK! I WALKED THROUGH THOSE MOUNTAINS WHEN I WAS A BOY TO GET TO WUHAN.
TO FIND MAMA?
YES... TO FIND YOUR MAMA.
WHOOOOAAA!

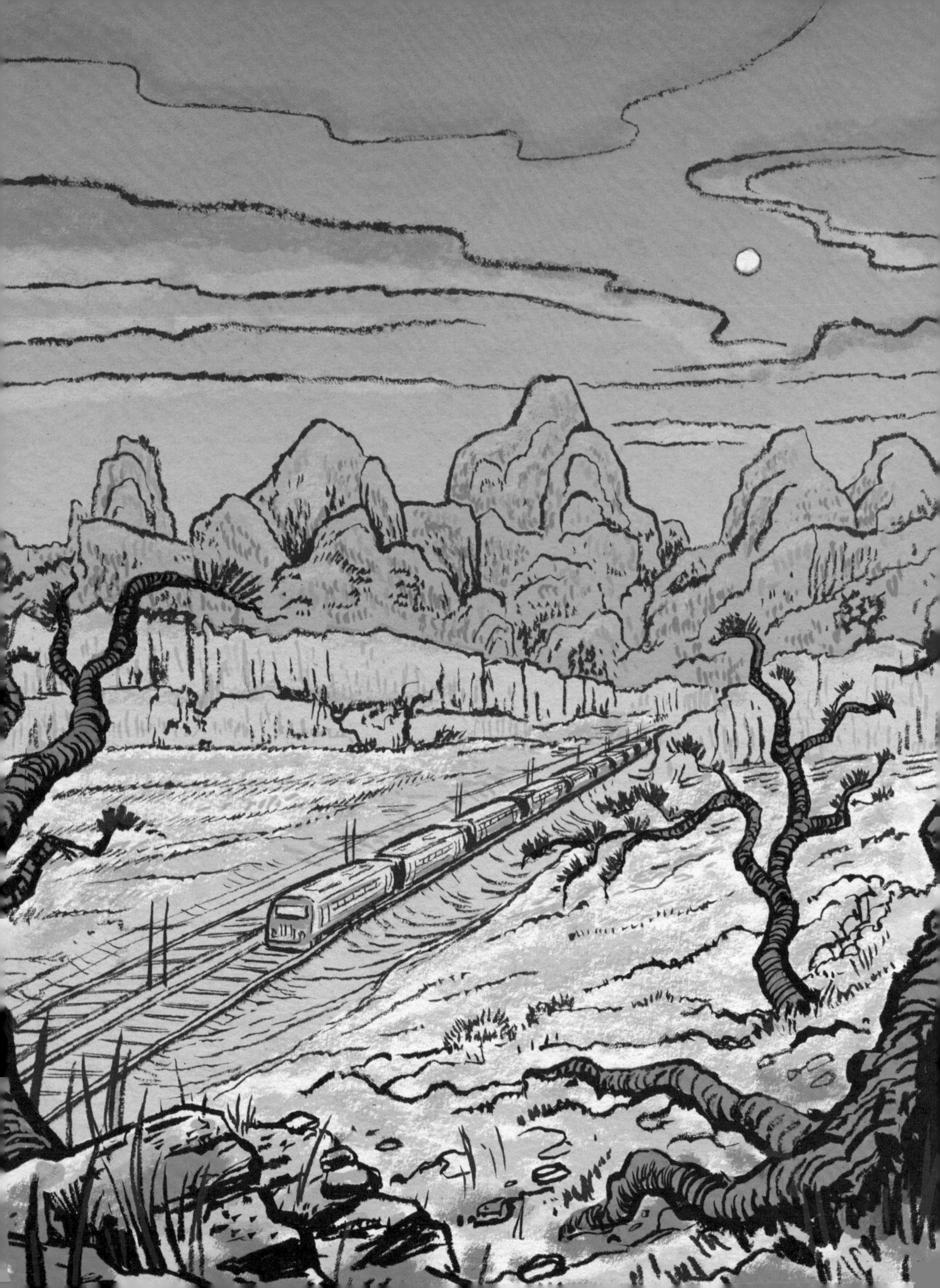

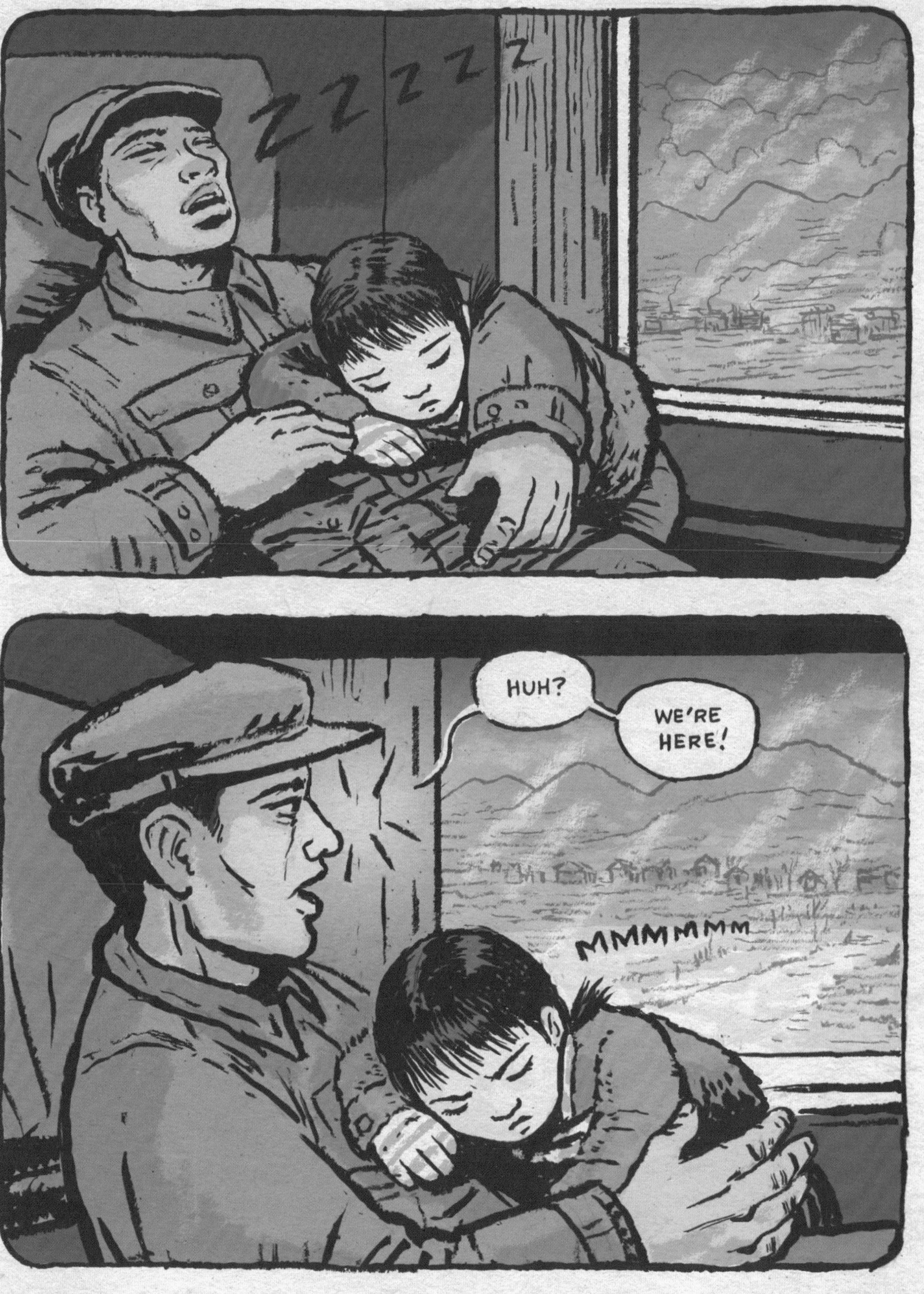
ZZZZZ
HUH?
WE'RE HERE!
MMMMMMM

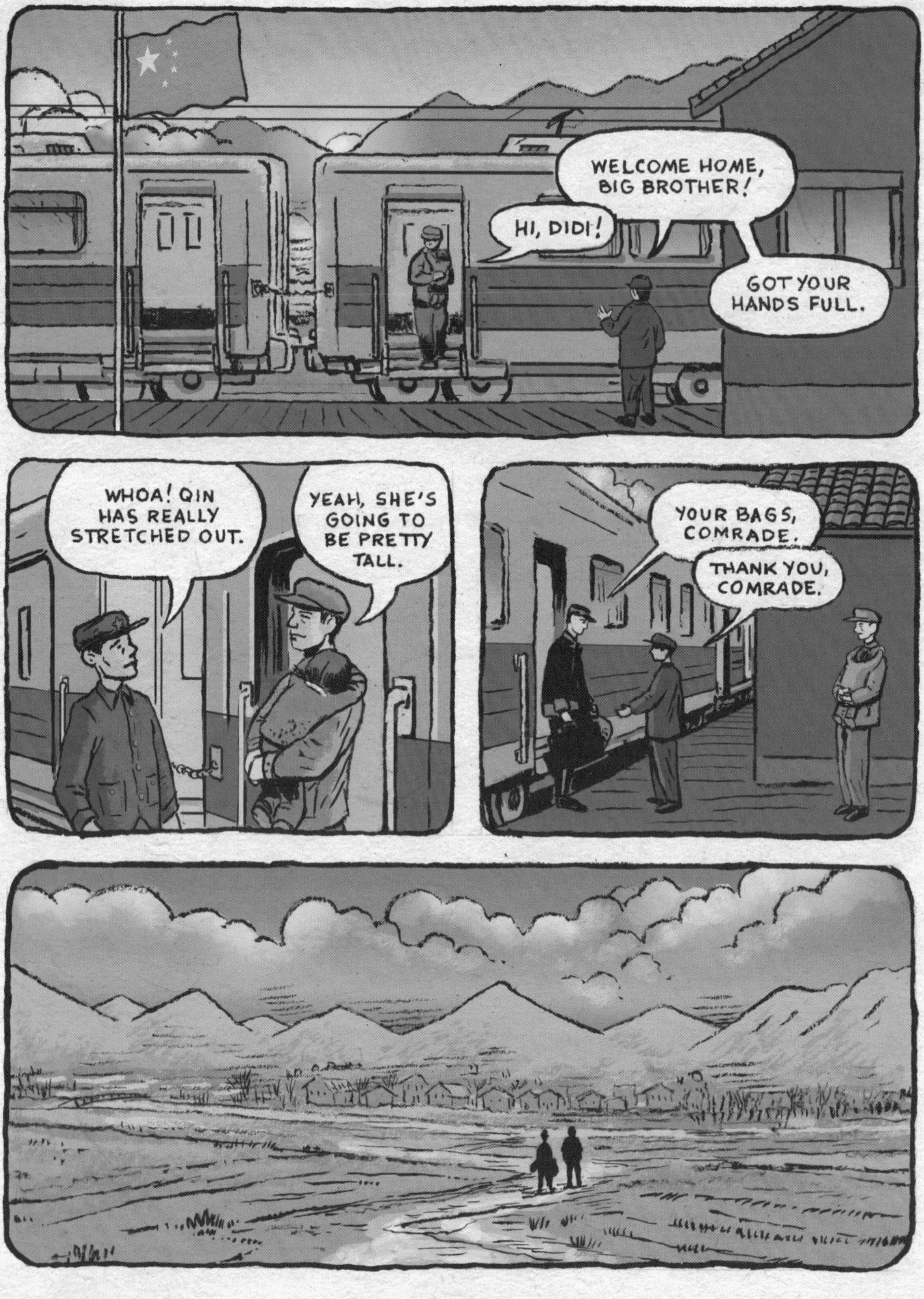
WELCOME HOME, BIG BROTHER!
HI, DIDI!
GOT YOUR HANDS FULL.
WHOA! QIN HAS REALLY STRETCHED OUT.
YEAH, SHE'S GOING TO BE PRETTY TALL.
YOUR BAGS, COMRADE.
THANK YOU, COMRADE.

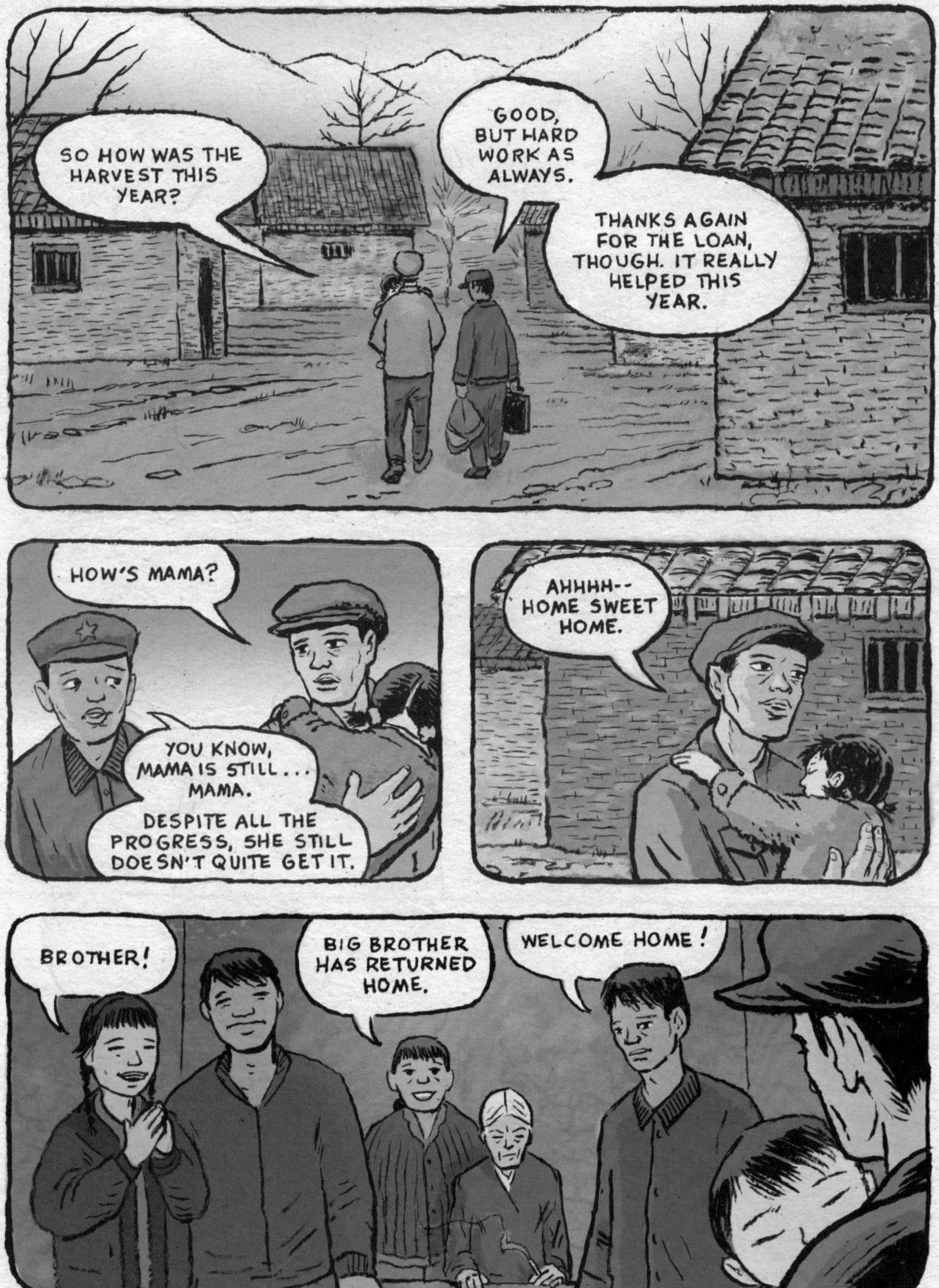
SO HOW WAS THE HARVEST THIS YEAR?
GOOD, BUT HARD WORK AS ALWAYS.
THANKS AGAIN FOR THE LOAN, THOUGH. IT REALLY HELPED THIS YEAR.
HOW'S MAMA?
YOU KNOW, MAMA IS STILL... MAMA.
DESPITE ALL THE PROGRESS, SHE STILL DOESN'T QUITE GET IT.
AHHHH-- HOME SWEET HOME.
BROTHER!
BIG BROTHER HAS RETURNED HOME.
WELCOME HOME!

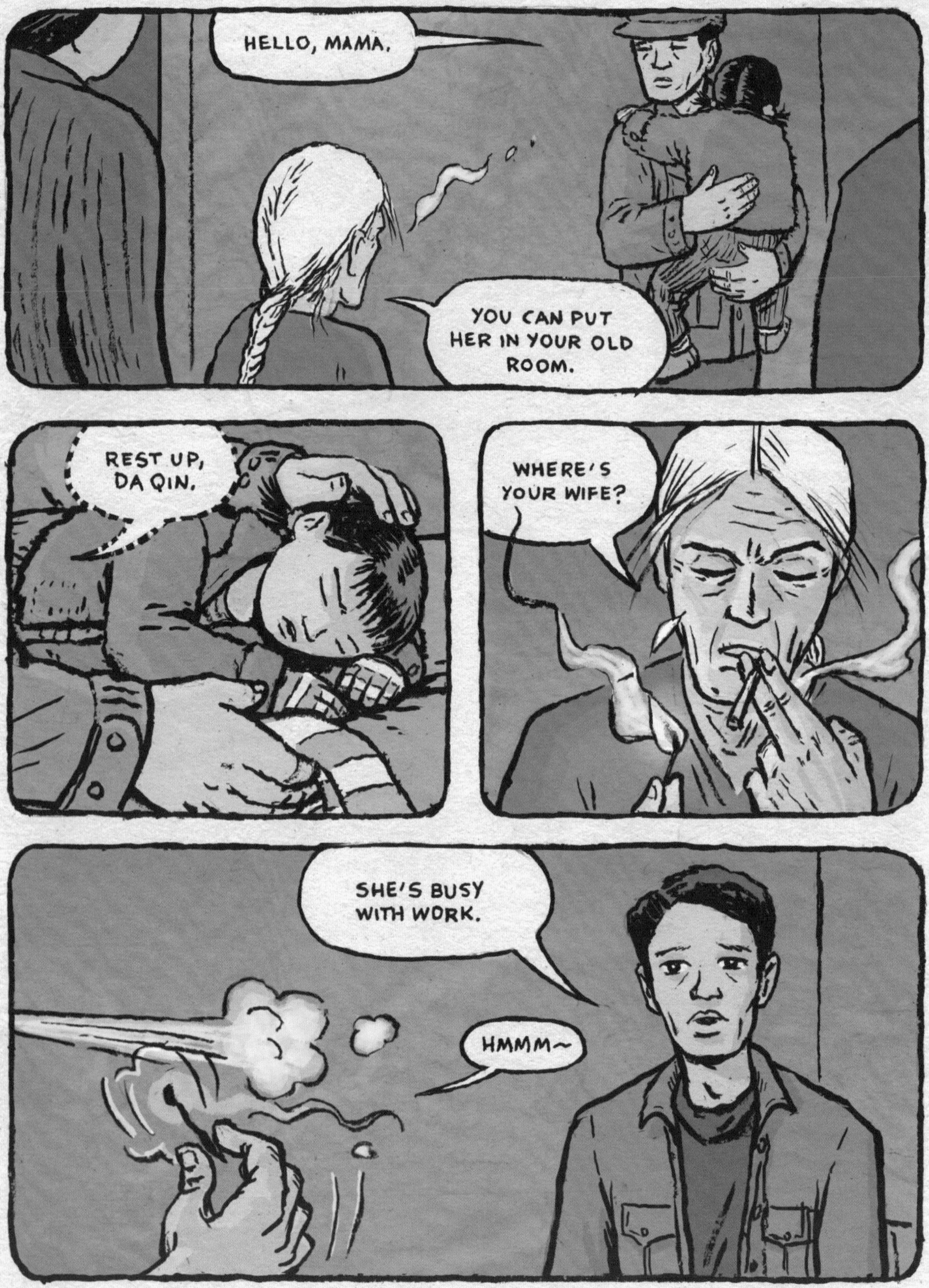
HELLO, MAMA.
YOU CAN PUT HER IN YOUR OLD ROOM.
REST UP, DA QIN.
WHERE'S YOUR WIFE?
SHE'S BUSY WITH WORK.
HMMM~

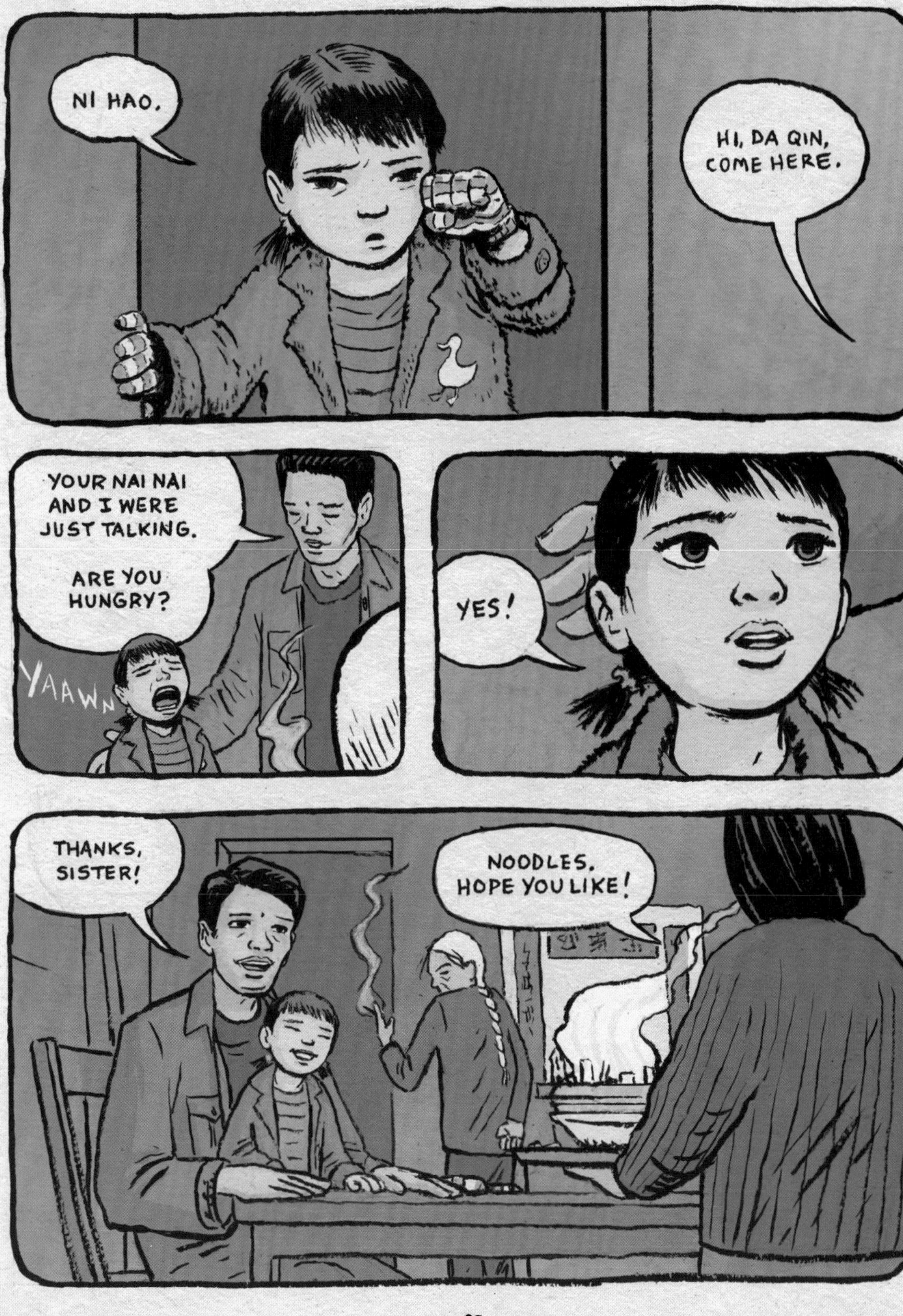
NI HAO.
HI, DA QIN, COME HERE.
YOUR NAI NAI AND I WERE JUST TALKING.
ARE YOU HUNGRY?
YAAWN
YES!
THANKS, SISTER!
NOODLES. HOPE YOU LIKE!

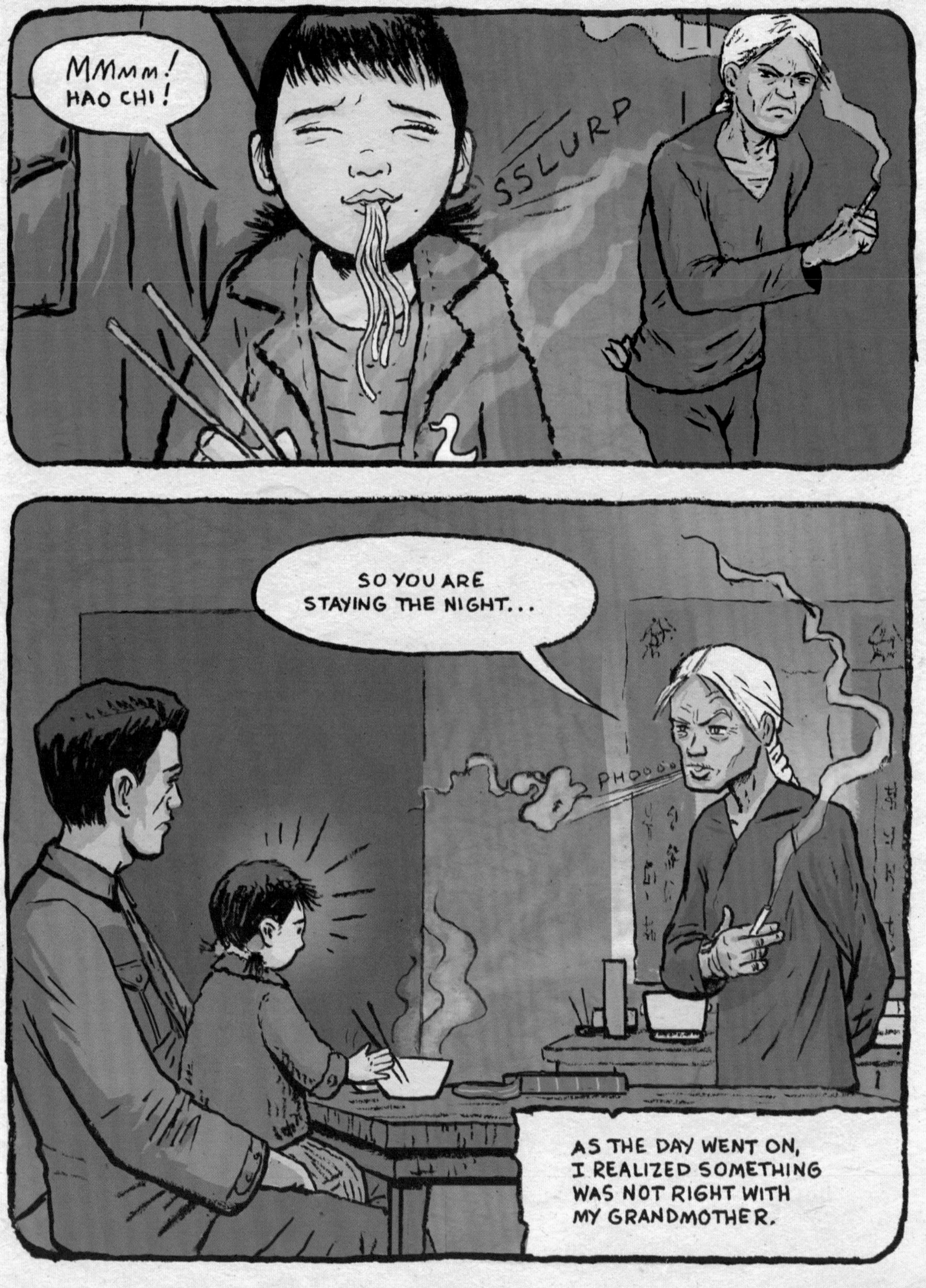
MMMMM! HAO CHI!
SSLURP
SO YOU ARE STAYING THE NIGHT...
PHOOOOO
AS THE DAY WENT ON, I REALIZED SOMETHING WAS NOT RIGHT WITH MY GRANDMOTHER.

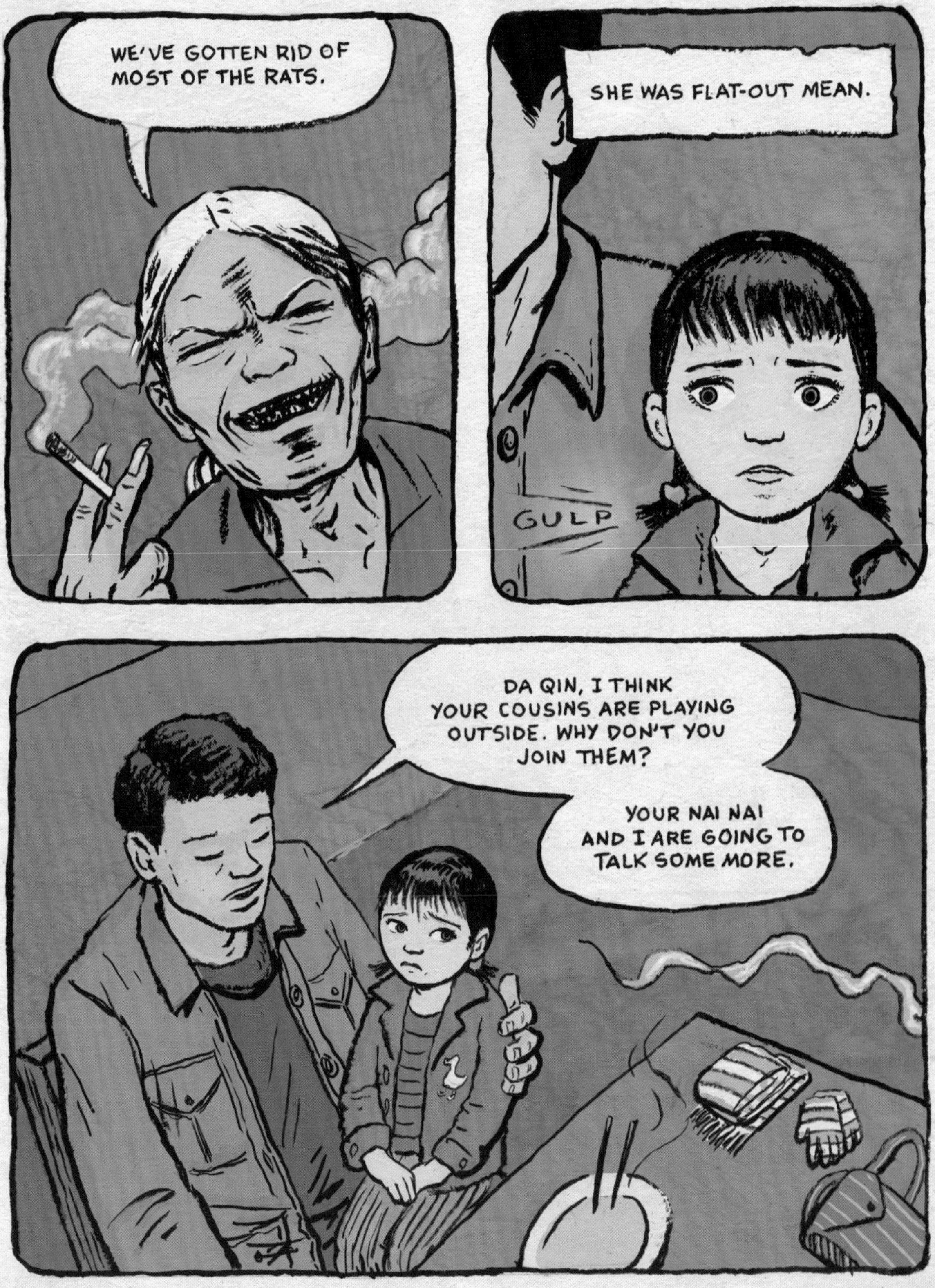
WE'VE GOTTEN RID OF MOST OF THE RATS.
SHE WAS FLAT-OUT MEAN.
GULP
DA QIN, I THINK YOUR COUSINS ARE PLAYING OUTSIDE. WHY DON'T YOU JOIN THEM?
YOUR NAI NAI AND I ARE GOING TO TALK SOME MORE.

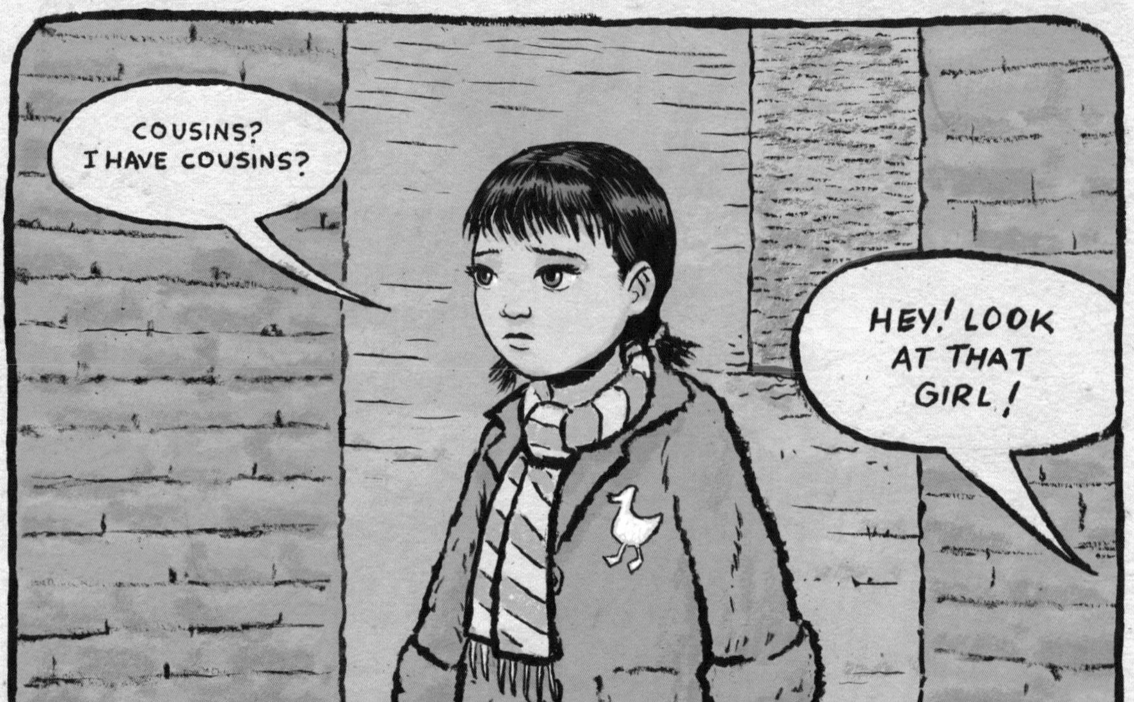
COUSINS?
I HAVE COUSINS?
HEY! LOOK AT THAT GIRL!

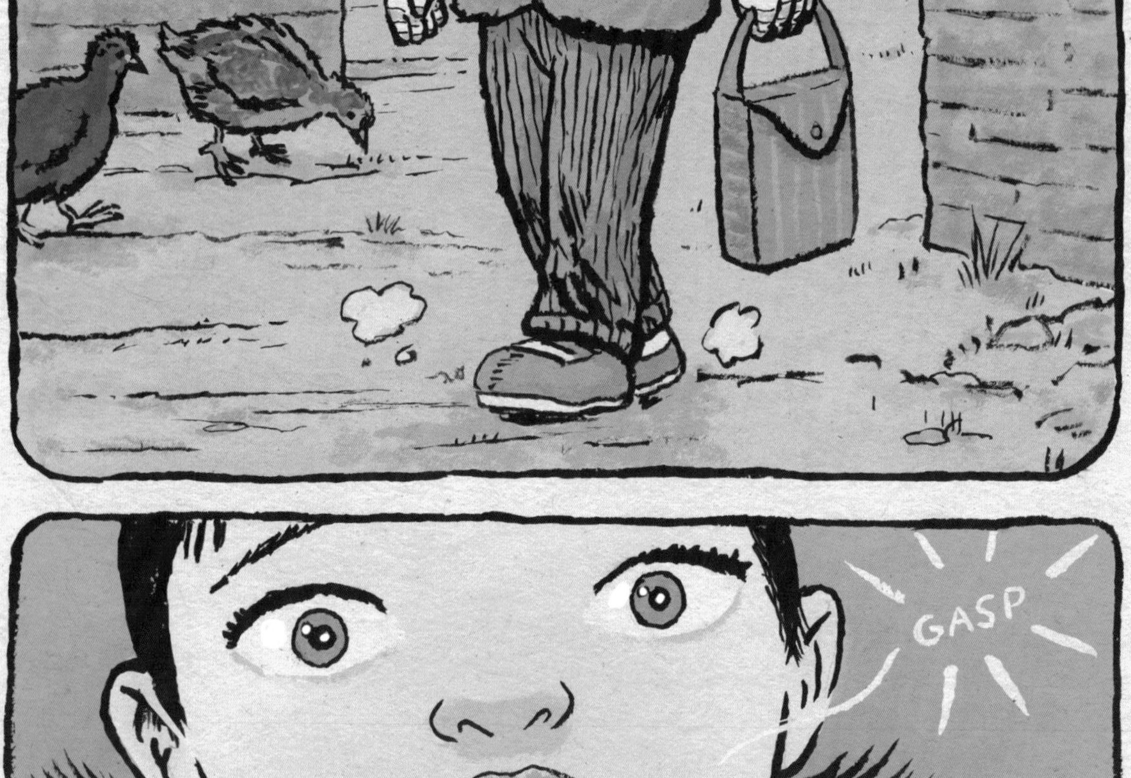
GASP

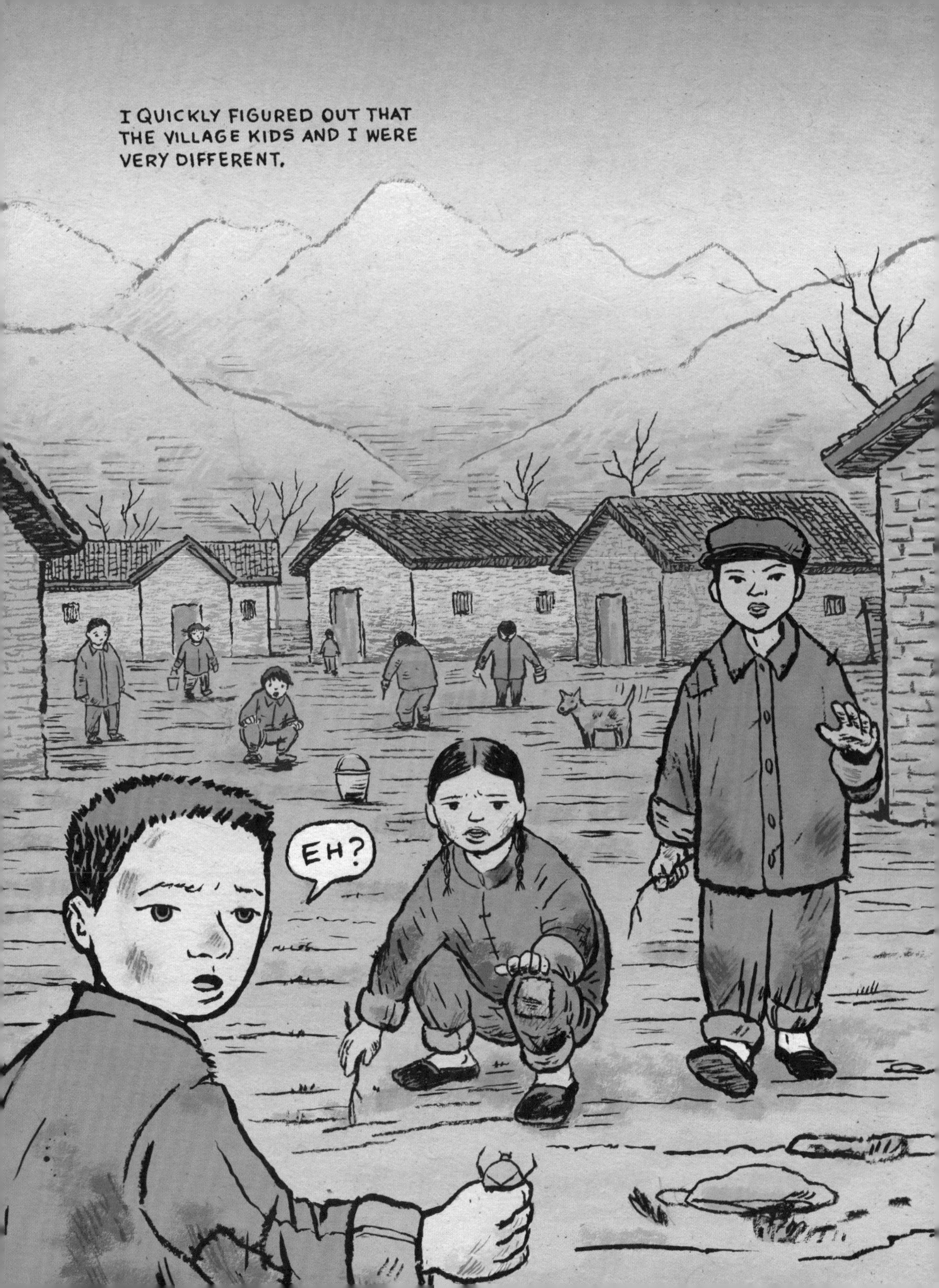
I QUICKLY FIGURED OUT THAT THE VILLAGE KIDS AND I WERE VERY DIFFERENT.
EH?

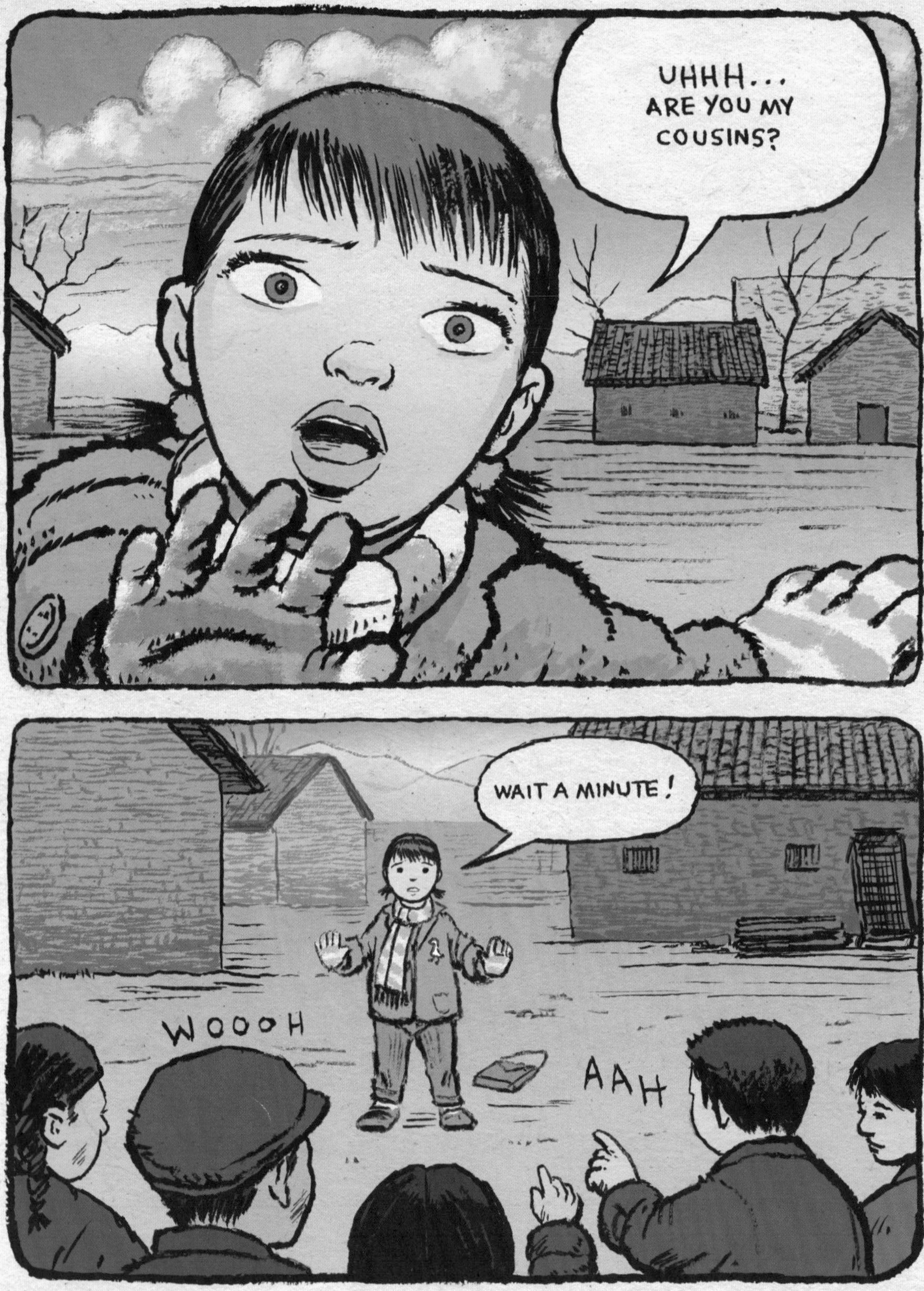
UHHH...
ARE YOU MY
COUSINS?
WAIT A MINUTE!
WOOOH
AAH

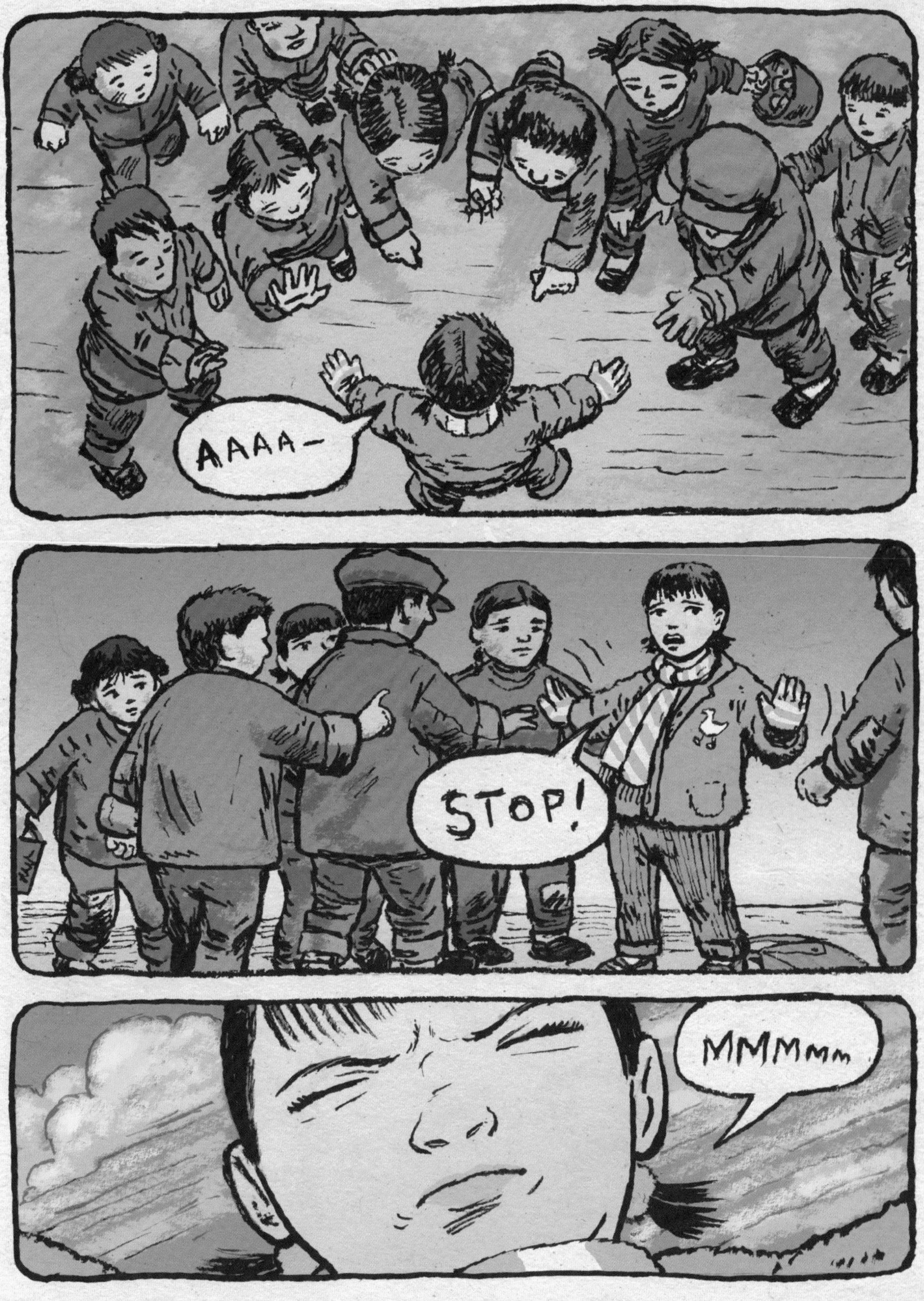
AAAA–
STOP!
MMMmm

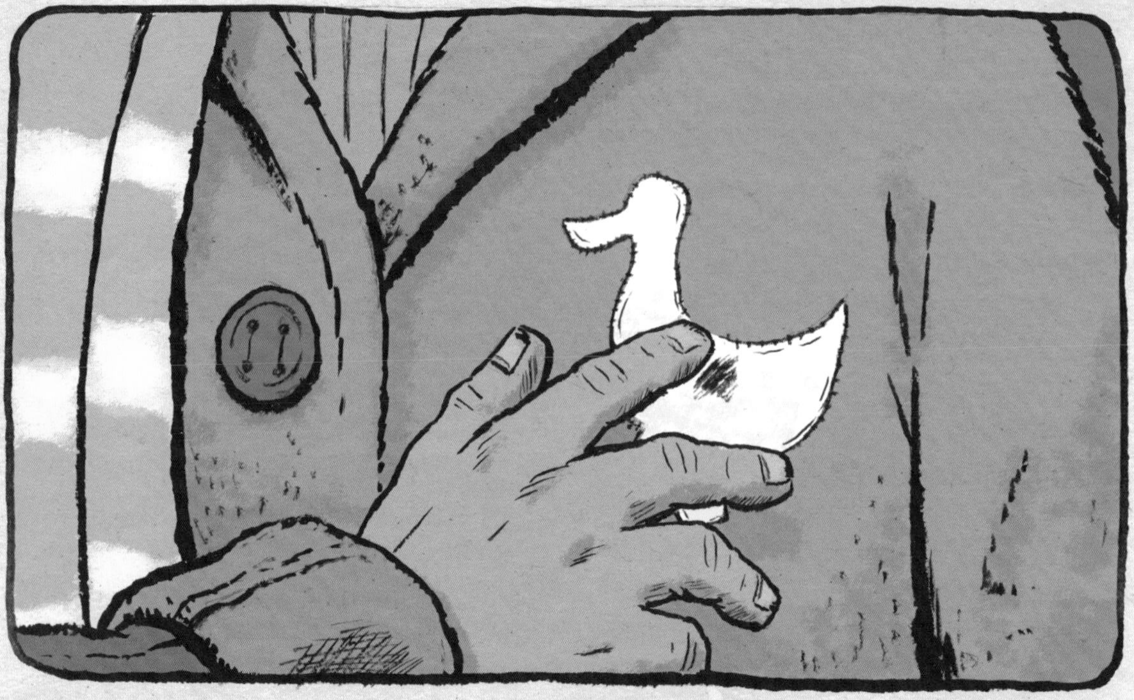

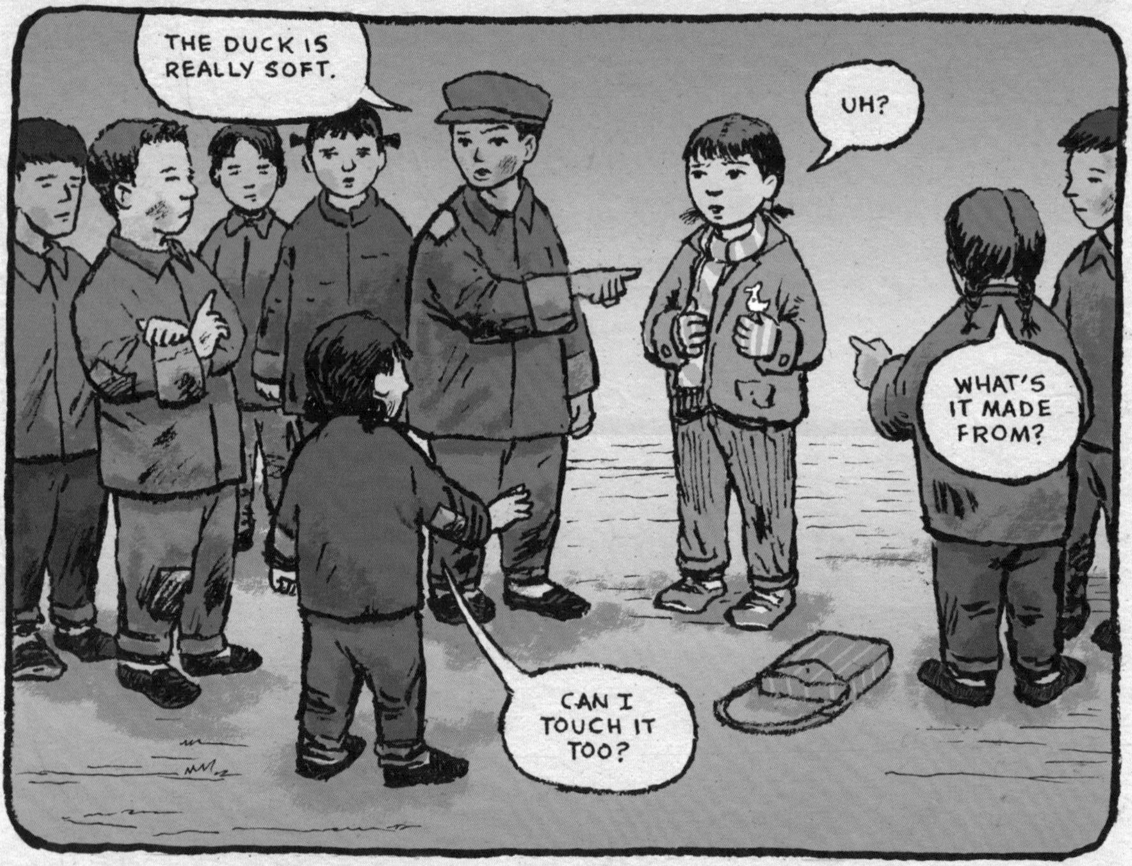
THE DUCK IS REALLY SOFT.
UH?
WHAT'S IT MADE FROM?
CAN I TOUCH IT TOO?

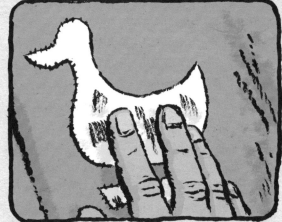

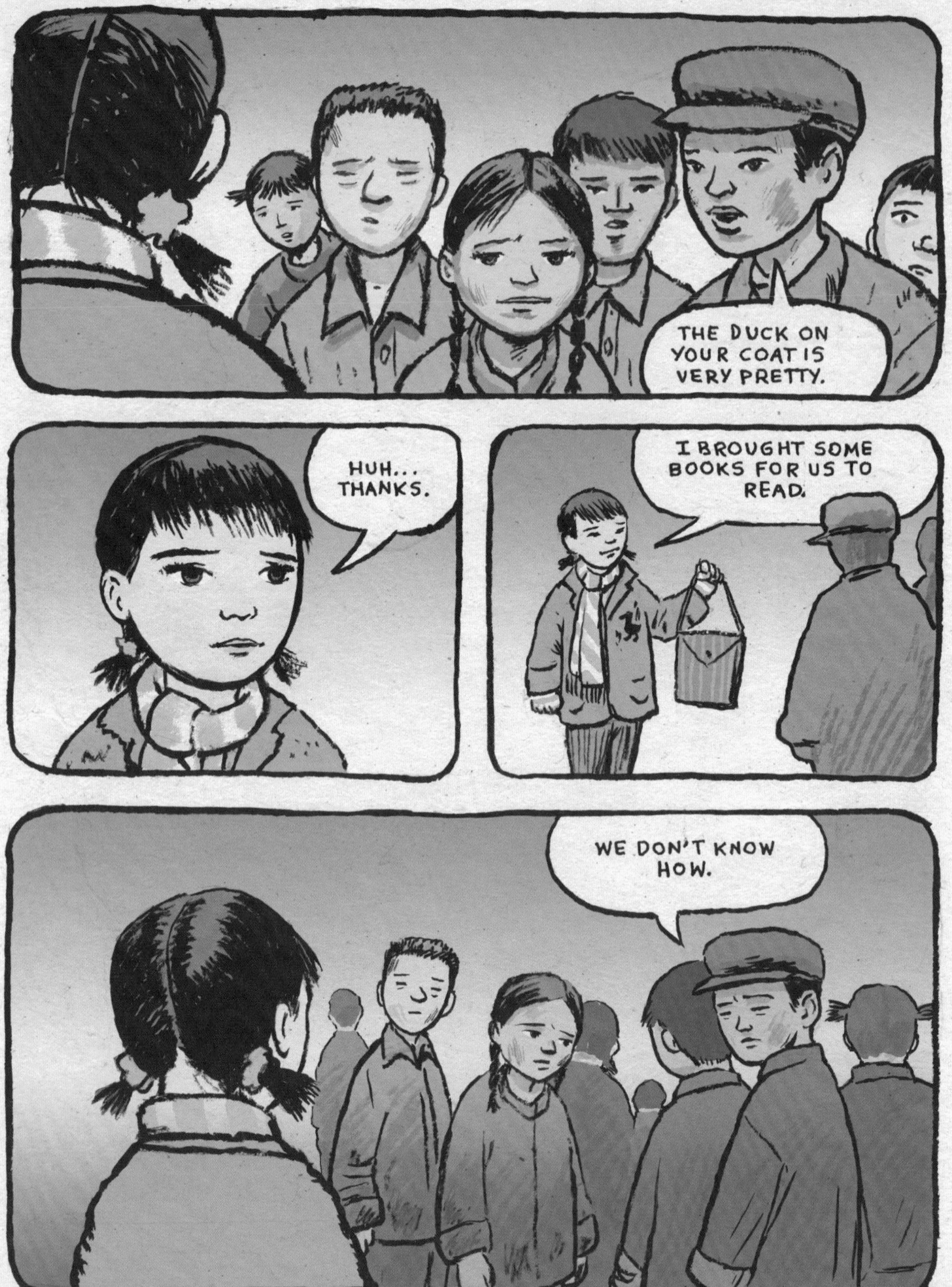
THE DUCK ON YOUR COAT IS VERY PRETTY.
HUH... THANKS.
I BROUGHT SOME BOOKS FOR US TO READ.
WE DON'T KNOW HOW.

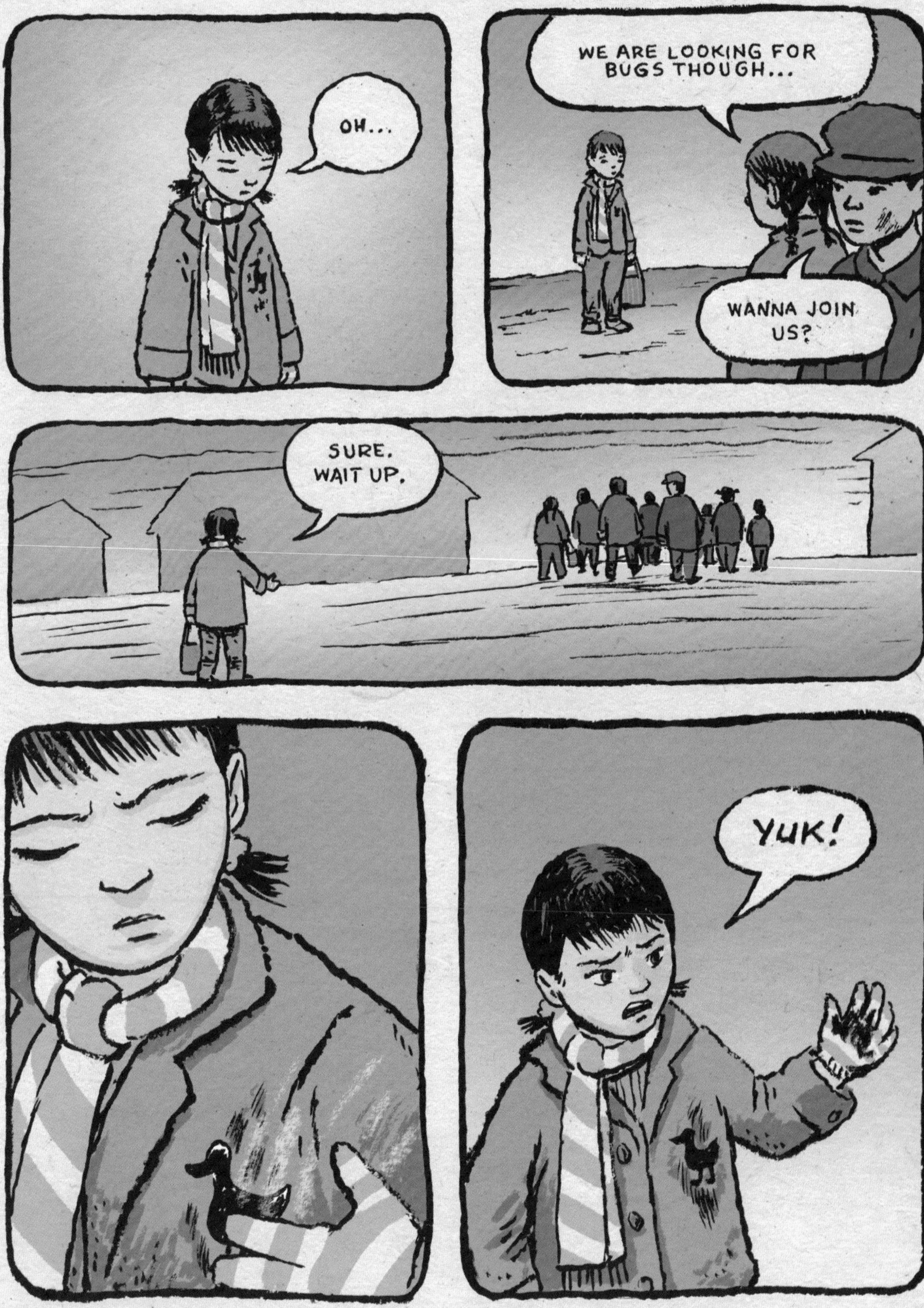
OH...
WE ARE LOOKING FOR BUGS THOUGH...
WANNA JOIN US?
SURE. WAIT UP.
YUK!

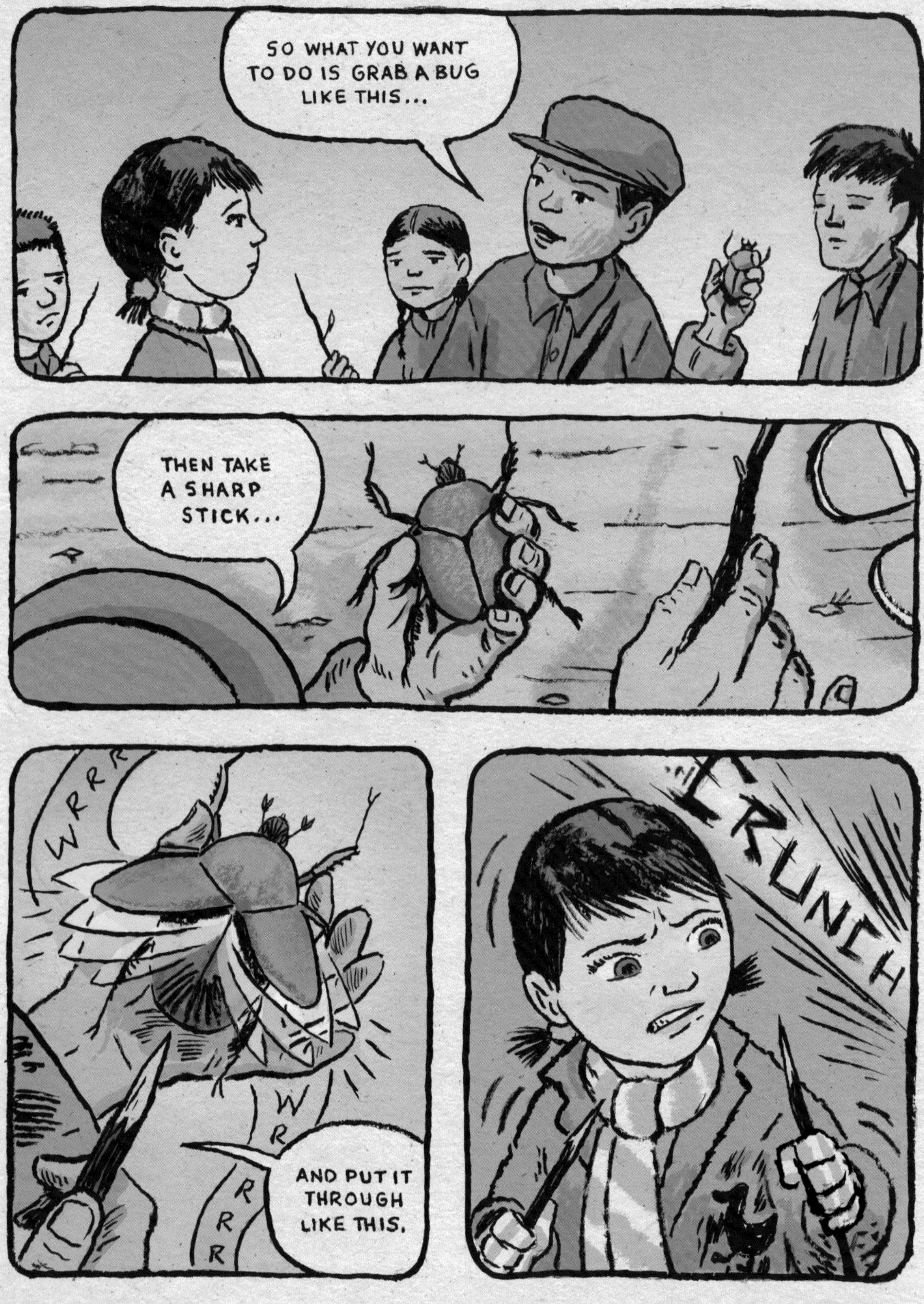
SO WHAT YOU WANT TO DO IS GRAB A BUG LIKE THIS...
THEN TAKE A SHARP STICK...
WRRR
WRRRRR
AND PUT IT THROUGH LIKE THIS.
KRUNCH

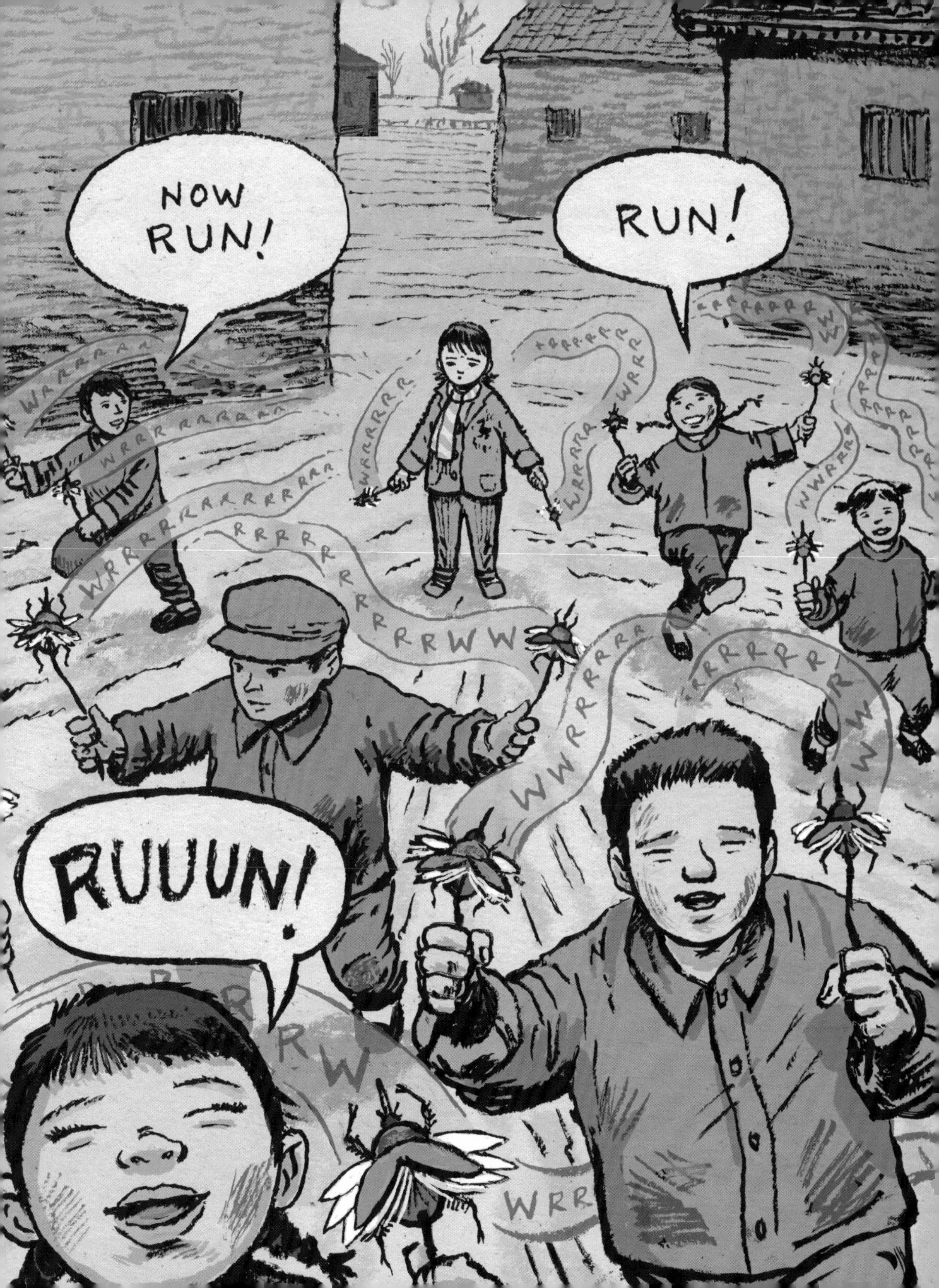
NOW RUN!
RUN!
RUUUN!

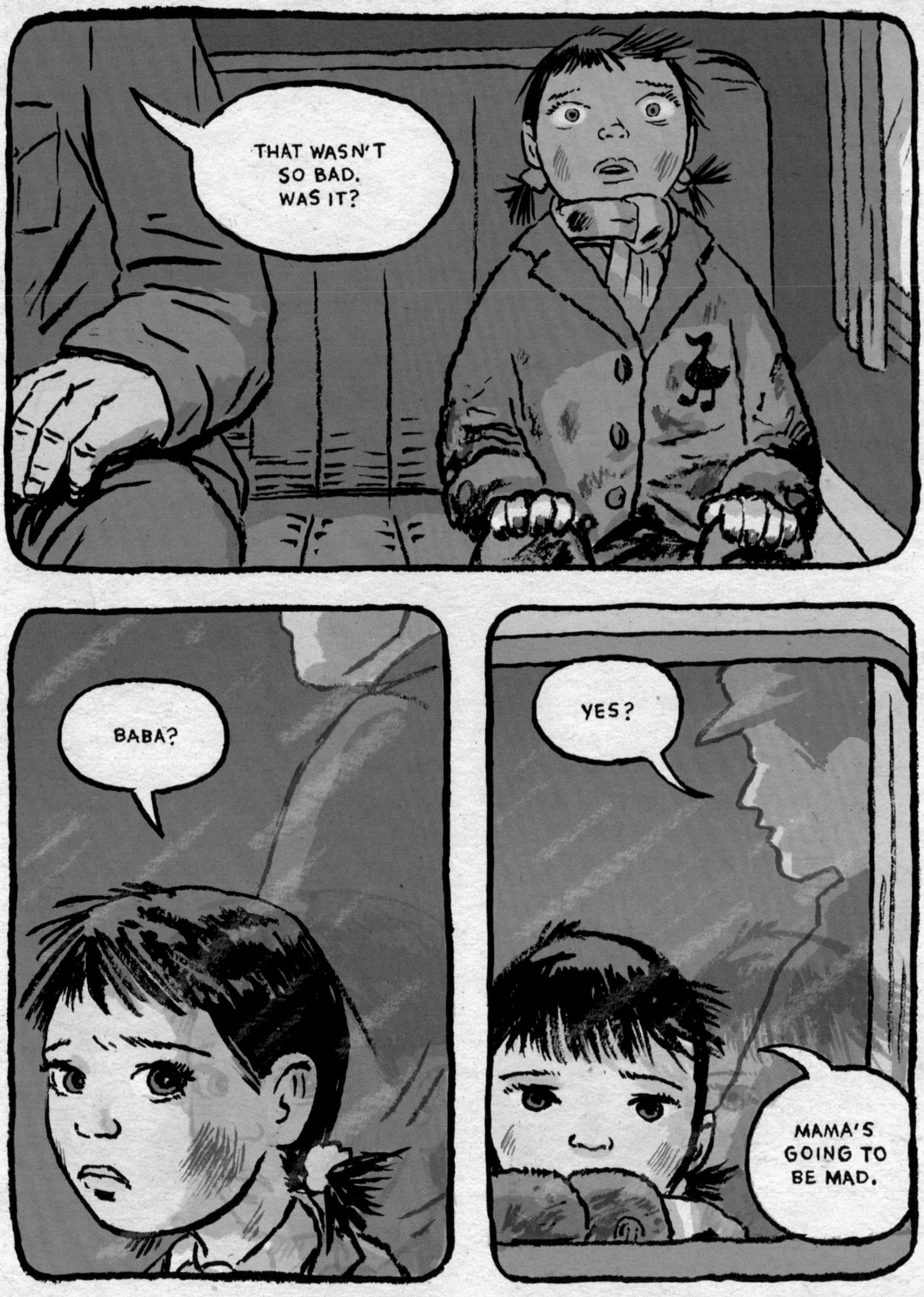
THAT WASN'T SO BAD. WAS IT?
BABA?
YES?
MAMA'S GOING TO BE MAD.

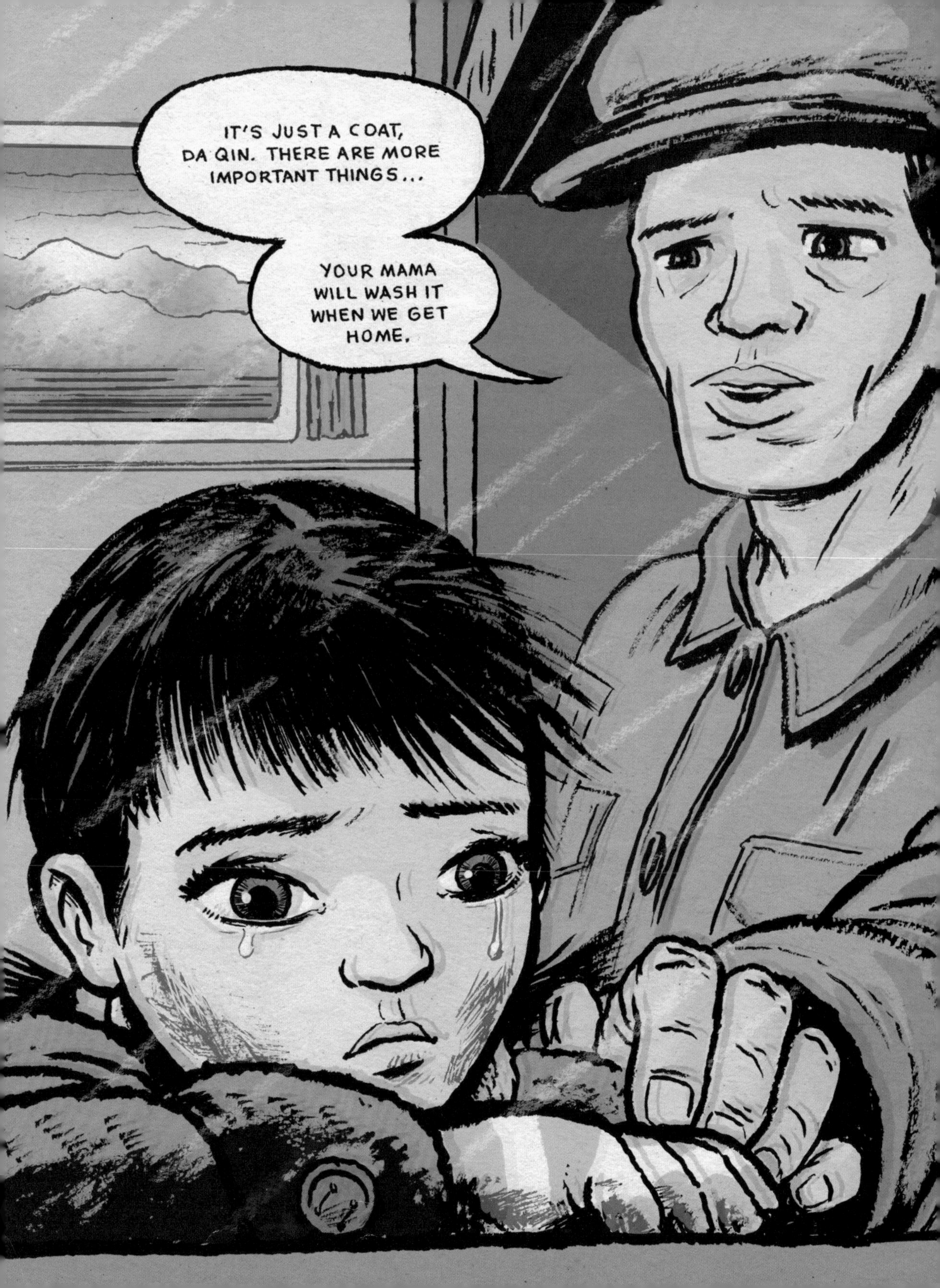
IT'S JUST A COAT, DA QIN. THERE ARE MORE IMPORTANT THINGS...
YOUR MAMA WILL WASH IT WHEN WE GET HOME.

I WAS SHOCKED SO MANY KIDS HAD NEVER SEEN SUCH A PRETTY COAT. I FELT REALLY BAD.

SNIF
SNIF

I WANTED TO LET THEM TOUCH MY COAT, BUT AT THE SAME TIME, I DIDN'T WANT THEM TO GET IT DIRTY.

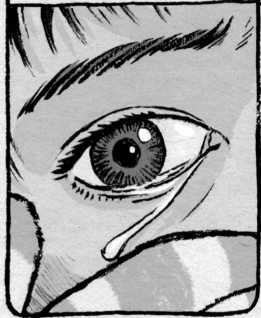

I READ IN THE WRITINGS OF CONFUCIUS THAT THERE ARE THREE WAYS TO LEARN...
FIRST: BY STUDYING HISTORY, WHICH IS THE BEST.
SECOND: BY IMITATING SOMEONE OR SOMETHING, WHICH IS EASIEST.
AND THIRD: THROUGH YOUR OWN EXPERIENCE, WHICH CAN BE HEARTBREAKING.

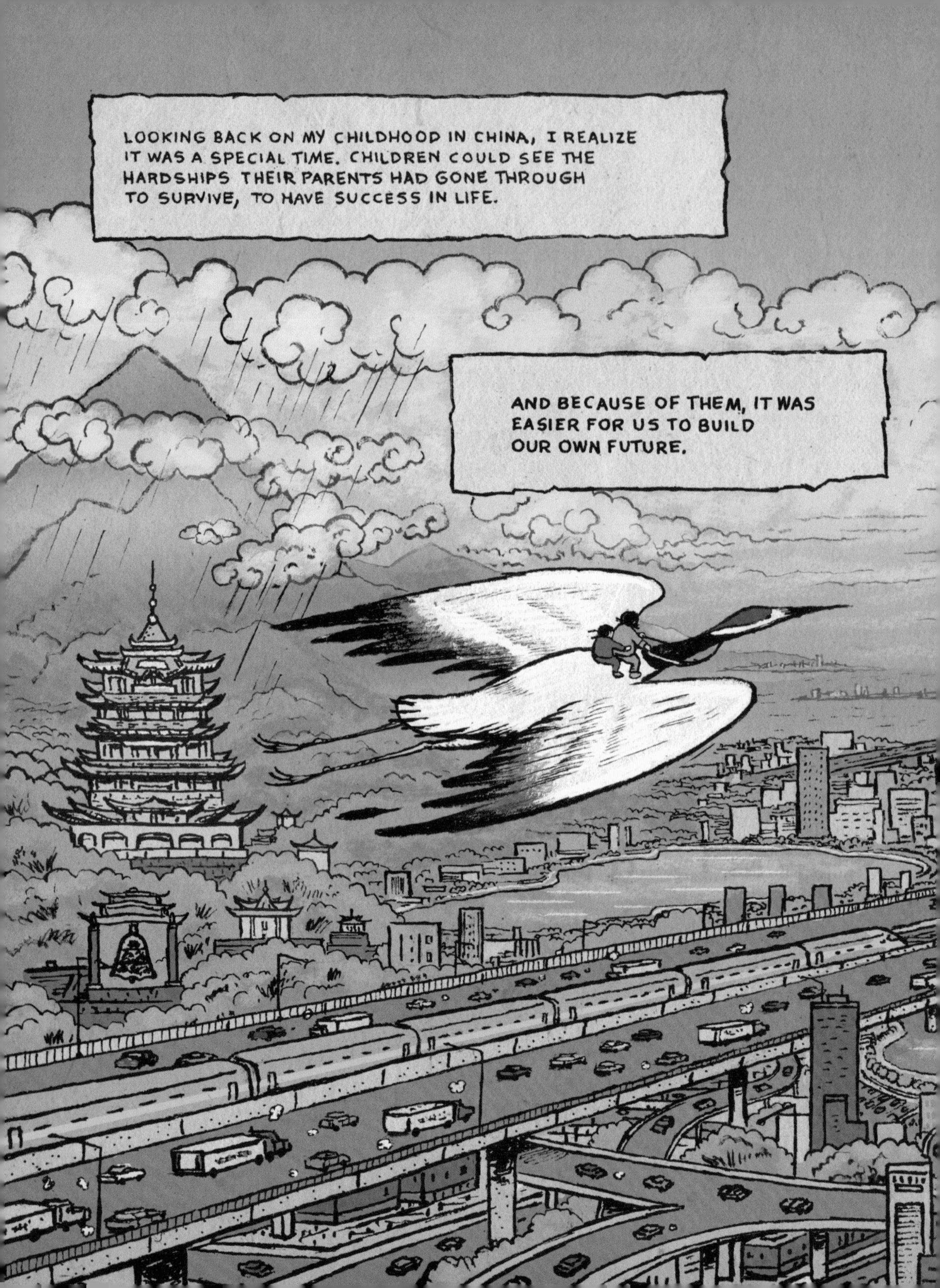
LOOKING BACK ON MY CHILDHOOD IN CHINA, I REALIZE IT WAS A SPECIAL TIME. CHILDREN COULD SEE THE HARDSHIPS THEIR PARENTS HAD GONE THROUGH TO SURVIVE, TO HAVE SUCCESS IN LIFE.
AND BECAUSE OF THEM, IT WAS EASIER FOR US TO BUILD OUR OWN FUTURE.

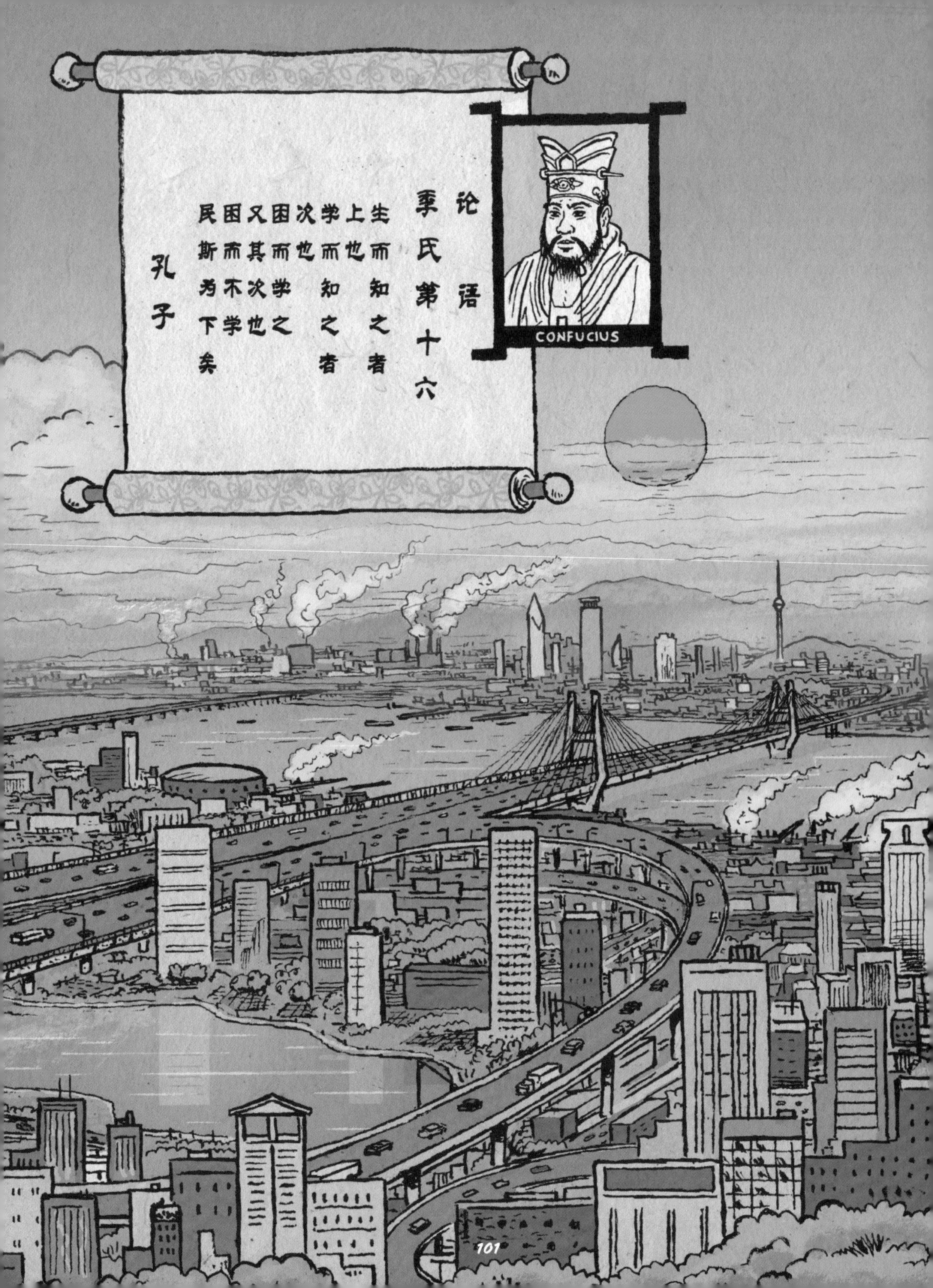
论语
季氏第十六
生而知之者
上也
学而知之者
次也
困而学之
又其次也
困而不学
民斯为下矣
孔子
CONFUCIUS

GLOSSARY OF MANDARIN CHINESE WORDS AND OTHER WORDS AND NAMES

baba: a word for "father," like papa

Chang: the world's third-longest river, running 3,915 miles (6,300 kilometers). Its name literally means "long river." Also called the Changjiang, Yangtze, or Yanzi.

Da Qin: Big Piano

didi: little brother

hao chi: delicious

hong bao: red paper envelopes filled with money, given to children on Chinese New Year. The red symbolizes life, happiness, and good luck.

jia jia: grandma, your mother's mother

jie jie: big sister

mama: just means "mama"

nai nai: grandma, your father's mother

Nian: a ferocious monster that, according to legend, attacked once each year until the people learned how to frighten it away. *Nian* also means "year."

ni hao: hello

polio: short for poliomyelitis, a dangerous disease that can cause muscle weakness or paralysis. A polio vaccine was developed in the 1950s.

Wuhan: the most highly populated city in central China, located where the Han and Chang rivers join.

Xiao Qin: Little Piano

xie xie ni: thank you very much

ye ye: grandpa, your father's father

TIMELINE

551 BCE

Confucius (Kong Fuzi), a philosopher who stresses personal morality and social justice, is born. His philosophy and way of life are still practiced by many in China today. He dies in 479 BCE.

246 BCE–1912 CE

The Imperial era, the longest period in China's more than 4,000-year history, begins with the first emperor, Qin Shi Huang. He rules from 246 BCE to 221 BCE. Among the most famous dynasties are the Han (206 BCE–220 CE), Tang (618–907), and Ming (1368–1644). The Qing dynasty is China's last dynasty before the establishment of the Republic of China. Puyi, the last emperor, steps down in 1912.

1927–1949

Civil war between the Chinese Nationalist Party and the Communist Party of China leads to the Communist Party winning control of the country.

1943

Mao Zedong, the son of a successful farmer, rises to power through his military leadership and political ideas, and becomes the leader of the Communist Party.

1949

The People's Republic of China is created. On October 1, the Communist Party takes over China. Mao Zedong becomes the country's leader. He is called the chairman.

1958–1961

During the Great Leap Forward, the Chinese government works to change the country from a land of farms to a nation full of factories and schools. The Four Pests campaign and the Great Chinese Famine take place during this time.

1962

Lei Feng, a hardworking soldier in the People's Liberation Army, dies in an accident on August 15 at the age of 22. The Chinese government makes him into an inspirational symbol.

1966–1976

During the Cultural Revolution, Chairman Mao encourages young people to root out old traditions and investigate their fellow citizens, including government officials, intellectuals, or anyone else they believe is not following communist ideas. The movement becomes violent, and hundreds of thousands of people are hurt or die.

1976

On September 9, Mao Zedong dies. Many Chinese believe Mao Zedong to be China's greatest leader of all time.

NA LIU'S BIOGRAPHY

My name is Na. Liu is my family name. In China the family name comes first: Liu Na.

The stories in this book are about my childhood in Wuhan, China, where I was born in 1973. The stories take place between 1976 and 1980. I moved to the United States much later, when I was in my twenties, to work in medical research. I married an American cartoonist from Texas—and this is where the idea for this book was born.

My husband, Andrés, says he loves to hear about my childhood in China. He says, "It's stuff I can't learn from books." Andrés likes books and, of course, he especially likes comic books. Soon after we found out that we were going to have our first child (our daughter, Mei Lan), we decided to create this book. It took some convincing from Andrés. But after living in the United States for more than ten years and recently going back home to see how much China has changed, I realized my childhood was pretty unique. I decided I should share my stories with more people.

China was going through major changes when I was a child. With the exception of Russia, China was pretty much closed to the influences of the rest of the world from the 1940s through the early 1980s. My parents grew up during a time when Chinese leaders wanted to put an end to old traditions and replace them with a nation where all people are treated equally. My parents benefited from the changes that took place. However, my sister and I are from a newer generation. We grew up when China was slowly opening up to the world both economically and culturally. This made for a much different childhood. We became a transitional generation—a generation caught in between one way of life and another, between the old and the new. Under the surface, my childhood stories reveal the drastic shift from how my parents grew up to how children of China live today.

China is still changing at a breakneck pace. Life in a large Chinese city is like life in any other city in the world, such as New York, London, or Tokyo. For the most part, modern Chinese children wear the same sorts of clothes, play the same video games, eat the same fast food, watch similar TV programs, and play the same sports, such as soccer and basketball, as children in those other cities. Material wealth is spreading quickly. The China I grew up in is disappearing. The China my parents knew is almost gone.

Not only is China changing, but our whole world is growing more connected. The way of life from one country to another is becoming more and more similar. After seeing China change so much and so fast in my lifetime, I believe it's possible that someday the only records we have of how cultures and countries were once very different from one another will be in books like this one. We can preserve our unique experiences of life through pictures and stories.

Xie Xie Ni!

TRANSLATIONS OF CHINESE CHARACTERS

page 10

Wide, wide flow the nine streams
      through the land,
Dark, dark weaves the thread
      from south to north.
Hazy in the thick fog
      of the misty rain
Tortoise and Snake
      hold the long river trapped.
The yellow crane is gone.
      Who knows where?
Only this tower remains,
      a roost for visitors.
I pour a toast to the rising torrent.
    —Mao Zedong, "Yellow Crane Tower"

page 11

My old friend said farewell to the west,
      here at Yellow Crane Tower.
In the spring cloud of willow blossoms,
      he's going down to Yangzhou.
His lone sail is a distant shadow slipping
      into a blue emptiness.
All I see is the Chang River flowing to
      the edge of the sky.
    —Li Bai, "Seeing off Meng Haoran
    to Guangling at Yellow Crane Tower"

pages 22–23

"Long Live Chairman Mao!"

More literally, this says, "Chairman
Mao for 10,000 years!"

pages 24–25

"We mourn the greatest leader,
Chairman Mao!"

pages 28 and 35

The signs in the classroom are a well-known
proverb that is easy to memorize. Roughly,
it means, "Study very hard and make
progress every day."

page 37

"Everybody come and kill a sparrow."

page 54

"We learn from Lei Feng. He is our role model.
Love the Communist Party. Love Communism
and love the people."

page 55

Upper right: "Study hard and become the next
Communist generation."

Lower left: "The Liberation Army serves the
people, and the people love the Liberation
Army!"

Lower right: "Revere the quotations of Chairman
Mao like Lei Feng does."

pages 60–69

The flags have the character that spells Nian, or
"year," the same as Nian the Monster's name.

The red banners around the doorways are
poetry with wishes for good fortune, such as
"Everything you try to do will be successful"
and "Every year will be better and better."

The characters on the chopsticks mean "spring."
Chinese New Year is also called Spring Festival.

The character next to the fish means "salt."

page 76

"Wuchang Train Station"

Wuchang is a borough of Wuhan.

page 101

This is the proverb that is given in English
on page 99. Here is a modern translation of
another saying from Confucius about knowledge:

Born with wisdom, first class citizen.

Acquire wisdom by learning, second class citizen.

Face difficulty and learn from it, third class
citizen.

Face difficulty and refuse to learn from it, the
lowest class citizen.

        —Confucius

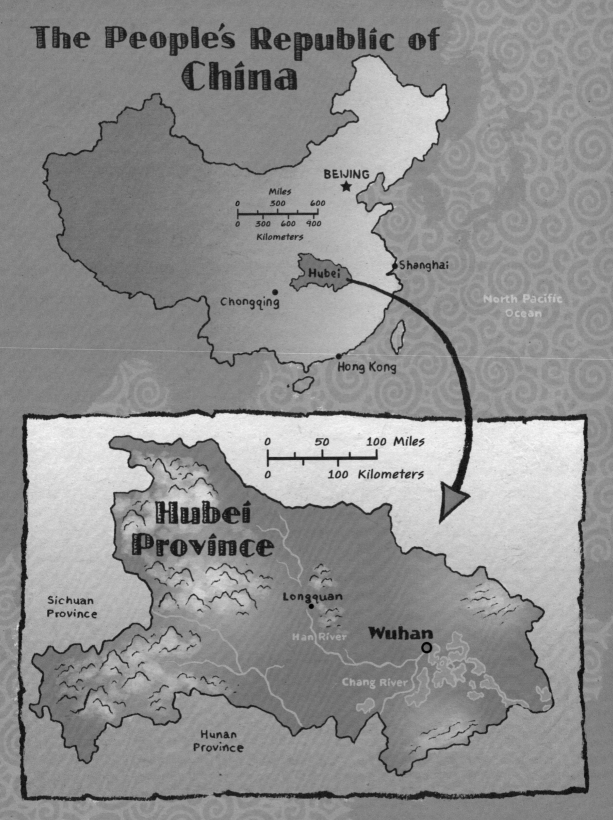

The People's Republic of China

BEIJING ★

Miles
0   300   600

0   300   600   900
Kilometers

Hubei

Chongqing •

• Shanghai

North Pacific Ocean

• Hong Kong

Hubei Province

0   50   100 Miles

0   100 Kilometers

Sichuan Province

Longquan •

Han River

Wuhan ○

Chang River

Hunan Province

107

ABOUT THE AUTHOR AND THE ILLUSTRATOR

Na Liu moved from Wuhan, China, to Austin, Texas, in 1999 to work as a research scientist for MD Anderson Cancer Center. Recently, she became a doctor of hematology and oncology. She met Andrés Vera Martínez, her husband, in Austin. He was born in Lamesa, Texas, and was raised in Austin. Growing up, he always wanted to be an artist. Andrés Vera Martínez has created comics and illustrations for Scholastic, Simon & Schuster, CBS/Showtime, and for the *New York Times,* and has received awards and recognition from the Society of Illustrators and *American Illustration.*

Na Liu and Andrés Vera Martínez live in Brooklyn, New York, with their daughter Mei Lan. They take annual trips to visit their families in Wuhan and Austin.